AREA HANDBOOK
for the
DOMINICAN REPUBLIC

Coauthors

Thomas E. Weil

Jan Knippers Black
Howard I. Blutstein
Kathryn T. Johnston
David S. McMorris
Frederick P. Munson

Research completed February 1973

Second Edition

Published 1973

(This handbook supersedes DA Pam 550-54, December 1966)

DA Pam 550-54

Library of Congress Catalog Card Number: 73–600179

For sale by the Superintendent of Documents, U.S. Government Printing Office
Washington, D.C. 20402—Price $7.15

FOREWORD

This volume is one of a series of handbooks prepared by Foreign Area Studies (FAS) of The American University, designed to be useful to military and other personnel who need a convenient compilation of basic facts about the social, economic, political, and military institutions and practices of various countries. The emphasis is on objective description of the nation's present society and the kinds of possible or probable changes that might be expected in the future. The handbook seeks to present as full and as balanced an integrated exposition as limitations on space and research time permit. It was compiled from information available in openly published material. An extensive bibliography is provided to permit recourse to other published sources for more detailed information. There has been no attempt to express any specific point of view or to make policy recommendations. The contents of the handbook represent the work of the authors and FAS and do not represent the official view of the United States government.

An effort has been made to make the handbook as comprehensive as possible. It can be expected, however, that the material, interpretations, and conclusions are subject to modification in the light of new information and developments. Such corrections, additions, and suggestions for factual, interpretive, or other change as readers may have will be welcomed for use in future revisions. Comments may be addressed to:

The Director
Foreign Area Studies
The American University
5010 Wisconsin Avenue, N.W.
Washington, D.C. 20016

PREFACE

Significant economic and political developments that have occurred since the election of President Joaquín Balaguer in 1966 underline the desirability of revising the *Area Handbook for the Dominican Republic.* Agrarian reform and increased exploitation of mineral resources point the way to important changes in the Dominican society.

After the text of this book had been completed, a small group of guerrillas landed on the beach about thirty miles west of Santo Domingo. According to official reports, their leader was Colonel Francisco Caamaño Deño, who in 1965 had led the rebel forces fighting against a military junta in an effort to reinstate Juan Bosch in the presidency. Colonel Caamaño was reported killed during the landing, and most of the other guerrillas were killed or captured.

While the armed forces were pursuing the guerrillas, the police raided the homes of Juan Bosch, leader of the country's largest opposition party, and the homes of other political leaders opposed to President Joaquín Balaguer's plans to retain the presidency after expiration of his second term of office in 1974. Hundreds of members of opposition parties were arrested, most for brief periods; a number of radio stations were closed temporarily, and the national university was surrounded by troops.

Bosch stated that his political party had had nothing to do with the raid and went into hiding. Early in May the armed forces, which had originally accused Juan Bosch of complicity in the attack, announced they would take no action against him. He came out of hiding and declared that his opposition to the president would continue.

This book supersedes the area handbook, published in December 1966, that was researched and written by Susan G. Callaway, Mary Elizabeth Carroll, Bela C. Maday, David S. McMorris, Elaine M. Themo, and John O. Weaver under the chairmanship of T.D. Roberts. It represents an effort to provide a compact and objective exposition and analysis of the dominant social, political, and economic characteristics of Dominican society. Consultants with firsthand knowledge of the country have provided data not available in printed sources. In this connection the authors are particularly grateful to Dr. Larman C. Wilson of The American University. The authors alone are responsible for the final draft.

English usage follows *Webster's Seventh New Collegiate Dictionary.* Spanish words and phrases, used only when adequate English equivalents are lacking, are defined at first appearance; if employed frequently, they are listed in the Glossary. Spanish words are based on *Appleton's New Cuyas Dictionary* (fifth edition). Unless otherwise stated, production and commodity tonnage figures are stated in metric tons.

COUNTRY SUMMARY

1. COUNTRY: Dominican Republic (República Dominicana).

2. SIZE, TOPOGRAPHY, AND CLIMATE: Land area of about 19,000 square miles comprises eastern two-thirds of Hispaniola, second-largest island in Caribbean; Haiti occupies western one-third. Rugged and mountainous terrain. Topography dominated by four parallel ranges extending in northwesterly direction in west of country and single range extending east to west in eastern part. Extensive valleys between major ranges and lowland plain cover most of eastern end of island. Numerous rivers and streams too shallow for navigation but important for irrigation and as hydroelectric power sources. Prevailing temperatures vary with elevation, and sea breezes temper tropical heat in coastal lowlands; little seasonal change. Complex rainfall pattern in which precipitation generally heaviest in north and east and diminishing toward south and west where mountains provide rain shadow, but considerable local variation. Two fairly well defined rainy seasons in much of country; maximum precipitation in late spring and fall.

3. POPULATION: Slightly over 4 million as recorded by the 1970 census; 40 percent in urban localities. Heaviest concentration in capital city of Santo Domingo and in Cibao Valley (Valle del Cibao). Census finding of 3 percent average annual growth rate lower than anticipated; attributed to substantial emigration during period. Birth rate among hemisphere's highest, however, and government supports active family-planning program.

4. ETHNIC GROUPS AND LANGUAGES: Population derived from white Spanish settlers and black African slaves whose extensive intermingling produced mulatto strain. In early 1970s this mulatto group constituted about 70 percent of the population. Remaining 30 percent formed by whites of European descent and by blacks. Since racial distinctions were not delineated in the last census, exact figures not available.

Spanish heritage well preserved and dominates all other elements of the culture. This is evidenced by the strength of Spanish customs, values, and institutions. Spanish, official language of the country, spoken by 98 percent of the population. Many of upper class are bilingual in another European language, and many of the lower class also speak Haitian Creole.

5. RELIGION: An estimated 98 percent of the people are Roman Catholic. There are also trace elements of Protestantism and voodooism.

6. EDUCATION: Enrollments at all levels gained rapidly during 1960s and early 1970s, but onrushing population growth presented severe challenge to educational program. Schools crowded, and teachers too few and poorly prepared. Secondary-school reform program initiated in early 1970s to increase emphasis on previously neglected secondary-level prevocational courses, to increase output of primary teachers from secondary-level normal schools, and to improve preparation of university matriculants.

7. HEALTH: Medical personnel and facilities concentrated in Santo Domingo and a few other major urban centers. Most of population depends on free public health service; separate program maintained by social security program for employed personnel insured under it. Heavy flow of emigration somewhat reduced number of physicians in practice during 1960s and early 1970s. Gastroenteritis, diseases of infancy, cancer, nutritional deficiency, heart disease, tetanus, and respiratory ailments principal causes of mortality. Effective campaign against malaria in operation since 1945.

8. GOVERNMENT: Constitutional democracy. Power largely centered in hands of president and military. Executive, legislative, and judicial branches. President elected to four-year term; nothing in constitution to preclude reelection. Legislature consists of twenty-seven-member Senate and seventy-four-member Chamber of Deputies. Supreme Court of Justice heads judicial system.

9. INTERNATIONAL MEMBERSHIPS: The country is a party to the Inter-American Treaty of Reciprocal Assistance and the Pact of Bogotá and a member of the Organization of American States, the Inter-American Development Bank, and the United Nations and many of its specialized agencies.

10. CURRENCY: Dominican peso; symbol is RD$. Official rate in 1972 was RD$1 equals US$1.

11. AGRICULTURE AND INDUSTRY: Based upon processing of a few agricultural export products—particularly sugarcane, followed by coffee, cacao, and tobacco. A wide range of crops grown for domestic use. A small mining industry also exists; nickel and bauxite, the leading minerals. Manufacturing comprises a small number of establishments, some of which are state owned. The food and beverage sector accounts for the largest proportion of manufacturing production and industrial employment.

12. LABOR: In 1970 some 1,102,000, or somewhat more than 27 percent of population, in labor force. Females made up 11 percent of total, one of lowest proportions in Latin America. Agricultural employment made up over 60 percent of total, and most of remainder were in services activities. High unemployment rate, particularly in fast-growing Santo Domingo.

13. TRANSPORTATION: Rapidly growing road network; over 6,600

miles in 1972. One government-owned rail line carries freight between La Vega and Sánchez. It is 137 miles long and has two different gauges: two feet, six inches and three feet, six inches. Fifteen cities are served by air transportation of the Dominican Aviation Company. All major seaports are being modernized and are adequately maintained. One major domestic line, the Dominican Steamship Line, offers coastal shipping and international shipping.

14. COMMUNICATIONS: Dial telephone service between major towns. Telegraph service is voice communicated between stations. Government and private firms provide international communications services.

15. IMPORTS AND EXPORTS: Exports are principally agricultural products. Sugar usually represents about half of all exports. Coffee, cacao, bauxite, and tobacco follow, in that order of importance. Imports are mainly consumer goods, including food, and capital goods, mainly machinery.

16. ECONOMIC AGREEMENTS AND AID: Dominican Republic is a member of the General Agreement on Tariffs and Trade (GATT) but of no other economic association. It receives foreign assistance from the United States, several international lending agencies, and other foreign governments.

17. ARMED FORCES: Security forces consist of army, navy, and air force numbering about 19,000 and police force of 9,000. Army by far largest branch, but all three services independent. Conscription authorized but not used, as ranks easily filled by voluntary enlistment. All branches, as well as the police, involved in civic action.

DOMINICAN REPUBLIC

TABLE OF CONTENTS

LIST OF ILLUSTRATIONS

LIST OF TABLES

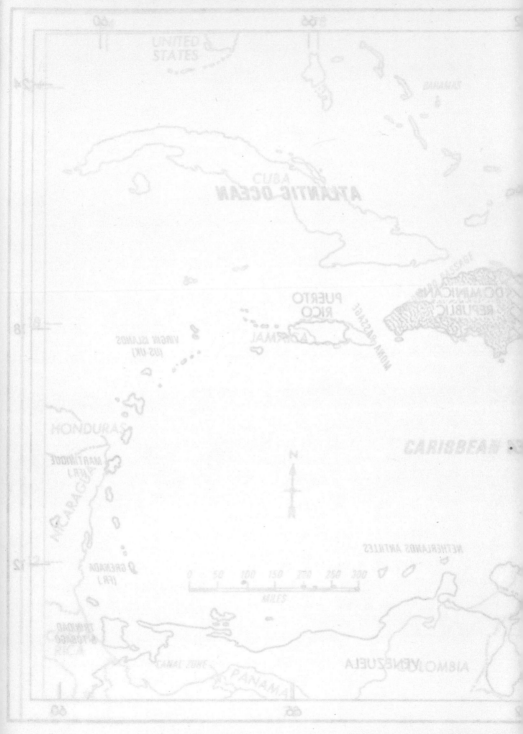

Figure 1. Dominican Republic (map).

xiv

SECTION I. SOCIAL

CHAPTER 1

GENERAL CHARACTER OF THE SOCIETY

In 1972 the people of the Dominican Republic lived under a government that was engaged in building public works, in expanding agricultural production, in promoting self-sufficiency in foodstuffs, and in carrying out reforms in the fields of health and education. After thirty-one years of life under a dictatorship (1930-61) and a decade of political turbulence marked by a civil war in 1965, the country was relatively tranquil, and the economy showed signs of substantial improvement. Firmly supported by the armed forces, the moderate, centrist government faced political opposition that comprised a number of parties and groups professing a variety of ideologies and objectives.

The country lies in the eastern two-thirds of Hispaniola, the second-largest island in the Caribbean; the western third is occupied by the Republic of Haiti. The Mona Passage, which separates Hispaniola from Puerto Rico, and the Windward Passage, which lies between Hispaniola and Cuba, are the principal water routes linking Europe and North America with Central and South America. The terrain is predominantly mountainous, but valleys between the larger ranges, coastal lowlands, and a plain covering most of the eastern part of the country provide soils suitable for agriculture and livestock. The surrounding seas, the trade winds, and the diversity of the terrain produce a great variety of climatic conditions, but in the populated parts of the country the climate is generally mild.

The European discovery of Hispaniola was accomplished by Christopher Columbus in 1492 when, searching for a route to Asia, he landed on the island and claimed it for the Spanish crown. Settlers from Spain subsequently colonized the land and brought with them the Hispanic culture, which is still admired in the Dominican Republic. Dominicans take pride in the fact that the capital of the Spanish colony, founded in 1493, is not only the oldest permanent European settlement in the Western Hemisphere, but is also the site of the first university and the first cathedral in the Americas.

The population, more than 4 million in 1972, is heaviest in the region extending in a northwest-southeast line across the country between two mountain ranges that parallel the northern coast and in the area around Santo Domingo—the capital—on the southern coast. The

1

population growth rate was high during the 1960s, but in 1972 much cultivable land remained available. Nevertheless, in the face of the high growth rate the government was committed to a substantial population control program.

More than half of the labor force was engaged in agriculture and related occupations in 1970, and most of the remainder were occupied with service activities. Only a small proportion of the labor force was engaged in manufacturing—principally food processing and light industry.

The primary importance of agriculture in the economy is a legacy of colonial times. When the Spaniards failed to discover gold and silver in appreciable quantities, those who did not leave for the mainland in search of treasure established ranches; subsequently—in the nineteenth century—plantations were developed.

Although the Spanish colony established models for economic, political, and ecclesiastical institutions throughout Spain's New World empire, it lacked a powerful elite of landowners, the military, and the Roman Catholic Church to control or guide political, economic, and social life. Not long after the founding of the colony, Spanish control and influence waned, and the cultural legacy of Spain was weakened by occupations of the country by France, Haiti, and the United States in the eighteenth, nineteenth, and twentieth centuries. Nevertheless, the people are proud of their Spanish heritage.

Throughout the history of the country the society had been plagued by civil wars, political turmoil, and assassinations, and many heads of government have assumed dictatorial powers. During the nineteenth century large numbers of the better educated people fled the country to escape the harsh rule of dictators, and it was not until the end of the century that the consolidation of a ruling elite evolved.

Among the elite are white descendants of Spanish settlers. The great majority of the people are mulatto—descendants of whites and Negro slaves brought from Africa. The indigenous Indian peoples were annihilated early and are not represented in the country's population. The turbulence that characterized the country's history militated against the growth of domestic political institutions and leaders. Not until the assumption of power by Rafael Leónidas Trujillo Molina, whose authoritarian rule lasted from 1930 to 1961, did the country have regularly organized military forces of any significance. In the past battles were fought by irregular forces recruited by regional political strongmen.

The history of the Trujillo regime was reflected to some extent by conditions existing in the country in 1972. The president, Joaquín Balaguer, and many of his supporters were former Trujillo adherents. The armed forces organized by Trujillo occupied a powerful position; and modern equipment introduced during his regime—in light industry, in radio and television stations, and in other fields—was in use. Trujillo's most prominent political foe, Juan Bosch, who served briefly as president in 1963, continued his open opposition to the Balaguer administration. In marked contrast to conditions under the Trujillo regime, freedom of expression, guaranteed by the constitution, appeared to be a reality.

In 1972 political and economic power was largely in the hands of a small number of leaders, and institutions still reflected the patterns of a colonial past; but dividing lines between classes were eroding, and new ideas and attitudes were manifesting themselves. Between 1930 and 1961 Trujillo had encouraged the growth of a middle class of industrialists, businessmen, military officers, and government employees and had forced a reevaluation of the position of the Roman Catholic Church and of the role of the extended family. He thus challenged the position of a small, educated, wealthy, and largely white elite that in the past had set the standards of social life, controlled the economy, and exerted a powerful influence on the political life of the nation.

Trujillo had forced many of the old elite into exile or political and economic impotence. He had created a group of newly rich that had gained extensive economic power and had laid the groundwork for the social structure that began to emerge after his assassination in 1961.

In 1972 the middle class was growing—largely as a result of increased industrial and agricultural production—but it still lacked cohesiveness and well-defined class consciousness. Members of the old elite who survived the Trujillo dictatorship had abandoned the traditional belief that direct involvement in commerce or politics was ungentlemanly and had begun to enter the professions or established business enterprises. Although family background, wealth, and a person's color continued to affect social status, class lines were not sharply drawn. A small elite, however, continued to preserve their Hispanic heritage and their social status on the basis of ancestry and intermarriage.

The majority of the population belonged to the lower class—uneducated, poor, mulatto, or black people who lived in both rural and urban areas. Many were almost completely outside the money economy and subsisted by bartering goods and services for provisions. In rural areas most people were tenant or independent farmers or migrant farmworkers. In urban areas, where many have gone to seek their fortunes, the lower class people had simply moved from rural to urban poverty.

The great majority of the people of all classes—approximately 98 percent—are Roman Catholics; most of the others are Protestants, and a number of lower class people practice voodooism—the Haitian-based religion derived from West African religions. During the early years of the Spanish colony the Roman Catholic Church had been the principal channel through which Spanish culture was brought to Hispaniola, and the clergy had distinguished themselves as sources of intellectual and humanitarian activities. The power and influence of the church, however, declined after the middle of the sixteenth century

3

and fluctuated through the years. During the Trujillo regime Roman Catholicism was recognized as the state religion, but Dominican churchmen subsequently opposed Trujillo. In 1972 Dominican churchmen were undertaking active roles in the process of social change.

The quality of Dominican living conditions is determined primarily by level of income and secondarily by location in rural or urban areas. In general, life in Santo Domingo, the capital, and in and around Santiago de los Caballeros in the Cibao Valley (Valle del Cibao) is apt to be more rewarding and varied than life in other parts of the country. During the Trujillo regime the movement of people from the countryside to cities and towns was effectively discouraged by the government, but after the collapse of the regime large numbers of people moved into urban areas. In 1972 the authorities administering social services faced the challenge of dealing effectively with a combination of accelerated urbanization and the significantly high population growth rate.

Members of the educated segment of the society read daily newspapers published in two cities, along with a number of periodicals. For the great majority of the population, however, the only mass medium at their disposal is radio, and people throughout the country listen to broadcasts—the most influential public information channel in the republic. As in the past, however, people of all classes value person-to-person exchange of news, gossip, and ideas—in coffeehouses, in marketplaces, and after church services.

The cultural life of the country is essentially Spanish in its origins, but reflections of North American and French influences are apparent in graphic arts, formal music, and literature. During the first half of the sixteenth century Spanish influence dominated literature, architecture, and the theater. Subsequently, however, development of creative and intellectual endeavors suffered from periods of tyranny, anarchy, and foreign intervention. It was not until the late nineteenth century and the early twentieth century that Dominican writers produced significant works. These dealt with a variety of subjects, including political satire and the social life and customs of the country.

In 1972 the arts and scholarly studies, which had been crippled during the Trujillo regime and had been adversely affected by the turbulence of the early and middle 1960s, were again making their contribution to the cultural life of the country. Favored subjects were folklore, the civil war of 1965, and political satire.

Writers' interest in political subjects stems from generations of political turbulence. Although twenty-five constitutions—promulgated between 1844, when the republic was founded, and 1972—guaranteed rights of the individual citizen and provided for a government of checks and balances, the law has rarely been strictly observed, and public officials have seldom been clearly responsible to the citizens. President Balaguer's proposed agrarian reforms announced in April 1972, however, promised significant changes in the economic and politi-

4

cal life of the country. His reorganization of the sugar industry and settlement of labor disputes had resulted in increased efficiency in production—in an industry responsible for a large portion of the foreign exchange earned by exports.

The government was endeavoring to meet one of the most challenging problems—improvement of the educational system—by improving and expanding institutions for training teachers for the crowded primary school system; by encouraging a massive increase in the number of students in prevocational fields; and by revising the curricula of academic secondary schools to improve the quality of university matriculants. These reforms were designed to overcome shortcomings of the public education system inherited from the Trujillo regime. Under that system teachers and classrooms had been in increasingly short supply, a large proportion of students were dropping out of school, and increasing numbers of families, disappointed in the public system, were sending their children to private schools.

As the first president since Trujillo to enjoy the full confidence of the armed forces, President Balaguer was in a strong position to carry out reforms, and indications were that he planned to run for election for a third term in May 1974. Opposition groups were fighting among themselves, and the only point on which leaders of the various factions appeared to agree was determination to oppose the reelection of President Balaguer.

In its efforts to strengthen the economy, the government was making use of substantial financial aid from the Inter-American Development Bank (IDB) and from the United States. The Dominican Republic maintained closer economic and political ties with the United States, a major trading partner, than with any other country.

In 1972 the Dominican economy was growing with new construction starts, increasing exports, and expanded investment. Landless peasants were looking forward to settling on land distributed by the government—from state-owned tracts and from unused, privately owned tracts. People of the middle class were enjoying the benefits of improved economic conditions, and there were indications that conservative rural society preferred the programs and practices of the government in power to those advocated by various opposition groups.

CHAPTER 2

GEOGRAPHY AND POPULATION

The approximately 19,000 square miles that make up the territory of the Dominican Republic occupy the eastern two-thirds of Hispaniola, the second-largest island in the Caribbean; the western one-third is occupied by the Republic of Haiti. Lying about 600 miles southeast of Florida, the island is separated from Puerto Rico on the east by the Mona Passage, and from Cuba on the west by the Windward Passage. Because these two seaways are the principal water routes linking North America and Europe with Central and South America, the Dominican Republic and Haiti have repeatedly been subjected to external influences (see fig. 1).

The Dominican Republic has a rugged and mountainous terrain in which the dominant relief features are four parallel ranges that extend in a northwesterly direction in the western part of the country and a single range of low mountains that extends from east to west in the eastern part of the island. Satellite ranges, extensive valleys between the larger ranges, narrow and broken coastal lowlands, and a lowland plain that covers most of the eastern extremity make up the remainder of the Dominican landmass.

Rivers and streams are numerous. They are generally too shallow for navigation but are important for irrigation and as sources of hydroelectric power. Although the country lies wholly within the tropics, temperatures are moderated by the surrounding seas and the prevailing trade winds, and topographic diversity results in a wide variety of climatic conditions. Mineral resources have yet to be fully exploited but are believed to be extensive, and the valleys and plains have deep alluvial soils suitable for intensive agriculture as well as shallower soils that provide good pasture. The relatively thin soils of the highlands that make up about 60 percent of the national territory have been subjected to considerable logging and slash-and-burn agriculture, which have resulted in erosion in many places. Cutting of timber, however, has been prohibited by law.

The population, with an average concentration of over 200 per square mile, is heaviest in the Cibao Valley (Valle del Cibao), which extends along a northwest-southeast axis across the country between two major mountain ranges along the Atlantic coast, and in the vicinity of the capital city on the shore of the Caribbean Sea. Although the settlement pattern is irregular, there are no frontier regions awaiting

7

settlement. Settlement in the highlands is sparse, and much arable or potentially arable land is unoccupied or ineffectively used. Colonization, which reached a peak during the regime of Rafael Leónidas Trujillo Molina (1930-61) consisted principally of the establishment of agricultural settlements in the relatively empty territory adjacent to the Haitian frontier.

The country has a high population growth rate, modified somewhat during the 1960s by a heavy stream of emigration. The 1970 census showed the population to be slightly in excess of 4 million persons. Urbanization had proceeded rapidly in the 1960s and by 1970 had reached approximately 40 percent of the total. In the country as a whole, males and females were about equal in number, and over half of the population was well under the age of twenty. Because much good farmland remained to be adequately exploited, the country had not yet reached the point of overpopulation. Sustained high birth rates and declining death rates, however, represented an emerging population problem, and in the early 1970s both the public and the private sectors were energetically pursuing family-planning programs.

Over half of the labor force in 1970 was engaged in agriculture and related activities, and a majority of the remainder was engaged in personal services and other service activities. Although a considerable number of laborers were employed as seasonal or regular workers on sugar estates and other large farms, most of those engaged in agriculture were subsistence farmers. The relatively small proportion of the labor force engaged in manufacturing showed little growth during the 1960s. Most of the limited number of female workers were employed in services activities. Few females were employed in industry, and the proportion was lower still in the agricultural sector.

BOUNDARIES AND POLITICAL SUBDIVISIONS

The 193-mile border between the Dominican Republic and Haiti, the island country's only international frontier, was agreed upon in a treaty signed in 1929. Some 80 percent of its demarcation was completed by 1930, and five remaining disputed border sections were settled by a 1936 protocol. For the most part, the frontier follows mountain ridges and courses of streams. There are also several short distances that follow straight lines, and in a portion of the interior highlands it is defined by a highway that parallels the course of the Libón River (Río Libón), a stream that had served as the border before the road was built.

Because of the dense rural population in Haiti and the relative emptiness of the frontier zone in the Dominican Republic, there has been considerable pressure on the border. During the nineteenth century the line in some places shifted substantially to the east, a circumstance that explains the occurrence of Spanish names such as Los Palos and Los Pozos for places on the Haitian Central Plateau (Plateau Central).

Haitian farmers occupying miniature farms close to the border have looked enviously at the relatively empty lands on the Dominican side, and the Dominican government has established a string of frontier-zone agricultural colonies in order to secure the border. The Haitian government, on its part, has endeavored to minimize friction by forbidding the construction of homes within one kilometer (0.62 miles) of the border in certain localities. Illegal migration of Haitians seeking employment in the neighboring country has continued, however, and at the middle of 1972 the border had been officially closed during a five-year period.

The Dominican Republic asserts sovereignty over a distance of six miles from the coastline and over a contiguous zone extending another six miles for purposes of fishing reservation. In addition, in mid-1972 the Dominican Republic was one of fifteen Caribbean countries that participated in a conference held in Santo Domingo, at which it agreed to a set of principles that called for patrimonial rights over a region extending to 200 miles from the coastline.

The Dominican Republic is divided into twenty-six provinces and a national district in which the capital city is located (see fig. 2). As defined in the 1970 census, the provinces were subdivided into seventy-seven municipalities and twenty municipal districts (see ch. 7).

The provincial and subprovincial borders reflect the natural features of relief and drainage that mark the terrain. For the most part, the internal boundaries have been determined by the east-west axis of highland ridges that have served to impede national development and to accentuate regionalism. President Trujillo's colonization and road-building programs, however, somewhat diminished the regionalism of earlier days.

NATURAL FEATURES

Landform and Drainage

The border between the Dominican Republic and Haiti follows an irregular line extending from north to south, but the relief features of Hispaniola follow an east-west axis (see fig. 3). As a consequence, the principal mountain ranges and intervening valleys are shared by the two countries. The laterally extending mountains have in the past made internal communication difficult. The arrangement of the intervening valleys, however, has served to furnish easy movement from one country to the other and has led to border incidents and illegal crossings of the frontier that have played important parts in the histories of the two nations.

The geography of the Dominican Republic does not lend itself readily to the division of the country into a few regions with similar characteristics of topography, climate, vegetation, and land use. A geomorphic study prepared by the Organization of American States divides the

9

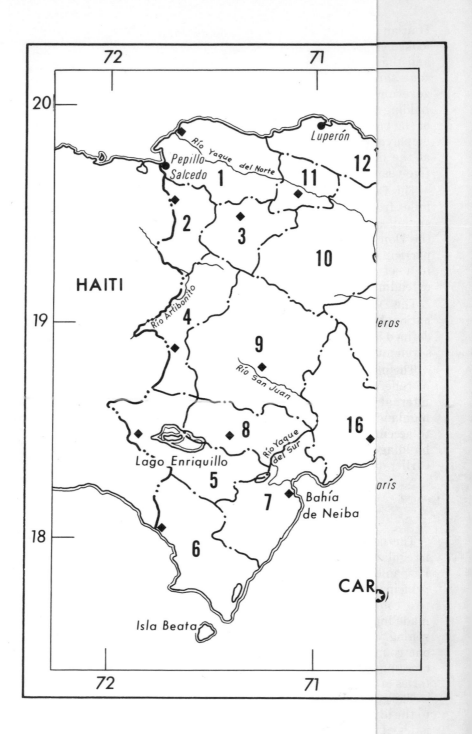

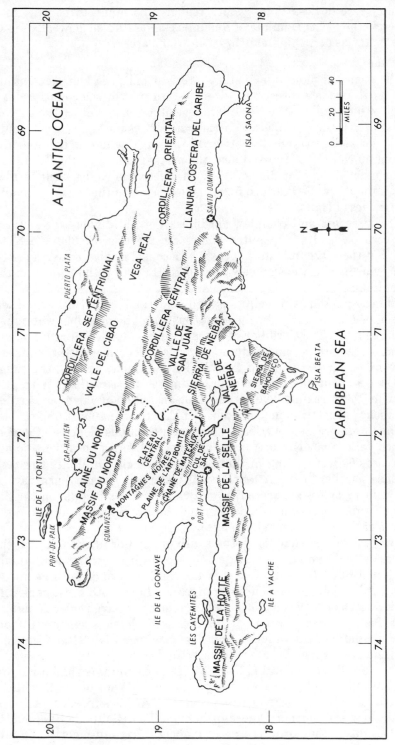

Figure 3. Dominican Republic, Relief Features of Hispaniola

11

country into no less than twenty regions, too many to be used in a general study. The Dominican Republic can be studied generally, however, in terms of its highland and its lowland areas.

Highlands

The principal mountain systems are four parallel ranges extending in a northwesterly direction in the western part of the country and a single minor chain—the Cordillera Oriental—in the east. The core of the system is the Cordillera Central, which rises in the east near Santo Domingo and veers northwestward into Haiti, where it becomes the Massif du Nord. It is flanked near the northern coast by the Cordillera Septentrional, and on the south by the Sierra de Neiba. Still farther south, the Sierra de Baoruco forms an extension of the southern mountain ranges of Haiti.

The dissected and complex Cordillera Central divides the country into two parts. Its convoluted ridges crest between 5,000 and 8,000 feet, but there are individual peaks with considerably greater heights. Pico Duarte, which has an elevation of 10,414 feet, is the highest in the West Indies.

The rugged slopes, precipitous and sometimes faceted, have gradients of as high as forty degrees and constitute the principal watershed of the country. The Cordillera Central is composed of a mixture of volcanic, metamorphic, and sedimentary rock. Together with the Massif du Nord in Haiti, including the various intermont valleys, the range makes up about one-third of the landmass of Hispaniola. Within it, innumerable streams have carved a jigsaw puzzle of yawning canyons and rocky gulches that in many places makes transit almost impossible.

The Cordillera Septentrional also has precipitous slopes and deeply etched valleys but is a less imposing range in which elevations do not exceed 4,000 feet. Rising in the west near the city of Monte Cristi, it extends parallel to the Atlantic coastline across the northern part of the country and is separated from a related series of hills on the Samaná Peninsula (Península de Samaná) by swamps that surround the mouth of the Yuna River (Río Yuna).

The two ranges that lie to the south of the Cordillera Central, the Sierra de Neiba and the Sierra de Baoruco, begin as escarpments flanking Neiba Bay (Bahía de Neiba) in the southwest and continue northwestward to join corresponding ranges in Haiti. Both crest generally at elevations of between 3,000 and 4,000 feet but have peaks as high as 6,000 feet. The eastern part of the Sierra de Neiba is separated from the remainder of the range by the Yaque del Sur River (Río Yaque del Sur) and is known as the Sierra de Martín García.

The Cordillera Oriental is less a range of mountains than a narrow band of hills representing an eastward terminal spur of the Cordillera Central. It extends westward some eighty-five miles from the Atlantic coast along the southern shore of Samaná Bay (Bahía de Samaná) to the foothills of the Cordillera Central about thirty miles north of Santo

Domingo. The western third of the range is rolling rather than craggy and permits fairly easy access from the capital city to the interior lowlands. The remainder is craggy and dissected by small streams that flow from its northern slopes to Samaná Bay and larger ones that flow southward to the Caribbean. Elevations are generally under 1,000 feet, except in the extreme east where a few isolated promontories rise to over 2,000 feet.

Lowlands

The country's lowlands consist for the most part of long valleys that, like the mountains that define them, extend in a northwesterly direction from origins close to the Caribbean Sea to corresponding lowlands in Haiti. In these, the fertile alluvial soils of their flood plains and terraces are suitable for intensive agriculture, and shallower soils provide good pasture.

The most extensive of the valleys, the Cibao Valley is the bread-basket of the country. Covering nearly 2,000 square miles, or 10 percent of the national territory, it has a longitudinal extent of about 140 miles from Samaná Bay on the east to the Haitian frontier; there, as the Northern Plain of Haiti, it continues into the neighboring republic. This heartland area lies between the Cordillera Central on the south and the Cordillera Septentrional on the north and has a valley floor width that varies between nine and seventeen miles. It breaks apart at the city of Santiago de los Caballeros. The portion to the east is known as the Vega Real, or the Royal Plain. This portion of the Cibao includes the country's richest and deepest agricultural land. The section on the western flank of Santiago is also fertile, but most of its land is arid and is becoming productive only as a result of the program for increasing irrigation.

Directly to the south of the Cibao, and separated from it by the crests of the Cordillera Central, is the San Juan Valley (Valle de San Juan), which extends across the frontier into Haiti as the Central Plateau. The valley, which is defined on its south by the Sierra de Neiba, has an extent of about 700 square miles and a length of seventy miles. It has a width of nearly thirty miles at the approaches to the Haitian border, but it narrows progressively to no more than five miles at its funnel extremity near the Caribbean Sea.

The third of the parallel valleys lies between the Sierra de Neiba and the Sierra de Baoruco and is known both as the Neiba Valley (Valle de Neiba) and as the Enriquillo Basin (Hoya de Enriquillo). It is about 750 square miles in extent, and most of the valley floor is below sea level. It extends about sixty miles from the Neiba Bay on the southeast to the frontier where it merges with the Cul-de-Sac of Haiti. The area is semiarid to arid, and the soils are generally of limited productivity. At one time this region was covered by a portion of the Caribbean Sea that separated the Sierra de Baoruco and the corresponding Haitian range from the mainland. At a later period, this strait was closed off at both ends by geological action, and gradual evaporation of the trapped waters has left brackish lakes and a series of ridge-like terraces on both flanks of the valley. The valley floor is made up of alluvial deposits with outcroppings of sedimentary and other rocks.

The largest of the other lowland regions is the Caribbean Coastal Plain (Llanura Costera del Caribe) that together with the foothills of the Cordillera Oriental mark its northern boundary. The plain covers more than 1,100 square miles. It is composed principally of a limestone platform formed by corals and alluvial deposition. Inland, there are calcerous soils of high fertility, and to the west of Santo Domingo there are infertile soils derived from acid clays. The region is the center of the country's cattle-raising and sugar industries.

In addition to the major lowland regions, there are numerous small valleys and basins, particularly in the Cordillera Central. Along the northern coastline, a discontinous coastal plain lies between the Atlantic Ocean and the Cordillera Septentrional. The soils are of good quality, but the lack of good passes through the mountains leaves the north coast relatively isolated from the rest of the country. In the far south, an arid coastal plain covers the lower part of the Pedernales Peninsula, and coastal plains of only moderate fertility surround the towns of Baní and Azua. In the northeast a narrow coastal plain separates the Cordillera Oriental and Samaná Bay. To its east, a low-lying area known as Los Haitises makes up most of San Cristóbal Province. It is composed of limestone and some alluvial soil and has altitudes reaching a maximum of about 800 feet.

Hydrography

The rivers of the Dominican Republic for the most part are shallow, subject to wide seasonal change in flow and consequently of little use for transportation. Flowing out of the several highlands in varying directions, they form a variety of drainage systems. The Cibao Valley has two systems. On its western flank it is drained into the Atlantic near Monte Cristi by the Yaque del Norte, the country's longest river; east of Santiago de los Caballeros in the Vega Real, the Yuna River drains eastward into Samaná Bay.

South of the Cordillera Central, the San Juan Valley is also divided between two hydrographic systems with opposite watersheds. Near the frontier it is drained by a tributary of the Artibonito River (Río Artibonito), a stream that continues westward across the border as the principal watercourse of Haiti; to the southeast, it is drained by the Yaque del Sur River, which flows into the Caribbean at Neiba Bay. The principal tributary of the Yaque del Sur, the San Juan, has a flow that increases fourfold between the driest and the wettest months.

Surface water in the arid Neiba Valley still farther to the south is lost through evaporation rather than runoff, although the Yaque del Sur River provides drainage for its southeastern portion as well as for the Neiba Valley. At the eastern end of the island, numerous rivers flowing southward from the Cordillera Oriental drain the Caribbean Coastal Plain. Among these, the Ozama River (Río Ozama), on which Santo Domingo is located, and the Macorís River (Río Macorís) are navigable for several miles from their mouths and are used for the transportation of sugar.

In 1972 dam construction was completed on the Yaque del Norte River at Tavera, located in the Cibao south of Santiago de los Caballeros, and was in progress on the Nizao River (Río Nizao) at Valdesia. The dams would create large artificial lakes; the first was to provide irrigation for an extensive acreage in the central Cibao, and the second was to supplement power and water supplies in Santo Domingo as well as to irrigate agricultural land along the Caribbean coast.

The largest of the country's natural lakes is Lake Enriquillo (Lago Enriquillo) in the Neiba Valley. A remnant of the strait that once occupied the area, its waters are 140 feet below sea level. Although it is fed by many streams from the surrounding mountains and has no outlet, the high rate of evaporation in the valley is causing its waters gradually to recede. The only other sizable body of inland water in the country is a smaller lake, located in the same valley near Neiba Bay. The most extensive marshland extends inland from the delta of the Yuna River on Samaná Bay. At the opposite end of the Cibao, there are salt marshes south of Monte Cristi Bay.

Coasts and Coastal Waters

Hispaniola, both in the Dominican Republic and in Haiti, is girded by an offshore rocky platform. On the Atlantic coast of the Dominican Republic, the platform is highly developed in the shallow waters of Samaná Bay, and continues in a westerly direction to the frontier, and along the Haitian coastline. Along the Atlantic coast it extends seaward from a few hundred yards to more than thirty miles at a maximum depth of 200 feet.

At irregular intervals the shelf rises to form tiny islands and jagged coral reefs that lie close to the surface, and represent hazards to navigation in waters to the east of Monte Cristi. The northern coast is marked by many sandy beaches and occasional rocky escarpments. Inland, the low but craggy ridges of the Cordillera Septentrional make access to the interior difficult. There are a few sheltered roadsteads, but the combination of dangerous offshore waters and the absence of ready access from the coast to the interior hinterland has discouraged port development, although most of the produce of the Cibao moves through these ports.

The Caribbean coast is better suited to port development. The submarine shelf is generally lower than along the northern coast, reefs and islets are relatively few, and access from ports to the interior is easier. A majority of the ports scattered along the thousand-mile coastline of the country are found on the Caribbean side. The best of the natural harbors are located on the broad estuaries of rivers that meet the Caribbean at Santo Domingo, San Pedro de Macorís, and La Romana.

Among the numerous islands scattered off the Dominican coastline, only three are permanently inhabited, and none is of significant economic importance. The largest, Saona Island (Isla Saona), has maximum dimensions of fifteen by four miles and is located at the southeastern tip of Hispaniola. The twenty square miles of Beata Island (Isla Beata) lie off the Pedernales Peninsula in the extreme west, and tiny Catalina Island (Isla Catalina) lies a few miles west of the sugar port of La Romana. In addition, off the coasts lie some 3,000 square miles of fishing banks with depths of less than 600 feet.

Climate

Located three to five degrees south of the Tropic of Cancer, the country enjoys, for the most part, a maritime climate in which the modifying influence of the surrounding ocean couples with the prevailing effect of the trade winds and the relatively high elevation of much of the terrain to provide generally pleasant conditions that are not characteristically tropical. The accumulated effect is one in which the variety of local climatic conditions is reflected in a corresponding variety in temperature, rainfall, and humidity patterns. These, in turn, result in a variety of conditions conducive to the growth of a wide variety of crops.

Average annual temperatures tend to differ principally in accordance with altitude of the locality. Averages of a little over 78°F are recorded in such widely scattered low-elevation locations as Santo Domingo at the western end of the Caribbean Coastal Plain, at Barahona on the southern coast at the foot of the arid Neiba Valley, at Pepillo Salcedo in the western extremity of the Cibao, and at Santiago de los Caballeros in the center of the country. In the town of San Juan, located in the foothills of the Cordillera Central at about 1,300 feet, averages are about three degrees lower. Above 3,600 feet frosts are common.

A moderate seasonal variation ranges from five to eight degrees in the capital city. In the winter months the temperature averages about 71°F; during the remainder of the year it rises to about 90°F during the daytime, but freshening trade winds make the nights comfortable.

The rainfall pattern is much more complex than that of the temperature. Precipitation tends to be heaviest in the north and east and diminishes to the south and west as these latter portions of the country are subjected, in varying degrees, to the rainshadow of the mountain systems that removes the moisture from the northeast trades. In general, rainfall is heavier in the relatively exposed Dominican Republic than in Haiti, which is to the west, where a further rainshadow effect is felt from the same mountains.

Heavy precipitation occurs on the entirely exposed Samaná Penin-

16

sula. At the town of Samaná, near its tip, it exceeds 100 inches annually; at Sánchez, near its base, it is about seventy-five inches. Along the northern coast the rain declines from nearly seventy inches annually at Puerto Plata to a scanty thirty-five inches at Monte Cristi, near the Haitian frontier. In the Cibao it declines to the west from some sixty-six inches at La Vega to forty inches at Santiago de los Caballeros. The weather station reporting the heaviest precipitation recorded is nearly 110 inches annually over a fifteen-year period on the northeastern slopes of the Cordillera Oriental. From there it drops to sixty-one inches to El Seibo in the middle of the Caribbean Coastal Plain and further to twenty-four inches at some places in the Neiba Valley. In most of the region adjacent to the Haitian frontier, excessively porous soils and a high rate of evaporation combine to make the moderate rainfall insufficient for the growth of crops without extensive irrigation.

The combined influences of the anticyclones and the trade winds bring about two fairly well-defined rainy seasons in much of the country, maximum precipitation occuring in the late spring and fall. On the northern coast between Puerto Plata and Luperón, however, rainfall is lowest in the summer months and heaviest in November and December; and in the vicinity of Lake Enriquillo the scanty rain occurs principally in three seasons that usually reach their maximums in January, May, and October. In the capital city about two-thirds of the annual precipitation falls in the May-to-November rainy season. A high year-round humidity, however, causes problems of mildew, mold, and oxidation of metal furnishings and appliances and contributes to respiratory ailments, skin irritations, and fungus.

The season of tropical weather disturbances extends from June through November and frequently generates squalls with winds of from thirty to forty-five miles an hour. Storms of hurricane velocity, however, do not ordinarily occur until August. The Dominican Republic lies in the general path of the hurricanes that generate in the southwest part of the Caribbean Sea. The two tracks of maximum intensity pass to east and west of the island country, but its exposed Caribbean coast sometimes feels their effect. In 1930 a hurricane with winds of up to 150 miles an hour killed some 2,000 people in Santo Domingo and caused an estimated RD$15 million (see Glossary) in damage.

Vegetation and Wildlife

The bulk of the natural vegetation belongs ecologically to the region of the low subtropical latitudes. Temperatures are influenced by elevation and degree of shelter from maritime influence. Sharp contrasts in rainfall between exposed coastal and deep intermontane valley localities in the lee of mountain ranges combine with varying soil conditions to make possible an enormous variety of vegetation. In all, there are nine basic and seven transitional vegetation zones. Because of a

17

generally good soil moisture in most of the country, the native species are subject to ready regeneration, and introduced species grow readily. Where the original forest cover has been cut away, second-growth scrub and guava thickets prevail.

Occupying nearly half of the national territory, the zone of sub-tropical moist forest is most nearly characteristic of the country's natural cover. In general, it includes the natural cover that occurs at lower levels in elevation. In the northwest it covers the floors and slopes of the valleys from which rivers empty into the Atlantic. It also includes most of the drainage system of the Cibao and of the river valleys that connect with the Yaque del Sur drainage system. In the east it covers most of the Samaná Peninsula and nearly all of the Caribbean Coastal Plain. In this extensive area much or most of the original forest cover has been removed for charcoal-making or for agriculture. Clearing for timber purposes has, for the most part, occurred at higher elevations.

Among the species characteristic of this zone are the mahogany and the royal palm. There is also the *capá*, a West Indian tree used extensively in shipbuilding. Small clumps of second growth that occur in pastures and along the courses of streams include the jagua palm, lancewood, yellowwood, cashew, and logwood. In savannas there are malpighia, ground oak, and other growths. Dragon tree, sea grape, and red mangrove abound in coastal marshlands and swamps.

In this vegetational zone and throughout the country, the royal palm is among the most conspicuous of the trees. It grows in clumps or in isolation at all but the highest elevations. It is encountered in most localities but is most frequently found in the Vega Real. Its nuts are useful as feed for hogs, its fronds are useful for thatch, and its trunk is used as a kind of soft, easily hewn lumber. Near the coast the natural cover in many localities has been replaced by eucalyptus and several kinds of pine.

Most of the remainder of the country is composed of lower montane and subtropical wet forest. It occurs principally on the slopes of the mountain ranges. Soils tend to be shallow and suitable only for forest or for plantation culture. In the flatlands, savanna grasses or dry forest prevail.

In the early 1970s the remaining natural pine forest cover constituted less than 5 percent of the national territory—most of it on the slopes of the Cordillera Central—and the balance, principally on the two parallel ranges to its south. A slightly smaller proportion remained covered by mixed forest, including various broadleaf species, such as cedar, ebony, mahogany, and almond trees, in the moist forests of the Cordillera Central and on the northern slopes of the Cordillera Oriental. Slash-and-burn land clearing by squatters had caused havoc in the forest areas of the mountains and had been coupled with overcutting of timber lands. The National Forest Service, established after the termination of the Trujillo regime, had discouraged forest clearing by squatters, however, and in 1967 national legislation made it—according to a Dominican tourist-trade issuance—a crime to kill a tree.

The Island of Hispaniola has no indigenous land mammals other than a few rodents, including a rare species called the *jutia*. Birdlife, however, is plentiful. A wide variety of tropical wildfowl with bright plumage is supplemented seasonally by visitations of ducks, doves, and several varieties of pigeon. Flocks of flamingos are found in the waters of Lake Enriquillo and in the delta of the Yuna River.

Although there are no indigenous snakes, alligators and marine turtles abound. Freshwater fish are not important, but coastal and offshore waters provide an enormous variety of marine life. Samaná Bay has mackerel, red snapper, kingfish, and shrimp. Bonito and tarpon are important game fish offshore (see ch. 9).

Fishing legislation enacted in 1962 protects some of the marine species. Marine turtles cannot be taken on beaches while nesting or while preparing nests. Spiny lobsters cannot be taken while spawning or when under a stipulated minimum in length; and the law prohibits seining with nets under a minimum dimension in mesh. Other provisions provide protection for additional species of fish as well as for mollusks, crustaceans, and aquatic mammals.

Minerals

The principal revenue-producing mineral exploited during the 1960s was bauxite extracted from the south slopes of the Sierra de Baoruco in Pedernales Province. There was a limited production of copper near San Cristóbal to the west of Santo Domingo, and in La Vega Province. Production of high-grade black magnetic oxide iron ore from a small deposit in Santiago Rodríguez Province ceased in 1961, but further exploration in the vicinity was reported in 1970. Salt and gypsum were produced in considerable quantity from deposits in the Neiba Valley; the salt comes from an almost inexhaustible supply contained in a ten-mile-long mountain of pure salt, and the almost pure gypsum deposits near the port of Barahona are of massive proportions. Production of ferronickel from a major nickel deposit at Bonao in La Vega Province commenced in 1972 (see ch. 9).

There has been intermittent and limited production of placer gold in Cordillera Central since early colonial days. Other minerals that have been mined from time to time include limestone, granite, marble, travertine, and common and glass sands. In Samaná Province a road ten miles in length is said to be paved with marble from adjacent deposits, and in 1969 the government was reported studying bids for exploitation of manganese deposits.

An official Dominican map shows the area having the greatest mining possibilities to correspond roughly to the Cordillera Central. The highlands skirting the southwest coast are also extensively mineralized, however, and few provinces are without known mineral resources of some kind. Minerals reported to exist in varying quantities, but not yet commercially exploited, include alabaster, amber, graphite, lead, magnesium, molybdenum, onyx, phosphates, pyrites, sulfur, tin, titanium, and zinc. Nineteenth-century records tell of findings of yellow quartz, carnelian, jasper, and agate.

Coal, reported in Puerto Plata and El Seibo provinces, has not been discovered in commercial quantities. Exploration for petroleum began in the 1860s, and seeps in Azua Province led to test drillings and a limited production from 1904 to 1907 and briefly in 1939, but followup prospecting in the 1940s and 1950s was unsuccessful. In the early 1970s some hope for the discovery of petroleum in commercial quantities persisted. Oil seeps had been reported in Barahona Province, and the sedimentary valleys and basins of the western part of the country had characteristics meeting the conditions necessary for the formation and storage of hydrocarbon fuels.

SETTLEMENT PATTERNS

In the early 1970s the country's population averaged about 220 persons per square mile, a proportion far greater than the thirty-five-per-square-mile average for nineteen Latin American countries but well below the average for other Caribbean countries. The population was unevenly distributed. There were no remaining large frontier areas of land awaiting settlement, and unused and imperfectly exploited lands remained in considerable quantity. These were scattered about the country in various localities—particularly along the north-facing piedmont of the Cordillera Central and along the north coast near Puerto Plata.

The public program for the settlement of these lands reached its zenith during the later years of the Trujillo regime, when more than 100,000 Dominican and immigrant colonists were placed in farm villages. Many of these colonies proved to be unsuccessful, however, and the colonization efforts made at later dates under 1962 agrarian reform legislation were secondary to settling of farmers on an individual basis (see ch. 9).

In 1972 the pattern of agricultural landholding remained one in which many small farmers lived in farm villages or on isolated farms alongside extensive plantations and ranches located principally in the Caribbean Coastal Plain and in the Cibao. In 1960, 45.4 percent of the cultivable land was controlled by 1 percent of the landowners, and in 1970 the Autonomous University of Santo Domingo estimated that 450,000 farmers were working unprofitably small plots of land.

In the early 1970s about half of the population was concentrated in the Vega Real portion of the Cibao Valley between the cities of Santiago de los Caballeros and San Pedro de Macorís, where the population exceeded 600 per square mile, and along the northern coast. One-

71,402
55,151
43,941
42,473
37,889
36,722
32,248
32,181
31,085
27,111
829

third was located in the capital city and on the sugar and cattle lands of the Caribbean Coastal Plain between the cities of La Romana and San Cristóbal. Most of the remainder was scattered along the southwest coast, in the extreme northwest and northeast, in the intermontane valleys of the Cordillera Central, and along the Haitian frontier.

Largely as a consequence of their relatively ready accessibility, the slopes of the Cordillera Central, the Cordillera Septentrional, and the Cordillera Oriental had been extensively cleared for agriculture. Because little or no consideration had been given to crop selection and soil maintenance, however, the soil had become depleted, and the population density remained relatively low. The foothill spurs of the Cordillera Central and the higher slopes of the Sierra de Baoruco and the Sierra de Neiba enjoyed climatic conditions well suited to human habitation, but the population remained sparse because of low fertility of the soils, poor communications, and the inability of settlers to develop effective techniques for the use of these lands.

The Trujillo regime established numerous agricultural colonies in order to increase and diversify agricultural production and to occupy more firmly the more sparsely settled and remote parts of the national territory. It also aimed at reducing urban slum problems by providing destinations other than the increasingly crowded urban localities for displaced excess farm labor and by endeavoring to attract members of the urban unemployed.

The most successful of the colonization efforts, and those that did most to alter the pattern of rural settlement, were carried out near the Haitian frontier. Strings of agricultural colonies established in previously underutilized lands had the effect of changing a poor grazing region not yet effectively incorporated into the national territory into an economically viable and socially modern section of the country. A colony was established on irrigated land north of Lake Enriquillo, and a string of colonies was planted along a new all-weather road following the line of the frontier in the mountainous interior. In the northwest, between the towns of Monte Cristi and Dajabón, the colonization program was assisted by the Jesuit Order of the Catholic Church, which established a frontier mission providing religious, educational, and social services in the area. In addition, irrigation projects made possible the extension of settlement along the flood plain and terraces of the Yaque del Norte River west of Santiago de los Caballeros. Roadbuilding, as well as irrigation, was an integral part of the colonization program, and each colony was made accessible to an all-weather highway; no colony established was more than eight hours distant from Santo Domingo by motortruck.

In 1970 Santo Domingo had more than 40 percent of all of the urban population and was more than four times the size of Santiago de los Caballeros, its nearest rival (see Population Structure and Dynamics, this ch.). It owed its size in large measure to its site on a protected harbor at the mouth of the Ozama River and to a strategic location having ready access to the Caribbean Coastal Plain, to the Cibao Valley, and to the smaller coastal plains surrounding the towns of Azua and Baní, to the west of the city. Several other major urban centers, such as Puerto Plata and Montecristi on the Atlantic Coast and San Pedro de Macorís and La Romana on the Caribbean, were located on good harbors. Because of the lack of navigable rivers, urban centers of the interior were not, for the most part, located on watercourses. Santiago de los Caballeros on the Yaque del Norte was the only important city situated on a major river. A majority of the urban localities of the interior had grown up as administrative and market centers for agricultural hinterlands of sufficient size and productivity to support them.

POPULATION STRUCTURE AND DYNAMICS

The country's population as counted provisionally in the 1970 census was 4,011,000. According to earlier census data, the totals had been 3,047,000 in 1960; 2,136,000 in 1950; and 1,479,000 in 1935. These figures reflect annual growth rates averaging 2.4 percent annually between 1935 and 1950, 3.6 percent between 1950 and 1960, and 3 percent between 1960 and 1970. The population total revealed by the 1970 census was somewhat lower than had been estimated, and authorities had predicted that an annual growth rate of as high as 3.6 would prove to have been continued during the 1960s. The lower reported rate may have reflected a census underenumeration or the heavy flow of emigration that occurred during the decade.

United Nations estimates show a crude birth rate of 48.5 per thousand of the population and a crude death rate of 14.7 for the 1965–70 period, an infant mortality rate of 61.9 per thousand for 1969, and a 1959–61 life expectancy at birth of 57.15 years for males and 58.59 years for females. Government estimates for 1960 showed the crude birth rate to have been 47.47, the crude death rate to have been 16.32, the infant death rate to have been 110.42, and life expectancy at birth for the population as a whole to have been 51.5 years. Both series of estimates on birth and death rates are much higher than the civil registration statistics, which are known to be incomplete, particularly in rural areas. Birth rates are estimated to have been underenumerated by 20 percent, and general mortality rates, by 40 percent.

Males and females are approximately equal in number. Census figures show males to have been in scanty majorities of 6,000 in 1950; 24,000 in 1960; and 33,000 in 1970 (see table 1). Under the age of fifteen, males outnumbered females; between the ages of fifteen and thirty-nine, females were in the majority. In the forty- to sixty-four-year age group, males were in the majority; and at the age of sixty-five or older, females again were slightly more numerous than males. The proportion of the population under the ages of fifteen rose from more than 45 percent of the total in 1950 to 46 percent in 1960 and 47 percent in 1970.

Population by Age Group and Sex, 1950, 1960, and 1970
(in thousands)

	Age Group							Total
	0–4	5–9	10–14	15–19	20–39	40–64	Over 65	
......	189	151	142	102	302	156	29	1,071
......	187	147	135	124	304	136	32	1,065
....	376	298	277	226	606	292	61	2,136
....	283	246	204	133	398	226	46	1,536
male..........	277	241	190	153	411	195	44	1,511
Total..........	560	487	394	286	809	421	90	3,047
1970								
Male.............	372	325	267	176	524	299	59	2,022
Female..........	364	316	251	201	541	256	60	1,989
Total[2]..........	736	641	518	377	1,065	555	119	4,011

[1] Figures for 1955 and 1960 as per censuses for those years; 1970 figures are from preliminary data.
[2] Structure of sex and age groups based on 1960 census.

Source: Adapted from Dominican Republic, Secretariado Técnico de la Presidencia,
    Oficina Nacional de Estadística, *República Dominicana en Cifras, 1970*, V, 1970,
    p. 14.

During these years, the proportion aged forty and over remained at between 16 and 17 percent of the total, and the median age declined from about eighteen years in 1950 to less than seventeen in 1970.

The urban sector of the population increased from 23.8 percent in 1950 to 30.3 percent in 1960 and to 40 percent according to the preliminary 1970 census figures. Urban localities are defined as administrative centers of municipalities and municipal districts that include some suburban zones of rural character. Urban migration was actively discouraged by the Trujillo regime, and the increase in the rate of migration registered during the 1960s reflected the lifting of this restriction. In 1970 there were fourteen urban centers with populations in excess of 20,000, but only the capital city and Santiago de los Caballeros were true cities (see table 2). The remainder were large market towns less concerned with such urban undertakings as industry than with the provision of services to their agricultural hinterlands. While the urban centers were growing in population, the number of small farms in the countryside was increasing through fragmentation.

The heaviest participation in urban migration was by girls and women. Between 1950 and 1960 the urban female population increased from 25.8 percent to 32.5 percent of the total, while the urban proportion of males increased from 21.8 to 28 percent. This sustained urban preponderance of females reflects a relatively large number of young

Table 2. Dominican Republic, Cities with Populatio[n]
1950, 1960, and 1970*

City	195[0]		
Santo Domingo	181,55[ ]		
Santiago de los Caballeros	56,558		
San Francisco de Macorís	16,083		
San Pedro de Macorís	19,876		
Barahona	14,654		
La Romana	14,074	2[2]	
San Juan	9,920	21,6[ ]	
Puerto Plata	14,843	18,530	
La Vega	14,200	19,830	
Mao	6,611	17,550	
San Cristóbal	9,723	16,580	25,[ ]
Baní	10,210	14,570	23,71[0]
Higüey	5,382	10,560	21,741
Bonao	4,723	12,090	20,159

*Figures for 1950 and 1960 as per censuses for those years; 1970 figures are from preliminary data.

Source: Adapted from Dominican Republic, Secretariado Técnico de la Presidencia, Oficina Nacional de Estadística, *República Dominicana en Cifras, 1970*, V, 1970, p. 15.

women who have been unable to find employment in rural localities and who have migrated to the cities and towns in search of jobs.

Exact measurement of the volume of external migration is made difficult or impossible by two factors. First, an undetermined but probably large number of Dominicans who leave the country as tourists never return or remain absent for protracted periods. Second, a substantial illegal migration of Haitian nationals has usually been tolerated because of the need for their services during the sugar harvest. According to the National Statistical Office, however, during the 1950s the number of persons entering the country to reside exceeded the number of long-term departures by 2,364. During the 1960s the trend was reversed, and a negative balance of 84,432 resulted. The effect of this recorded shift of population dynamics was intensified by the fact that most of the Dominican emigrants were between the ages of twenty and forty years, the population group with both the highest rates of fertility and the lowest of mortality.

Immigration had a substantial effect on the composition of the population during the Trujillo regime. Beginning in the late 1930s and continuing through the 1950s, the regime sponsored the immigration of certain alien elements, principally as agricultural colonists. These included Spanish Republicans, Jewish refugees from Europe, Hungarians, Japanese, and some others. In general, this series of experiments was not a success. A majority of the Japanese eventually returned to their homeland, and the Spanish Republicans, to Mexico. In 1963 the

Israeli consul general in Santo Domingo reported that no more than 160 out of 506 Jewish families who had entered as agricultural colonists remained in the country. In the late 1960s the reported flow of legal immigrants was no more than about 300 annually. Earlier data were not of significance because they had included returning residents.

In the 1960s the principal alien element in the country was composed of Haitians who were estimated to include anywhere from 20,000 to as many as ten times that number. Most had entered illegally, many had taken Dominican wives, and the presence of so many Haitians in the country represented a continuing cause of tension between the two nations.

During the 1960s the effect of emigration on the population structure was much more important than that of immigration. The approximately 100,000 Dominicans entering the United States legally from the Dominican Republic represented the highest per capita immigration to the United States from Latin America during the decade. An undetermined additional number are believed to have entered the country illegally or to have remained after having entered temporarily on tourist visas.

Most of these migrants have gone to New York City. Informal canvasses have revealed that most of these have left the country for political reasons or in order to accumulate savings. Most intended to return to their country. Estimates of the number clustered in New York City during 1971 ranged from the 100,000 estimated by the Dominican consulate general to the 200,000 estimated by local Dominican community leaders. Whatever the actual figure, New York must have at least the third largest, and probably the second largest, Dominican population of any city in the world.

POPULATION PROBLEMS

In 1972 both the Dominican government and the better educated portion of its population had become aware of the problem implicit in the country's high rate of population growth. During the Trujillo era, however, the historical fear of Haitian invasion coupled with the availability of much unoccupied land had given rise to an attitude that encouraged rather than discouraged untrammeled population growth. A more thoughtful attitude began to emerge after the Trujillo downfall, but the old views remained alive among conservative elements of the population, and the first family-planning initiatives were private in inspiration and deliberately low-key in presentation.

A beginning was made in 1965 when a few Protestant religious leaders and professional people formed an informal group called Friends of Family Planning (Amigos de Planificación Familiar—APF) with financial help from the Church World Service organization. It joined forces with an evangelical church organization in opening the country's first family-planning clinic in Las Minas, a working-class suburb of

Santo Domingo, and in distribution of contraceptive devices in Santo Domingo and elsewhere in the country.

A reluctance to appear too closely associated with Protestant churches led in 1966 to a restructuring of the APF as the Dominican Association for Family Welfare (Asociación Dominicana Pro Bienestar de la Familia—ADPBF); its directorate included a broad participation of academic and professional communities, including several prominent Catholic physicians. The restructured organization became affiliated with the International Planned Parenthood Federation.

Relations between the ADPBF and the Dominican government were amicable, if distant, and the Church World Service was given authorization to import contraceptives on a duty-free basis by classifying them as religious educational materials. During 1966 and 1967 the government refrained from formulating a population-control policy. President Joaquín Balaguer on several occasions acknowledged the existence of a serious demographic problem, however, and at the end of 1967 the Dominican Republic joined twenty-nine other nations in subscribing to a declaration that was sponsored by the United Nations and which placed the signatory states clearly among those favoring family planning. At the same time, Dominican family-planning services were added to the maternal and infant care activities of the public health program.

An executive order issued in February of 1968 created a public entity named the National Population and Family Council (Consejo Nacional de Población y Familia—CNPF) to study all aspects of population growth. The secretary of state for public health was to serve as ex-officio president. The organization had already been activated when a five-year program for it was approved in late 1968. The basic goals for achievement by 1973 were a birth rate reduced to thirty-seven per 1,000 coupled with a population growth rate down to 2.7 percent.

By the end of 1968 there were nine government-sponsored family-planning clinics, and by the end of 1970 there were thirty-three, including five in Santo Domingo, two in Santiago de los Caballeros, two in La Romana, and one in each of twenty-four places scattered about the country. A goal of 100 clinics was set for mid-1973.

The initial record of accomplishment in family planning was modest in terms of cases. By the end of 1968 the clinics had assisted a little more than 4,000 patients in beginning birth control practices, and by the end of 1970 the number had risen only to about 37,000. The public CNPF, however, had maintained an effective working relationship with the private ADPBF in the training of personnel and in the development of sex education.The program included lectures and television programs and the publication of a monthly newsletter by the ADPBF. In 1970 legislation was enacted exempting contraceptives from customs duties and prescribing the fixing of prices.

The Roman Catholic Church furnished little initial opposition; in general, its reaction was one of stressing the importance of responsible parenthood as opposed to direct birth-control measures. Several Catholic organizations cooperated with the ADPBF in development of sex education programs. After the Dominican government officially interested itself in family planning, however, the church became concerned over the alleged CNPF policy of giving preference to the distribution of contraceptives over education in responsible behavior. As a consequence, at the end of 1970 the Roman Catholic bishops of the country asked the government to discontinue family-planning programs in the numerous public hospitals where nuns were employed.

Opposition came also from the political Left and from some public officials who disputed the indispensability of population control as a concomitant to national economic and social development. Opposition was generally minimal, however. At the end of 1970 it was estimated that only about 4 percent of the women of childbearing age were receiving family-planning assistance; nevertheless, the framework of a substantial program had been established, and the number of participants was growing. Almost all of the service was provided in urban localities, but in 1971 the British government had contributed three mobile units designed for bringing family planning to the countryside as well.

LABOR FORCE

The labor force was estimated to have increased from 881,000 economically active persons in 1960 to 1,102,000 in 1970 by the International Labor Organization (ILO), which also projected an increase to 1,421,000 in 1980. These figures represented participation rates (percentages of the total population) of 28.52 percent in 1960, 27.43 percent in 1970, and 26.35 percent in 1980.

The most recent actual count of the labor force available in 1972 was that taken in connection with the 1960 population census, which showed the total to have been 820,710 persons aged fifteen and over. The discrepancy between the ILO esimate for 1960 and the census figure is partially accounted for by the fact that the census was a count of economically active persons aged fifteen and over and did not include about 35,000 working young people who were under that age.

The census showed that by sector of employment some 61.4 percent were engaged in agriculture and related activities; 11.4 percent, in industry; 20.4 percent, in personal and other service occupations; and 6.8 percent, in occupations not adequately described. It was later determined, however, that at least 1.5 percent of those counted in occupations not adequately described were engaged in the manufacturing industry. Scattered estimates in the late 1960s and early 1970s indicated that there had been little change in these proportions other than a slight gain in the urban employment sectors, principally in services, at the expense of agriculture as a consequence of the substantial migration of working-age people from rural to urban localities during the 1960s.

The census also showed some 0.9 percent of the working population to have been employers; 43.9 percent, self-employed; 44.1 percent, wage and salary earners; and 11.1 percent, unpaid family workers. Some three-fourths of the employers and self-employed were in the agricultural sector; nearly half of the remainder were engaged in commercial services, and the manufacturing industry ranked third. Almost all of the unpaid family workers were in the agricultural sector, with the exception of a small number in commercial services. Among wage and salary earners, the proportions were somewhat more evenly distributed. Agriculture represented the largest with about one-third of the total. Personal services came next and was followed in order by manufacturing industry and commercial services.

Relatively few women are economically active. According to the ILO estimates, females made up about 10.3 percent of the labor force in 1960 and 11 percent in 1970 and were expected to reach 11.8 percent in 1980. The gradual increase in participation coincided with the continuing migration of young rural women to urban localities where job opportunities for them were relatively more plentiful. According to a 1963 estimate, the proportion of females in the urban labor force had more than doubled since 1950.

Data from the 1960 census showed that the bulk of the economically active females were engaged in the service sector—60 percent of the total in personal services alone and 13 percent in commercial services. Some 13 percent were employed in the manufacturing industry (primarily in textiles and clothing) and 10 percent in agriculture. The remaining few were scattered in other industrial and service occupations or were in occupations not identified.

The census shows also that the median age for economically active women in 1960 was about thirty years; for men it was in the mid-thirties. The median was older for men because a relatively larger proportion continued active after middle age. In the fifteen- to nineteen-year age bracket, the participation rate was 70 percent for males and 9 percent for females. Men maintained a near maximum participation rate averaging 95 percent or higher between the ages of twenty and sixty-five. For women, participation declined irregularly after maintaining a maximum averaging a little more than 12 percent between the ages of twenty and forty-nine. Over the age of sixty-five years, the rate was over 68 percent for men and 4.3 percent for women. ILO estimates for 1970 and 1980 show a gradually decreasing proportion both of younger and older working people of both sexes.

High unemployment is chronic. No statistics are available, but it was estimated by the Secretariat of Labor to have reached 31 percent in 1965 and to have remained at over 20 percent during later years of the decade. Other estimates during the late 1960s and early 1970s range as

high as 35 percent nationwide and 50 percent went for the slum neighborhoods of Santo Domingo, which were flooded with unskilled
migrants from the countryside. In the early 1970s the lowest of the
estimates available was 15 percent.

Unemployment is probably the country's most serious socioeconomic
problem. New jobs are created slowly, and these are to a large extent
offset by dismissals resulting from streamlining of operations and
modernization of equipment while the population growth calls for the
creation of 40,000 or more new jobs a year. Less pressing, but also
serious, is a chronic underemployment rate estimated to be at least 20
percent of the labor force. In the countryside it is seen principally in
excessive availability of family labor on the small farms and in the
seasonal nature of employment on the plantations. In urban localities
it is seen in the many workers—frequently unskilled migrants from
the countryside—employed as peddlers or in marginal personal services occupations. To meet the current unemployment and underemployment problems and to make provision for the rapidly increasing
working-age population, the 1970-74 National Development Plan called
for the creation of 211,500 new jobs—about 20 percent of the 1970 total.

CHAPTER 3

HISTORICAL SETTING

Throughout its history the society of the Dominican Republic has reflected conditions that developed during the colonial period; and Santo Domingo, as the first permanent Spanish settlement in the New World, set the pattern for economic, political, and ecclesiastical institutions in all the Spanish American colonies. An economy based primarily on agriculture is a legacy of colonial times when, failing to find gold and silver in substantial quantities, Spaniards who did not move on to Mexico and Peru became ranchers.

The colony occupied a potentially strategic position in the Antillean chain of islands between the Atlantic Ocean and the Caribbean Sea and the Gulf of Mexico. But when it became apparent that it lacked significant amounts of natural wealth that could be exploited, adventurers sought their fortunes on the mainland, and the colony became little more than a way-station between Spain and the conquered lands on the continent.

The colony, unlike most others in Latin America, lacked a strong tripartite ruling elite of landowners, the Roman Catholic Church, and the military to manage the political, economic, and social life of the country. After the first half of the sixteenth century Spanish influence and control were neither strong nor continuous, and occupations of the country by France, Haiti, and the United States weakened the cultural legacy of Spain.

Economic problems as well as political turmoil, civil wars, assassinations, and authoritarian rule have plagued the society from the beginning. Large-scale emigrations of the better educated, white elements of the population and members of the Roman Catholic clergy prevented the consolidation of a ruling elite until the late nineteenth century and militated against the accumulation and perpetuation of economic and political power in any single group or class.

The total absence of an Indian population in Hispaniola is traceable to cruel treatment of the indigenous people and to diseases brought by the settlers, which virtually wiped out the Indians after the colony was established by Christopher Columbus in 1493. The largely mulatto population is descended from the Spanish colonists and the Negro slaves imported to work on the plantations. In the latter half of the twentieth century many were illiterate, but progress was being made in the development of educational facilities.

Before the assumption of power by Rafael Leónidas Trujillo Molina, who ruled from 1930 to 1961, the country never had a regularly organized military establishment of any consequence. Irregular forces, recruited from idlers and the unemployed, were maintained by local political leaders. Persistent internal political conflicts, long periods of repression under dictators, and military occupation by alien forces hampered the formation of purely domestic political institutions and development of responsible domestic leadership. In the countryside, civil disorders and foreign incursions ravaged the land and repeatedly destroyed the agricultural economy.

The assassination of Trujillo in 1961 was followed by a period of turbulence. The growing political power of the urban and rural lower classes was demonstrated by the election to the presidency in 1962 of the exiled leader Juan Bosch, but he was deposed and deported after barely seven months in office. A civil war, which broke out in April 1965, ended after the United States and the Organization of American States (OAS) intervened, utilizing both military force and negotiation in efforts to restore order. In January 1966 Joaquín Balaguer, a former follower of Trujillo supported by a group that included other former Trujillo adherents, was elected to the presidency.

THE SPANISH COLONY, 1493–1795

Hispaniola (La Isla Española), now divided between Haiti and the Dominican Republic, was sighted by Columbus in 1492 toward the end of his first voyage of discovery. Columbus and his companions found the island inhabited by a large population of friendly Taino (Arawak) Indians who made the explorers welcome. The land was fertile, but of much more importance to the Spaniards was the discovery that gold could be obtained either by barter with the natives or by extraction from alluvial deposits on the island.

After several attempts to plant colonies along the north coast of Hispaniola, Spain's first permanent settlement in the New World was established on the southern coast at the present site of Santo Domingo, capital of present-day Dominican Republic. Indications of the presence of gold and of tractable natives who could be used as laborers attracted many newcomers from Spain during the early years. The greater part were adventurers—fortune seekers who at least initially were more interested in acquiring sudden wealth than in settling on the land. Their relations with the Taino Indians, whom they ruthlessly maltreated, deteriorated from the very beginning. Aroused by continued seizures of their food supplies, other exactions, and abuse of their women, the Indians rebelled—only to be crushed decisively in 1495.

Columbus, who ruled the colony until 1499, attempted to put an end to the more serious abuses to which the Indians were subjected by prohibiting foraging expeditions against them and by regulating the informal taxation imposed by the settlers. This milder form of exploitation caused active opposition on the part of the settlers. To meet their demands, Columbus devised the *repartimiento* system of land settlement and native labor under which a settler, without assuming any obligation to the authorities, could be granted in perpetuity a large tract of land together with the services of the Indians living on it.

The *repartimiento* system did nothing to improve the lot of the Indians, and the Spanish Crown changed it by instituting the system of *encomienda* in 1503. In theory, all the land became the property of the crown and the Indians were considered tenants on royal land. The crown's right to service from the tenants could be transferred in trust to individual Spanish settlers by formal grant. Those awarded such grants were entitled to certain days of labor from the tenants who became their charges and, in return, were obligated to provide for their physical well-being, instruct them in Christianity, and pay the crown a tribute. In theory an *encomienda* did not involve ownership of land, but, in practice, possession was gained through other means.

The hard work demanded of the Indians and the privations they suffered proved the undoing of the *encomienda* system on Hispaniola, although it was to flourish for many years in the mainland colonies. The Indian population died off rapidly from exhaustion, starvation, disease, and other causes. By 1548 the Taino population, estimated at about 1 million in 1492, had been reduced to approximately 500. The consequences were profound. A new labor force was required, a need accentuated by the expanding cultivation of sugarcane. Importation of Negro slaves began in 1503; by 1520, Negro labor was used almost exclusively.

The early grants of land without obligation under the *repartimiento* system resulted in a rapid decentralization of power. Each landowner possessed virtually sovereign authority. In addition, the island was dominated by its capital city, Santo Domingo, which was the seat of government for the Indies and drained the more vital elements from the surrounding countryside. Santo Domingo was oriented outward— toward continental America, which provided gold for the crown, and toward Spain, which provided the administrators, supplies, and immigrants for the colonies. There was little contact between the city of Santo Domingo and the hinterland. Any local government thus lacked vitality, and for practical purposes the countryside was privately ruled by the big landowners.

When the landowners demonstrated their power in the early years by conspiring against Columbus, the Spanish crown appointed Francisco de Bobadilla chief justice and royal commissioner in 1499. Bobadilla sent Columbus back to Spain in irons, but Queen Isabella soon ordered him released. Bobadilla was not successful in his administration of the colony and was replaced in 1503 by Nicolás de Ovando, who was appointed governor and supreme justice. Because of his success in initiating reforms desired by the crown—the *encomienda* system being among them—de Ovando was awarded the title of Founder of Spain's Empire in the Indies.

In 1509 Columbus' son, Diego, was appointed governor of the colony. Diego's ambition and the splendid surroundings he provided for himself aroused the suspicions of the crown. This resulted in the establishment of the *audiencia*, a new political institution in the colony in 1511 intended to check the power of the governor. It was established throughout Latin America. The first *audiencia* was simply a tribunal composed of three judges with jurisdiction extending over all the West Indies. In this region it formed the highest court of appeals.

The tribunal's influence grew, and in 1524 it was officially made the Royal Audiencia of Santo Domingo with jurisdiction in the Caribbean; the coast of Central America and Mexico; and the northern coast of South America, including all of Venezuela and part of Colombia. As a court representing the crown, the *audiencia*'s powers expanded to include administrative, legislative, and consultative functions; and the number of judges increased greatly. In criminal cases the *audiencia*'s decisions were final, but important civil suits could be appealed to the Royal and Supreme Council of the Indies (Real y Supremo Consejo de las Indias) in Spain.

The Council of the Indies, created by Charles V in 1524, was the Spanish crown's main agency for directing colonial affairs. Spanish power over the American colonies was vested in the crown, and the Council of the Indies was subject only to the crown. During most of its existence, the council had almost absolute power in making laws, administering justice, controlling finance and trade, supervising the church, and directing armies.

The agency of the Council of the Indies that dealt with all matters concerned with commerce between Spain and the colonies in the Americas was the House of Trade (Casa de Contratación), organized in 1503. Trade was regulated primarily in the interests of the mother country. Monopoly seaports on either side of the Atlantic Ocean were designated to facilitate control by the Casa de Contratación and the collection of taxes. During most of the colonial period, overseas trade was confined largely to annual convoys between the monopoly ports. No trade was allowed between the colonies and countries other than Spain. Trade between the various colonies themselves was severely restricted. The effect was to hamper economic activity in the New World and to encourage contraband traffic.

The Roman Catholic Church became the primary agent in spreading Spanish culture in the Americas. The ecclesiastical organization developed for Santo Domingo and later established throughout Spanish America was based on a union of church and state that was closer in the Americas than in Spain. This affiliation of the church and the Spanish crown, independent of that existing in Spain, was known as the Royal Patronage of the Indies (Real Patronato de las Indias or, as it was called later, the Patronato Real).

The crown's jurisdiction over all ecclesiastical affairs was delineated in several pontifical documents issued between 1493 and 1508. These gave the Spanish crown dominion over the Indies, the responsibility of Christianizing the natives, the right to found churches and benefices, the right to the tithes of these churches, and the privilege of universal patronage over the church in the Indies. The first representatives of the Roman Catholic Church arrived in the New World with Columbus on his second voyage in 1493. In 1511 a bishopric was created in Santo Domingo, dependent upon the archbishop of Seville. This was the first Roman Catholic see in the New World. In 1547 it was made an archbishopric, also the first in the New World.

Santo Domingo's prestige began to decline in the first part of the sixteenth century with the conquest of Mexico by Hernán Cortés in 1521 and the discovery there, and later in Peru, of great wealth in gold and silver. This coincided with the exhaustion of the alluvial deposits of gold and the dying off of the Indian labor force in Santo Domingo. Large numbers of colonists left for Mexico and Peru, and new immigrants from Spain bypassed Santo Domingo for the greater wealth to be found in lands to the west. The population of Santo Domingo was greatly reduced; agriculture languished; and Spain soon became preoccupied with its richer and vaster colonies on the continent.

The stagnation that prevailed in the colony of Santo Domingo for the next 250 years was interrupted on several occasions by English and French attempts to breach Spain's economic and political monopoly in the New World. In the early years Santo Domingo had been the first port of call for Spanish ships. It therefore became the first place where the English and French attempted to establish a stronghold. In 1586 the English admiral, Sir Francis Drake, captured the city of Santo Domingo and collected a ransom for its return. In 1655 an English fleet commanded by Sir William Penn arrived at Santo Domingo in an attempt to occupy the island. After sustaining heavy losses, however, the English moved on to Jamaica.

The colonial government then abandoned the northern port cities of Puerto Plata, Monte Cristi, and Cap-Haïtien, where smugglers had based their operations. This opened the way for French buccaneers, who had a base on Tortuga Island (Ile de la Tortue) off the northwest coast of present-day Haiti, to move to Hispaniola in 1641 and found Port Margot, the first settlement on the western end of Haiti. The Spanish destroyed the buccaneers' settlements several times, but each time they returned.

The settlements on the western third of the island were finally stabilized in 1664 when the French government commissioned the French West India Company to colonize the area permanently. There was intermittent warfare between the French and Spanish settlers over the next three decades, but Spain, hard-pressed by warfare in Europe, did not maintain a strong enough garrison in Santo Domingo to secure the entire island against encroachment. In 1697, under the Treaty of Ryswick, Spain ceded the western third of the island to France. The exact boundary of this territory (Saint-Domingue—modern Haiti) was not established at the time of cession and remained in question until 1929.

During the first years of the eighteenth century the Spanish colony stagnated. Landowners did little with their huge holdings, and the sugar plantations along the southern coast were abandoned because of pirates. Trade was nearly nonexistent, and the small amount of domestic commerce was limited to the capital city.

After the Bourbon dynasty replaced the Hapsburgs in Spain in 1700, innovations—especially economic reforms—were introduced that gradually began to revive trade in Santo Domingo. The rigid controls and restrictions on commerce between the mother country and the colonies and among the colonies themselves were progressively relaxed. The last convoys sailed in 1737, and the system was abolished shortly thereafter. By the middle of the century immigration had increased, and more slaves were being imported.

In 1765 the Caribbean Islands were opened to almost unlimited trade with Spanish ports, and in 1774 trade was authorized between the Spanish colonies in America. Duties on many commodities were greatly reduced or removed altogether. By 1790 traders from any port in Spain could buy and sell anywhere in Spanish America, and by 1800 Spain had opened colonial trade to all neutral vessels.

As a result of the stimulus provided by these reforms, the population of the colony of Santo Domingo increased from about 6,000 in 1737 to approximately 125,000 in 1790. Of this number, about 40,000 were white landowners; about 25,000 were freedmen; and some 60,000 were slaves. The increased agricultural and commercial wealth supporting this population, however, could not match the opulence of the colony's neighbor on Hispaniola, French Saint-Domingue, where approximately 500,000 Negro slaves constituted the labor force. The Spanish did not attempt the intensive exploitation of the land that the French did and, as a result, the slave population was much smaller and subjected to a relatively mild form of servitude.

HAITIAN DOMINATION, 1795–1844

Racial tensions and discontent in French Saint-Domingue were catalyzed by news of the French Revolution of 1789. The slaves, led by Toussaint Louverture revolted in 1791, and a confused civil war ensued. At first Toussaint joined his Negro and mulatto army with Spanish forces based in Santo Domingo who were fighting against the French in Saint-Domingue. In 1794 he learned of the decree abolishing slavery in all the French colonies and decided to shift his allegiance. The French colonial forces and Toussaint together succeeded in driving the Spanish out of Saint-Domingue. Spain ceded Santo Domingo to France in 1795, and the French Convention made Toussaint governor of the French colony of Saint-Domingue.

In 1801 Toussaint marched into Santo Domingo, forced the surrender of the governor, and promulgated a constitution for the entire island, granting freedom to all the slaves. This caused many of the Spanish colonists to emigrate to neighboring Spanish colonies in Puerto Rico, Cuba, and Venezuela. It is estimated that in the decade beginning in 1795 the Spanish colony lost more than one-third of its population (over 40,000 people), the primary representatives of the country's wealth, education, and cultural tradition. By 1819 the population had diminished to about 63,000 people, many of whom were Negro.

In 1802 Napoleon Bonaparte, then ruling as First Consul of France, decided to tighten French rule on the island. He dispatched a powerful force under General Charles Victor Emanuel Leclerc, who established French control over Santo Domingo and captured Toussaint, sending him back to France in irons. Leclerc was defeated in Saint-Domingue in 1803 by Negro and mulatto forces led by Jean Jacques Dessalines, who had replaced Toussaint. On January 1, 1804, Dessalines proclaimed the independence of Saint-Domingue, which he renamed Haiti.

Although the French were driven out of Haiti, they remained in control of Santo Domingo until 1809 when, aided by the English, the Spanish colonists revolted and reestablished Spanish sovereignty. In 1814 Ferdinand VII came to the Spanish throne. Under his rule economic conditions deteriorated. Cash crops no longer were planted in the colony, and poverty was widespread. In 1821, under the leadership of José Núñez de Cáceres, the colonists rebelled. They deported the Spanish governor, declared their independence from Spain, and requested admittance to Simon Bolívar's newly formed Republic of Gran Colombia. Before the request could reach Bogotá, Haiti's president, Jean-Pierre Boyer, occupied the colony in 1822 and declared it subject to the laws of Haiti.

The 1822-42 period was an epoch of degradation for the country's people and institutions. Emigration increased as the remaining white Spanish colonists were victimized both by a tyrannical bureaucracy and by unpaid Haitian soldiers who lived off the land. The Haitian government pursued the policy of turning the entire island into a Negro state and, therefore, encouraged the emigration of white landowners while confiscating their property. All slaves were emancipated; government posts were filled with French-speaking mulattoes; and Haitian Negroes were settled in Santo Domingo.

President Boyer attempted to reestablish prosperity by enacting the Rural Code (Code Rural), which in essence established a combined system of forced agricultural labor and production incentives. Most Dominicans ignored the code, and President Boyer did not enforce it with any vigor. The production of sugar and tobacco was paralyzed, and the people were reduced to subsistence farming. The University of Santo Domingo was closed; all church properties were seized by the state; foreign clergy were deported; and the remaining clergy were cut off from papal supervision. Under these conditions the economy deteriorated, and the influence of the church was drastically reduced.

In spite of the terror and oppression there was no attempt to oust the Haitians until the return from Europe in 1833 of a young student, Juan Pablo Duarte. To accomplish his goal of making Santo Domingo independent and liberally governed, Duarte formed in 1838 a secret society, La Trinitaria, that had pledged to put an end to the Haitian occupation. Duarte was aided by Francisco del Rosario Sánchez and Ramón Mella; and many young Dominicans joined this revolutionary group.

The Haitians ignored the movement until President Boyer was replaced in 1843 by the more astute Charles Hérard-Rivière, who took steps to arrest the spreading disaffection. Duarte went into hiding and then escaped to Caracas, where he sought aid for his cause. The remaining Trinitarios (members of La Trinitaria), led by Sánchez and Mella, continued to organize the plot against the oppressors. Fearing that they were about to be betrayed, they seized the Ozama fortress in the capital on February 27, 1844, the date Dominicans designate as Independence Day. Surprised, the Haitian garrison of Santo Domingo offered little resistance and evacuated the city. The main provincial centers capitulated within a few days, and a provisional government representing the conspirators took control of the country.

INDEPENDENCE, 1844–1916

The newly independent Dominican Republic of the mid-nineteenth century differed substantially from the Spanish colony of Santo Domingo of the early sixteenth century. The native population of Indians had disappeared. Two substantial waves of emigration—one of which took place the middle of the sixteenth century and the other at the beginning of the nineteenth century—had weakened the landed, white, educated sector of the population who were the main representatives of the Spanish cultural tradition. The Haitian occupation had introduced a significant Negro element. The economy was paralyzed and the agricultural land neglected. The church had lost influence; its estates had been allowed to go to ruin; and its clergy had been reduced in number. There was no responsible leadership and no economic base or unified military power to support it.

Small groups contended for power. Duarte, Sánchez, and Mella—the liberal leaders of the revolutionary movement—initially held power and were intent upon maintaining the country's independence and building a constitutional and democratic government. They were opposed by a military faction led by General Pedro Santana who, still fearing Haitian invasions, supported the idea of placing the republic under the protection of some major power. In September 1844 Santana and his troops captured the capital. He then exiled the liberal leaders and proclaimed himself supreme chief of the republic.

Buenaventura Báez emerged as another strong leader who favored making the country a protectorate and challenged the power of Santana. These two men alternated in power until Santana's death in 1864. Their rivalry kept the country in almost continual turmoil, and their authoritarian and opportunistic rule set the pattern for Dominican politics in the latter half of the nineteenth century.

Successive Haitian invasions persisted until 1855, and fear of Haiti kept alive the desire to sacrifice national sovereignty for greater security under the flag of Spain, France, England, or the United States. All these powers refused to accept the Dominican Republic as a dependency until Spain, ruled by Isabella II and spurred by ambitions for new imperial greatness, again made the Dominican Republic a Spanish colony in 1861. Santana, then in control, was appointed captain general. Spanish officers took charge of Dominican troops, and high government and ecclesiastical posts were filled by Spaniards. Business deteriorated, taxes increased, and the ensuing discontent led to revolt and to a two-year struggle for the restoration of independence, which ended in 1865 when the Spanish forces left the country.

By this time the economy was seriously weakened. Years of invasions, revolutions, and guerrilla warfare had reduced the export trade to some hardwoods and a little tobacco. Food production was meager because of conscription of able-bodied farmers and destruction of crops by passing armies. In the cities commerce was stagnant because of a worthless currency. Neither independence nor Spanish occupation had arrested the economic decline that had begun with the Haitian occupation.

The withdrawal of the Spanish left the country under the control of revolutionary generals who competed for power. Between 1865 and 1882 there were seven successful revolutions and sixteen chief executives. The two major factions were headed by Báez, whose followers formed the Red Party, and by General Gregorio Luperón, whose followers formed the Blue Party. The continuing changes in regimes did not mean significant shifts in policy. Most governmental attention was devoted to securing new funds, usually in the form of foreign loans, in order to replenish the treasury and pay the current president's supporters. One attempt to secure financial aid was an offer to sell Samaná Bay (Bahía de Samaná) to the United States.

Some order was established in the country's political and economic affairs when General Luperón, assisted by his lieutenant, Ulises Heureaux, assumed the presidency in 1879. His regime, like that of his successor, Archbishop Fernando Arturo de Meriño, was devoted to reconstruction. The army was reorganized, salaries paid, foreign claims adjusted, and measures taken to promote economic recovery. For the first time in two decades the countryfolk could plant their fields without danger of being impressed into military service or having their crops destroyed.

Ulises Heureaux became president in 1882 and dominated the country for the next seventeen years as an unscrupulous dictator. Although the country was relieved of the political instability it had experienced since 1844, Heureaux's regime incurred a very large foreign debt that had serious consequences for the country in the twentieth century.

Heureaux's first two-year term was deceptively uneventful because of the restraint exercised upon his power by a united Blue Party leadership under Luperón. Because he could not succeed himself constitutionally, Heureaux supported the election of General Francisco Billini to the presidency, while attempting to destroy the unity of the Blue Party leaders. When Billini proved not to be a docile figurehead, Heureaux mounted an intrigue against him and forced his resignation. Vice President Alejandro Wos y Gil assumed office and appointed Heureaux commander in chief of the army. Heureaux was reelected to the presidency in 1886 and inaugurated in January of 1887, this time to hold office until his assassination in 1899.

To reduce the strength of the various political parties, Heureaux began a policy of blurring, if not eliminating, the distinctions between them. Leaders of all parties were included in his cabinet. Lower ranking party members were made government officials, and military leaders were urged to forget their nominal party affiliations through bribes. Those who persisted in political partisanship were either exiled or assassinated. Heureaux also encouraged young talent in his administration—individuals having no political loyalty except to the president. The only remaining political problems—the limitation on his term of office and the rule of no reelection—were overcome by a constitutional amendment drawn up by a subservient constitutional convention.

Heureaux maintained iron-clad control and in so doing stifled political, social, and economic initiative and responsibility. Once again, upper class white families began to emigrate to neighboring islands, but the number of those leaving was relatively small compared to the number involved in previous emigrations.

Heureaux quickly depleted the treasury and attempted to replenish it by exacting loans from private citizens, by printing large amounts of unsupported paper money, and by floating bond issues. Loans were obtained from European banking houses. Both were secured by hypothecating the country's customs revenues, and both were defaulted. Three loans then were obtained from a group of New York financiers, and again customs receipts were pledged. All three loans were defaulted. Heureaux attempted to settle his financial difficulties by offering either to sell the Samaná Peninsula (Península de Samaná) to the

United States or to make the entire country a United States dependency. Both proposals were rejected; and when Heureaux was assassinated in 1899, the Dominican Republic was approximately RD$32 million (1 peso equals US$1—see Glossary) in debt to foreign creditors—ten times the size of the debt when Heureaux first assumed office.

The assassination of Ulises Heureaux initiated another period of political turmoil during which two main factions, composed of the supporters of Horacio Vásquez and those of Juan Isidro Jiménez, contended for power, and the country went still deeper in debt. General Carlos F. Morales succeeded to the presidency in 1904. Confronted by the possibility of armed intervention by European powers to collect debts owed to their nationals, Morales turned to the United States for protection and financial assistance. His efforts to negotiate a treaty placing his country under direct United States protection for fifty years were unsuccessful. He did, however, reach an agreement with the United States for a customs receivership under which United States agents collected the duties and disbursed part of the revenue to the Dominican government and part to the foreign creditors.

These measures put the government's finances on the road to recovery but provoked accusations that the Morales government was pro-American and led to sharp political differences over the issue of United States "imperialism." Fearing loss of control, President Morales late in 1905 attempted a coup to oust dissidents in his own regime. The attempt failed, and Morales was given asylum in the United States legation. Ramón Cáceres was inaugurated president about a month later and remained in office until 1911. During his regime the country enjoyed a period of relative peace and prosperity. Order was maintained; the economy prospered; most of the foreign debt was liquidated; and civil liberties were respected. Cáceres, however, was assassinated in 1911. Civil war broke out and continued sporadically until 1916.

In 1914 the United States made an effort to put an end to the civil disorders that plagued the Dominican Republic by persuading the contending factions to accept a truce and by arranging to supervise national elections held in that year. Jiménez became president and, in a conciliatory move, he included representatives of nearly all political factions in his cabinet. Consequently, there was continual disagreement, particularly over policy toward the United States. Jiménez was threatened with impeachment by a hostile congress even though he refused to accept a United States proposal to appoint a financial adviser and create a national constabulary to be trained and commanded by United States officers. Revolts broke out in several regions of the country; rebel forces entered the capital and fighting began.

As Jiménez was rapidly losing control of the situation, United States Marines landed at Santo Domingo in May 1916 and occupied key areas in the country. Jiménez resigned, but his successor, Francisco

Henríquez y Carvajal, refused to accept a United States proposal that the United States help stabilize the situation by taking control of the government's finances and operating the constabulary. Unable to reach agreement with the Dominican government and unwilling to withdraw its forces at the almost certain expense of another outbreak of domestic violence, the United States installed its own military government.

UNITED STATES OCCUPATION, 1916–24

The military government that ruled the country between 1916 and 1924 was headed by an officer of the United States Navy, who was appointed governor. His cabinet was drawn from the United States forces because no Dominican would accept a portfolio. During the first two years of the occupation, the military government initiated the training of a National Constabulary; organized the public treasury; reduced the public debt from RD$12 million to RD$3.5 million and straightened out a confused land-claim situation. In addition, it instituted an ambitious roadbuilding and sanitation program and expanded primary education.

Upper class Dominicans would have nothing to do with an alien occupation force. They did not participate in the central government, nor did they join the officer corps of the National Constabulary. For this reason most of those recruited were individuals having fewer advantages, who sought a chance for advancement and power.

Trujillo was one of the early recruits in the newly organized constabulary. Through its ranks he rose to become chief of staff of the National Army and, eventually, the country's dictator.

Resentment of the occupation forces was widespread, and guerrilla fighting broke out in the eastern provinces. Part bandit, part insurrectionist, these bands occupied the attention of the marines for over five years.

Growing Dominican opposition to continuance of the occupation was aided by the victory of the Republican Party in the United States elections of 1920. The new administration put into effect a plan for gradual withdrawal. The first conciliatory step was the removal of an unpopular military governor. The second was the preparation of a detailed program of evacuation. Initially, the Dominicans were disappointed over the suggested length of time involved in the withdrawal. But negotiations between General Horacio Vásquez, his leading political rival, Federico Velásquez, and the United States Department of State established mutually acceptable plans for the selection of a provisional president and a schedule for elections and evacuation by the marines. In elections held in March 1924 General Vásquez was chosen president. With his inauguration in July 1924, the last of the United States forces left the country.

Dominican sovereignty had been restored. The finances of the country were in good order; an improved system of roads and sanitation had been built; educational facilities and public works had been expanded; and constitutional reforms had been introduced. Dominicans, however, had not taken part in governing their country during the occupation, and the old political habits and patterns of instability had not changed.

THE TRUJILLO ERA

Trujillo's rise to power occurred during the six years of the Vásquez administration. Vásquez' first four-year term was relatively uneventful, although the economy stagnated and the government went deeply into debt. Before his term expired, Vásquez amended the constitution to prolong the presidency to six years and later repealed the ban on reelection. These maneuvers not only created a split in his party but general disapproval throughout the country.

As the elections of 1930 approached, the country was nearing a political crisis. The elections were to take place in May, but it is probable that a secret alliance was completed in February between Trujillo, who was then commander of the reorganized armed forces, and the local political leader of Santiago, Rafael Estrella Ureña. Toward the end of February, Estrella Ureña proclaimed a revolution and, with a small band of followers, marched on the capital. The revolutionaries could have been easily crushed by the armed forces, but Trujillo suddenly declared his "neutrality" in the dispute. With no army willing to defend the government, Vásquez and his vice president were forced to resign, and Estrella Ureña was made provisional president.

At this point, Trujillo declared his own candidacy for president in the forthcoming elections. In his campaign he made elaborate promises of efficient government and a prosperous economy. He also adopted violent measures to eliminate much of his opposition and to intimidate the Central Electoral Board. As a result, on May 16, 1930, Trujillo was elected president, unopposed.

Shortly after Trujillo's inauguration as president, a severe hurricane hit the island, killing some 2,000 people and leveling many buildings in the capital city. Trujillo very efficiently organized medical aid, housing, and food and set about rebuilding the city. This was the beginning of an impressive record of material achievement in the country.

After assuming office, Trujillo quickly consolidated his power. Some of his political opponents disappeared. He extended his control over the legislature, the bureaucracy, and the courts by filling posts only with those persons loyal to him and by revamping systems when necessary. Through control of the communications media, he was able to manipulate public opinion. Opposition political parties were not allowed. Critics of the regime, even those who obtained asylum in foreign countries, were eliminated by Trujillo's efficient secret police. Elections were held regularly, but when Trujillo himself did not occupy the presidency, the chiefs of state were merely puppets who carried out his wishes.

Progressive establishment of a near monopoly in many sectors of the economy accompanied Trujillo's consolidation of political power. At the high point of monopoly in the late 1950s, the Trujillo family and close associates controlled well over half the country's sugar industry and virtually all other agricultural exports. They owned about one-third of all cultivable land and practically all of the main commercial houses and manufacturing plants. The actual value of the family fortune at the time of Trujillo's assassination is unknown, but estimates run over half a billion dollars.

Although Trujillo and his followers managed to accumulate great personal wealth, the era was not without material benefit to the public at large. Many buildings, public works, highways, harbor facilities, plants and factories, schools, hospitals, and clinics were constructed. A forced peace ended the lawlessness, banditry, and civil strife that had plagued the country since independence and helped to stimulate agriculture and industrialization. By 1957 the foreign and domestic debts had been liquidated; the economy had experienced substantial growth; and government finances were in order. The benefits of these accomplishments, however, were largely negated by the rapid growth of the population and the expatriation of capital, which became particularly pronounced toward the end of Trujillo's rule. In addition, material progress was bought at the cost of civil liberties.

The tyranny of the Trujillo regime stimulated another exodus of Dominicans from the country. Many of the emigrants were from the upper classes—forced to leave because they opposed the government, because they owned profitable enterprises or lands that Trujillo and his clique wanted, or because they were members of the higher social strata who would not accept Trujillo into their ranks. Expansion of the government bureaucracy as well as that of commerce and industry created a new urban middle class in significant numbers. A class of newly rich, whose members held great economic and political power even though they did not have distinguished family backgrounds, began to develop. Many of the newly rich continued to maintain their position after Trujillo's assassination.

The mid-1950s saw the beginning of mounting foreign pressures against the Trujillo regime. Relations between the United States and the Trujillo administration became strained, and hemispheric opposition to Trujilloism became vocal. In 1959 a group of Dominican exiles aided by Cubans invaded the country; Trujillo responded with mass arrests and indiscriminate prosecution. Many prominent citizens were jailed. At this point, the Roman Catholic Church, which previously had at least tolerated Trujillo, turned against him. In January 1960 the six bishops issued a pastoral letter, read in all Roman Catholic churches throughout the country, protesting the denial of human rights and stating that these rights constituted a higher law than that of any state. Many people from the upper and middle classes turned to the church for leadership in their opposition to the Trujillo regime.

Early in 1960, Venezuela requested that the OAS investigate denial of human rights in the Dominican Republic. The Inter-American Peace Commission was assigned the task; and its report, issued in June 1960, was an indictment of the Trujillo regime. Shortly thereafter, Venezuela accused Trujillo of attempting to engineer an assassination attempt against its president, Rómulo Betancourt. The Organization of American States Council convoked the Meeting of Consultation of Foreign Ministers in August 1960 and, by a vote of nineteen to two, the foreign ministers adopted a resolution condemning the Dominican Republic for acts of aggression and intervention against Venezuela. All member states were urged to break off diplomatic relations with the Dominican Republic, and limited economic sanctions as well as a ban on all arms shipments were recommended.

Trujillo's reaction was ineffectual. With his island republic isolated, the country suffered economic difficulties, and Trujillo's control of the domestic situation steadily diminished. In May 1961, less than a year after the OAS recommended the sanctions, a small group of high military officers and civilians assassinated Trujillo. The political, economic, and social systems built by Trujillo began to disintegrate soon after the assassination. New forces unleashed by his death shaped events in a society reacting to the enforced order and fear of the Trujillo years, in a country that never had experienced sustained internal peace and prosperity.

DEVELOPMENTS, 1961–66

The Trujillo regime was unchallenged for thirty years, and its legacy of institutional bankruptcy dominated the early 1960s. Trujillo's armed forces and secret police permitted no dissent; indoctrination was carried on by the schools and the communications media; and membership in the official Dominican Party (Partido Dominicano—PD) was virtually mandatory. Trujillo permitted no effective opposition parties and controlled labor, student, professional, and business associations. Those who did not praise the dictator risked economic deprivation and social ostracism.

Trujillo's death released President Balaguer from the dictator's overriding control; Balaguer courted popular support by reducing the price of basic goods; increasing freedom of expression; allowing the formation of opposition parties; and permitting exiled leaders to return. Trujillo's son, armed forces commander Rafael Trujillo, Jr. (known as "Ramfis"), accepted these reforms; and he served as a buffer between his uncles, who opposed any modification of the Trujillo system, and President Balaguer. Aided by lower ranking officers and a show of force by the United States, Balaguer survived a coup d'etat attempted by the older Trujillos. The Trujillo family, including Ramfis, then fled the country.

President Balaguer restored the old name of the capital city, Santo Domingo, which Trujillo had changed to Ciudad Trujillo. The president outlawed the Dominican Party; and began to confiscate Trujillo's property. With these confiscations, the state possessed at least as large a proportion of the country's wealth as did any Latin American counterpart. President Balaguer also distributed sizable quantities of Trujillo's movable property to the poor. Prolonged negotiations between the president and the opposition produced the Council of State government in January 1962. One of the members of the council, General Antonio Imbert Barrera, was to play an important role in the crisis of 1965.

The OAS then lifted its sanctions. When anti-Balaguer riots broke out, Balaguer resigned the presidency of the council and went into exile. With United States support, the council survived two attempted military coups d'etat. Led by Rafael F. Bonnelly and composed chiefly of Dominican businessmen and professional men who had lived in the country during the Trujillo regime, the council received substantial economic assistance under the Alliance for Progress program. It concentrated on maintaining order and preparing for national elections.

Juan Bosch, a political leader who had formed the Dominican Revolutionary Party (Partido Revolucionario Dominicano—PRD) in 1939 and had long been in exile, returned and, pledging social and economic reform, was elected president in December 1962. In February 1963 he embarked on a program of economic development that combined domestic austerity and foreign economic aid. His initial support soon dissipated. Labor leaders became uneasy over President Bosch's proposal to combine the unions into a single labor alliance, and agricultural workers lost interest when promised large-scale land reforms did not materialize.

Clerical, business, military, and landowning elements generally had opposed Bosch's election. Their acceptance of his victory grew tenuous when armed hostilities with Haiti nearly developed and the president secured enactment of a new constitution, which was more explicit than previous documents in committing the government to involvement in the economic and social order. The traditional elite resented President Bosch's persistent criticism of them and generally withheld their support from his administration. The president's refusal to curtail the civil liberties of leftists and Communists, considerable numbers of whom he permitted to return from exile, unified the opposition. On September 25, 1963, armed forces officers, led by air force Colonel Elías Wessín y Wessín, deposed and deported Bosch, whom they accused of administrative incompetence and laxity toward communism. Some 500 persons accused of being subversives were sent to jail; and the United States suspended recognition and terminated its aid programs.

46

Installation of a three-man civilian junta, the Triumvirate, to rule the country encountered little organized opposition. The Triumvirate promptly disbanded congress; it continued earlier reforms and initiated programs designed to further the country's social and economic development. But Donald José Reid Cabral, the leading member of the Triumvirate, lacked Bosch's appeal and failed to gain wide support. Moreover, he adopted unpopular austerity measures, suspended civil liberties in response to repeated strikes, and alienated military officers by rotating commands and attempting to curtail their privileges. A coalition of minor political parties assisting the Triumvirate withdrew its support when it became uncertain that the promised elections would be held.

On April 25, 1965, the military deposed Reid. Many younger officers then joined civilians in demanding the restoration of Bosch. With Bosch's approval, Colonel Francisco Caamaño Deñó led a grouping of military and civilian factions known as the Constitutionalists, who controlled part of the city of Santo Domingo, against the forces of General Wessín and of General Imbert y Barrera, who had formed the Government of National Reconstruction. Despite a cease-fire agreement and intervention by United States marines and the Inter-American Peace Force dispatched by the OAS, fighting continued sporadically throughout the summer, claiming nearly 4,000 lives. Each faction accused the other of atrocities and claimed that it would have achieved military victory if the intervention had not occurred. When communist leaders, many of them trained in Cuba, gained increasing influence in the revolutionary movement, Imbert supporters declared that the Constitutionalists were communist-dominated. The Constitutionalists called Imbert's adherents reactionary. Both sides formed governments, but neither was recognized by any foreign government.

Negotiations conducted by the papal nuncio and officials of the OAS and the United States produced a provisional government. Provisional President Héctor García Godoy, who was installed on September 3, 1965, reintegrated the Constitutionalist Sector into the national territory and asked the Inter-American Peace Force to help maintain order and collect the weapons that had been distributed during the civil war. Amid terrorism and strikes, the Provisional Government recognized the revolutionary council that had seized the University of Santo Domingo, removed several regular military officers from positions of power and sent leading officers abroad. By spring 1966, Constitutionalist soldiers had not been reincorporated into the regular armed forces ranks. Bosch and Balaguer, former presidents who had returned from exile, became the leading presidential candidates in the election campaign, which was of consuming national interest. Balaguer, winning over 57 percent of the votes, defeated Bosch, who received only 39 percent of the total. In September 1966 the United States marines and the other units of the Inter-American Peace Force were withdrawn.

Together with those members of the traditional elite who had actively cooperated with Trujillo, a new administrative elite recruited from the military and the lower and middle classes filled the industrial and governmental posts created by the expanding economy and public bureaucracy. Unlike the Trujillo family and top-ranking military officers, many of the civilian administrators had retained their positions after the regime fell. They then vied with the traditional elite to fill the vacuum of political leadership. In addition, the urban lower class, returning exiles, and revolutionary youth effectively pressed for greater influence.

Of outstanding importance was the introduction of the urban and rural lower class to political power. Their overwhelming numbers had secured Bosch's election in 1962. In addition to getting out the urban lower-class vote, party organizers and politically oriented labor leaders developed strikes and demonstrations into determinants of public policy. The urban lower class displayed considerable political consciousness and organization, and unemployed elements were particularly volatile. Urban laborers and the unemployed supported the Constitutionalists and had favored Bosch's candidacy in 1966.

Except for the politically organized employees of government-owned sugar plantations, the political activity of the far more numerous rural lower class had previously been virtually confined to voting. Unlike urban workers, rural laborers had been favorably inclined toward Trujillo's paternalism. In the post-Trujillo period their initial demands for land reform became increasingly tempered by their traditional concern for peace and stability. In the 1966 election the rural lower-class vote was sought by both Balaguer and Bosch (see ch. 7).

CHAPTER 4

SOCIAL SYSTEM

The structure of the Dominican social system and the problems facing it are similar to those facing many developing nations. A small elite rules the great majority of the people, and the institutions and values are based on the life-styles of a colonial past. Although steeped in tradition, the country is experiencing the disequilibrium of a society in transition. Social groups are becoming increasingly diversified and fragmented, and the historic customs are being undermined by new and challenging values.

The similarities between the Dominican social system and those of other Caribbean countries are particularly marked. As a historic entity, the Caribbean area experienced the early annihilation of its indigenous peoples followed by repopulation by white European landowners and black African slaves. As a socioeconomic region, it can be defined in terms of its plantation heritage and its subsequent polarized class structure. In this system of stratification color and physical differences are status markers, and status is differentiated by access to land, wealth, and political power. As of 1972, the majority of the Caribbean nations were characterized by large numbers of unintegrated peoples and by the absence of a common ideology.

Despite similarities, several features distinguish the society of the Dominican Republic from the social systems of its Caribbean neighbors. The tenacity of Hispanic values and institutions, the ethnic background of the population, and the regime of Rafael Leónidas Trujillo Molina shaped a society that is in some respects unique in configuration and composition. Dominicans boast the purest Spanish traditions in the Western Hemisphere, and statistics buttress their claim. Ninety-eight percent of the population are Spanish-speaking Roman Catholics, and the family structure and the values further reflect the Spanish heritage.

Furthermore, the Dominican Republic is one of the few Caribbean countries in which blacks do not constitute a majority. Its population is largely mulatto, the result of extensive intermarriage between blacks and whites. The Dominican Republic is particularly sensitive about its racial status because it shares the island with predominantly black Haiti. Traditional animosity between the two neighbors has given rise to mutual suspicion replete with racial overtones.

The thirty years of the Trujillo dictatorship were to alter the face of

Dominican society more than any other event in recent history. His regime had the effect of a controlled experiment in which political elements were kept constant while social and economic elements were indiscriminately imposed from above. Trujillo encouraged the creation of a middle class of businessmen, industrialists, military personnel, and government workers that challenged the position and the values of the old elite. He forced the reevaluation of such institutions as the Roman Catholic Church and the extended family, and in doing so he profoundly altered the face of Dominican society. All these changes were introduced without letting traditional sectors adjust and adapt. Under his leadership the country experienced accelerating and conflicting pressures that erupted when he was assassinated, leaving the society fragmented and disoriented (see ch. 7).

In pre-Trujillo days, the Dominican Republic presented the profile of a traditional and rigidly segmented society. Class lines and established values had divided the country into factional groups with fixed boundaries. Since Trujillo's death there has been growing evidence that the nature and the patterns of class loyalties have been changing. Divisive forces were causing fragmentation both within and among classes, while conflicting ideologies, values, and goals were forcing a restructuring of the social system at the national level.

ETHNIC GROUPS AND LANGUAGES

The vast majority of the Dominican people are Spanish-speaking mulattoes whose ancestors were black slaves from Africa and white settlers from Spain. The early and extensive mixing of these two races resulted in a strain of people who mainfest the physical characteristics of both. In 1972 the amalgamation was so widespread that figures estimating racial percentages were hazy at best, especially as ethnic groupings are not mentioned in the national census. The mulattoes composed at least 70 percent of the population, with the whites and blacks forming the remaining 30 percent. Although the issue of race is not as vital to the question of social status as those of family background and wealth, a person's color is indicative of his position in the society. The lighter his skin, the higher his social position is apt to be.

As a consequence of the early extirpation of the native populations, the Indian influence on Domican racial composition and cultural heritage is minimal (see ch. 3). The pattern of extermination and amalgamation of this racial strain left the population to evolve from the remaining two groups—Spanish colonists and black slaves.

The first black slaves were brought from Spain in 1502, and direct importation from Africa began soon afterwards. By the mid-sixteenth century blacks outnumbered the whites fifteen to one. With the introduction of slavery, the process of miscegenation began. The disequilibrium of the sexes, the paucity of white females, and the lack of stigma against concubinage aided in the evolution of the mulatto as a racial type. The degree of miscegenation was so extensive that a system of nomenclature was established to identify the parentage of the individual. By 1650 the mulatto had successfully come to dominate the Dominican ethnic scene and to form the base for the future population.

The basis for future race relations was also formed during this period. The economic dichotomy between the propertied class and the landless, between the slaveowner and the slave—or, after the emancipation, the planter and the indentured servant—began to orient the economy along racial lines. During the colonial period, politics became tied to economic pressures as wealthy planters, who formed the most powerful group of constituents, sought to maintain traditional ties between land ownership and government. Finally, prevalent theories of white supremacy also influenced ethnic patterns throughout the colonial epoch. The belief that Indians and Negroes were inferior beings led to the justification of their enslavement and oppressed position in the society.

Throughout the remainder of Dominican history, the ethnic pattern and racial relations established by the Spanish planters and their black slaves was reinforced by outside influences. The slave revolt of 1791 brought independence to Haiti and resulted in a series of disorders that, accompanied by the intervention of foreign powers, disrupted all of Hispaniola for several decades. The rapid and confused interplay of Spanish, French, English, and Americans for influence over the small island kept white people in powerful positions during much of the nineteenth century.

Even more important in the total picture of ethnic history was the Haitian occupation (1822–44). The Haitian influence was more lasting and has remained far more evident, both in ethnic composition and in life-style patterns, than that of the Europeans or Americans. Racial prejudice developed during the Haitian occupation that would significantly reinforce colonial values concerning the inherent inferiority of blacks in general, and Haitians in particular, and which would affect future relations with their Western neighbors. During its twenty-year rule the Haitian government pursued a policy of turning the entire island into a black state. Mulattoes from Haiti participated in the administration of the country, and black slaves were emancipated to become a free labor force. Black Haitian settlers flooded into the rural areas. During this repressive period racial violence was rampant, and mass exodus of whites to other Caribbean countries was common. In fact, most of the white people who remained during the Haitian occupation were those who had nothing to lose.

This period is referred to by Dominican patriots as the "ethiopianization" of their country, and fear of reconquest has influenced attitudes in that country more than any other event since its colonization (see ch. 3). After the occupation many of the white elite families returned to what had become the Dominican Republic. Once again a very small group of the wealthiest whites emerged at the top of the social structure, although many did not regain their land, which had been made state property during the years under Haitian domination. The strong Hispanic identification of this segment of the population and of the society in general assured this white aristocracy of their elite status. Bitter memories and bias generated by the Haitian occupation relegated the darker skinned individuals and especially the blacks to the bottom of the social and economic ladder.

Contemporary Ethnic Composition

Mulattoes, regarded as a separate race by most Dominicans, constituted the largest group in 1972. Blacks were the next largest, followed by whites of European descent. There were also trace elements of Middle Easterners and Asians. These groups could be distinguished by status, and by economic and geographic variables, as well as through physical and ancestral differences.

The mulattoes exhibit the greatest diffusion throughout the social structure. They are not limited to one geographic area or economic stratum but are found in both rural and urban settings. They have gained almost exclusive control of the armed forces. Traditionally, mulattoes have served as a combination synthesis and buffer between the white and black communities; and blacks desiring to move upward have looked to this intermediate racial strain to propel their offspring into higher socioecomomic strata through intermarriage and racial assimilation. The history of the Dominican mulatto portrays his slow consolidation of power in the economic and political arenas after becoming a racial majority early in colonial history. Trujillo was the archetype of a mulatto of middle class origin who gained the recognition of the traditional white elite and ascended to the most powerful position in the country.

The black portion of the Dominican society has evolved from three main sources—Africa, Haiti, and the United States—and of these, the most dominant in the contemporary society is the Haitian. The century and a half of migration of Haitians (1822-1972) was seriously interrupted only once, when Trujillo ordered the massacre of several thousand immigrants at the Haitian border. The Dominican government then established an immigration law imposing a tax of the equivalent of US$500 upon non-Caucasian immigrants. Temporary permits were given to those employed on the sugar plantations or in the mills; but many Haitians simply did not go back to their country and have chosen to remain along the border and in the southern provinces, where they are still concentrated today.

These individuals have retained their lower class and rural status and have remained at the bottom of the social structure. The Haitian immigrants have little affected the Dominican culture on a national scale. Nevertheless, numerous cultural parallels exist between the

52

lower classes of the two countries. Food, houses, and other items of material culture, as well as certain Haitian beliefs about the supernatural, have been readily assimilated into the lower class Dominican life-styles.

A miniscule percentage of the black population is made up of descendants of former American slaves. Their ancestors came to Hispaniola from Baltimore and Philadelphia during the early part of the nineteenth century and settled along the northern coast in the Samaná Peninsula (Península de Samaná). They formed an aloof Protestant community of English-speaking peoples who only recently have begun to intermarry with their Spanish-speaking neighbors.

The whites are numerically the smallest of the three groups, yet their influence in the realm of values, customs, and institutions far outweighs that of the other two. This tiny elite has been formed by the consolidation of original Spanish colonists and later European settlers. From this group arose the landed aristocracy and civilian leadership, who controlled the economics and politics of the country while maintaining the Hispanic tradition and ethic. Although once plantation owners, the majority of the whites now reside in the urban areas and larger cities. Santiago de los Caballeros, founded in 1500 and now the second-largest city, claims to have a population of the purest Spanish blood in the Western Hemisphere. Because only those of unmixed Spanish descent were once allowed to settle there, its inhabitants are lighter in color than the average for the country. The region considered to have experienced the least racial intermixing is that surrounding the town of Baní, on the southern coast, which was first populated in the early 1800s by white families from the Canary Islands.

The only group of whites to remain relatively unassimilated is that of German Jews who immigrated during the 1930s, forming agricultural colonies along the northern seacoast at Sosúa. The original number has decreased, and those remaining have stayed territorially isolated.

The remaining ethnic strains, the Middle Easterners and Asians, constituted a minimal percentage of the total Dominican population in 1972. Except for the Lebanese, neither group was particularly well integrated into the mainstream of Dominican culture, and there was little intermarriage; both, however, participated in entrepreneurial activities. The Chinese virtually monopolized the bar and restaurant trade, and Lebanese and other immigrants from the Middle East owned many businesses. They have concentrated themselves in large cities, such as Santo Domingo and Santiago de los Caballeros. Only certain Japanese settlers have departed from this pattern. Coming to the Dominican Republic after the Second World War, they established two agricultural colonies along the Haitian frontier. Twenty years later, only one of these colonies was still operating successfully (see ch. 9).

Race Relations

Dominicans generally maintain that there is no racial discrimination in their country. Nevertheless, there is a positive value attached to persons of white ancestry and a concomitant negative value attached to those of black ancestry. Furthermore, the concept of Haitians as cane cutters has become so established that it is nearly impossible to divorce the two in the Dominican mind. Even the lowest class of Dominicans feel that cutting cane is beneath them and that it is fitting work for these immigrants. Consequently, most of the recognizable prejudice is directed against Haitians in general, who are perceived as fit only for work in the cane fields, and not against black people per se.

The value attached to physical appearance is particularly manifest, in that there is an emphasis on whitening of individuals and the population as a whole. The desire to pass as a white person developed in response to the slave heritage and to the evolution of the mulatto and was supported by the undercurrent of prejudice against Haitians and the darker skinned peoples. Expressions such as "light mulatto," "washed Negro," "Indian color," "cinnamon type," and "good hair" have developed to describe certain physical characteristics and also reveal the Dominican's aspiration to be considered white and European. Women go to great lengths in their usage of lightening cosmetics, and in photographs negroid features are shaded and skin tones are lightened to make the subject appear more Caucasian.

Although race is an important determinant of social status, blackness in itself does not restrict an individual to a lower class position. Upward mobility is possible for blacks who manage to accrue wealth or acquire an education.

Languages

Spanish is the official language of the Dominican Republic and is also the spoken language of about 98 percent of the people. Of the remaining 2 percent, most speak Haitian Creole, English, Chinese, or Japanese. Among the Spanish-speaking Dominicans, there are few regional dialects and consequently no bars to communication. There are certain spoken nuances, expressions, and taboos that are strictly Dominican, but for the most part, the Spanish spoken in 1972 bore a great resemblance to that spoken by the first Spanish settlers in 1493.

The original colonizers were seafarers and navigators, and the Spanish they brought to the island was the dialect of their home, Andalusia. Castillian gentlemen, bringing their own dialect and mannerisms, arrived much later and had a lesser effect on the development of speech patterns. Spanish quickly took over the language spoken by the native population, and few vestiges remain of the original Indian tongue. (The Indian words that did survive, however, did not take root in the Dominican vocabulary alone but found their way into many European languages as well. Some commonly used words of this unique origin are: cannibal, canoe, hurricane, hammock, potato, maize, savannah, and tobacco). If the Indian languages suffered when pitted against the invading Spanish, the African dialects fared even worse. Early evolution of the Dominican patterns of speech paralleled development of its culture—domination by the Spanish and the sublimation of the Indian and Negro.

Although three regional dialects exist, the only one of any importance is Cibaeña, which is spoken by mainly rural lower class people of the northern Cibao Valley. The geographic isolation imposed by the surrounding mountains, coupled with the lack of communication from outsiders and consequent lack of new elements, has caused the development of a distinctive dialect. Archaic speech patterns predominate, and individual words may be phonetically altered through slurring, consonant omissions, or nasality.

Haitian Creole has had the greatest effect on lower class Dominicans and on those living near the Haitian border through the cultural drift experienced in this area. English has also had an effect on the language, especially the vocabulary. As in other Latin American countries, such English words as "bar" and "leader" (*líder*) are used because of the lack of equivalent Spanish terms, whereas other English terminology for food and sports has gained popularity through the movies and extensive contact with the United States. The trend towards americanization of Dominican Spanish is likely to persist through continued cultural and commercial interaction. The upper class finds English especially useful in their communication with the business world, and middle and even lower sectors have also found that their job potential increases directly with their mastery of English. Many who can barely write Spanish are taking correspondence courses in English.

Because Spanish is the language spoken throughout the society, the outsider may not see the fine distinction between class speech patterns. Tremendous differences do exist between the speech of the uneducated rural masses and the educated urban elite, and oratory and rhetoric are integral parts of a good education.

STRATIFICATION

The class system in the Dominican Republic reflects the conflict between a strong Spanish colonial tradition and the plantation heritage and the new values and life-styles of the twentieth century. The consequence of this struggle is the breakdown of traditional class boundaries and the emergence of a new criterion for stratification. Despite the fact that a middle class is evolving, its functions outside the economic realm are limited. The country still functions as a two-class society consisting of a small elite at the top and a large mass of poor at the bottom. The most important variables emphasized in defining the social classes are ancestry, wealth, family background and, to a lesser degree, education and occupation. Ethnicity, which Dominicans view as being based on skin color, also influences social position, although not in the same degree as wealth or ancestry. Generally, the poor, uneducated cane cutter of Haitian descent falls into the lowest category, whereas a lighter skinned businessman with a long pedigree is most likely to be a member of the elite.

The divisions between classes have been historically rigid; there was little or no overlap in life-styles or customs between the elite and the lower class. These class boundaries are becoming increasingly obscure as the single ruling aristocracy gives way to the rising middle sector. This change has been brought about by the thirty years of the Trujillo regime and the increased contact with foreign influence and ideas that have conflicted with the traditional Hispanic values. The Dominican middle class is still the most diverse and heterogeneous group in the country, and membership in this noncohesive group is not well defined. Many in the middle sector find themselves in transition from the lower stratum, and the newly rich are trying to move into the elite.

The Lower Class

At the bottom of the Dominican social pyramid lies an amorphous group of mulatto or black, uneducated, poor people who inhabit both rural and urban areas. The Spanish colonial heritage left an indelible mark on the class structure of the society and played a particularly large role in the formation of the values, institutions, and general composition of the lower class. It led to the development of a social configuration of two distinct and rigid classes: one white, free, and powerful; the other black, slave, and powerless. The large gulf between these two classes led to the evolution of parallel cultural systems that served the divergent needs of the two groups. The Spanish colonists set down ideals and precepts of behavior that have been followed by the upper class and aspired to by the rest of the society for nearly 500 years. This stringent pattern left the slaves and the poor to adapt their own culture as best they could around a style of life that had little relevance to their poor and harsh existence.

Even after the abolition of slavery there was little opportunity to change the patterns and relationships established during early colonial times. Social mobility between classes was still practically impossible. Education, wealth, and political power were jealously guarded by the elite, who maintained their power despite numerous invasions and setbacks. The Haitian invasion and subsequent illegal immigration of many lower class Haitians has served to perpetuate the original slave dichotomy. These immigrants and their descendants continue to occupy low status positions, not only because of their color, but also because of their alien language and culture.

There are certain characteristics of the lower class that apply throughout the poorer stratum. Besides being generally darker skinned than persons in the middle or upper classes, lower class persons have little education, low prestige jobs, or no job at all. Illiteracy may be as high as 80 to 90 percent in the rural areas, and figures for the urban areas are only slightly better (see ch. 5). Employment is difficult to find everywhere, and those who have a steady income, no matter how small, command significantly higher prestige in both regions. A great many who have no fixed wages live almost completely outside the money economy, surviving by bartering goods and services in exchange for provisions.

The poor masses of the Dominican Republic have remained largely outside the dominant culture, and their participation in the political process has been historically low. They have generally followed the upper class lead in politics and rarely question hierarchical authority. Although claiming to represent the interests of this segment of the population, most Dominican politicians have worked only to undermine further the political position of the poor. The dual favoritism-intimidation method used by ex-President Trujillo and many others kept the peasant and his urban lower class counterpart submissive and fearful subjects.

Of all the members of the lower class, the peasant is the least integrated into the national society. He produces little, consumes little, has little say in politics, and generally maintains a life-style similar to that of his ancestors. Outsiders view him as conservative and backward. This perception is enhanced by the peasants' traditional segregation in zones least favorable for cultivation and by the prevalent social attitudes favoring large agricultural enterprises over small subsistence farming. The peasant is engaged in a wide variety of rural occupations, among them tenant or independent farming or migrant work during harvesttime. The poor of the small villages may also be itinerant merchants or day laborers in construction. Wages depend upon the job, and income estimates vary. In 1968 a cane cutter could earn RD$0.90 (1 peso equals US$1—see Glossary) per ton and he could average two tons a day; but this job might only last two months, leaving him unemployed and penniless at the end of the season.

The peasant may build his home on unused public or private property, thus risking eviction. His home is built of palm planking with palm or banana leaf roofing, and it is patched together with thatch, mud, old newspapers, and leaves. He usually has a miniscule plot of land next to his hut on which he grows beans and yucca for home consumption. His social life is centered on the village nearby and his own immediate family. A marketplace, a church, a bar-restaurant, and a radio may become the focal points for social interaction among peasants in the villages.

To the casual observer, the Dominican countryside may appear more semiurban than rural. This is caused by the high density of the population accompanied by the low degree of rural isolation. Increased pressure for farmland coupled with expectations for a better life in the city has caused many peasants to seek their fortunes in crowded urban areas (see ch. 5). Few have moved up in status, however, and many have only realized a move from rural poverty to urban poverty.

When a peasant arrives in the city, he may be helped financially by relatives who have preceded him and who have some employment. He may find temporary work as a stevedore, peddler, or bottle collector, whereas the female migrant may become a housemaid or a prostitute. As time goes on these individuals may move into higher paying and more prestigious work, becoming carpenters or factory workers. These vocations are more permanent, but may not pay much more than rural occupations. The minimum wage for an unskilled laborer in 1971 was RD$0.25 per hour, amounting to about RD$50 a month, which does not differ greatly from the cane cutters' wages. Nevertheless, urban workers are better organized than their counterparts in the country, and the labor union movement is growing.

The Middle Sector

As of 1972, no cohesive middle class existed in the Dominican Republic, although 15 to 30 percent of the population was categorized as such by various Dominican scholars. Being neither peasant nor elite, this transitional sector could be distinguished only in terms of the other two strata. The members did not share concurrent goals, values, and heritage—all the things that make up class consciousness—and really held little in common with each other except a desire to emulate the life-style of the elite. Wealth became the major criterion for membership in this sector, although a person's education, color, and occupation also helped define his status. The middle sector was in evidence in both urban and rural areas and engaged in the full scale of occupations—landholding and renting, business and commercial enterprises, industrial and managerial posts, professions, the military, and white- and blue-collar jobs.

The middle sector has been in existence since colonial times, although it remained insignificant until the middle of the last century. During this period new groups began to form around a merchant ideology, but their influence and power were minimal before 1930, when Trujillo began his rise to power. With the advent of his dictatorship, significant changes took place in the social structure. The army became the most popular avenue for socially mobile individuals seeking higher status. Army officers and favored civilians developed into a wealthy segment—the newly rich—that rivaled the elite for power and prestige. Finally, the elite themselves, under the economic and political pressure of Trujillo, also began to look to nontraditional avenues of economic activity, forming a high class bourgeoisie involved in the professions, in real estate, and in the import business.

The middle sector has retained the traditional Hispanic values dictated and preserved by the elite, while experiencing great economic and occupational diversification. Physical characteristics and family heritage are of paramount importance in determining individual status within the group. Even the slightest gradation of color may affect interpersonal relationships, and persons in this group want all their associates and relatives to be as light-skinned as possible. Family background may be a large consideration in the search for a suitable spouse, as it is for the elite.

Displaying the traditional elitist disdain for manual labor, the middle sector demonstrates a desire to move into the most prestigious kind of position. A blue-collar worker will attempt to move into a white-collar position, even if his present position pays more. College students want to be doctors, lawyers, engineers, and architects, which are considered to be the gentlemanly professions, rather than technicians or scientists, which are equated with manual labor. Nevertheless, continued modernization of their country, coupled with the rising prestige of science and technology, has made careers in these fields increasingly appealing to young, middle-class Dominicans.

In spite of their strict adherence to elitist precepts, this middle sector is the vanguard of social change in the Dominican Republic. Members of this stratum are in a state of transition between the two dominant classes, and they express a certain feeling of insecurity about the future. They are not as bound to tradition as the elite and demonstrate greater willingness to change and adapt to societal change than does the upper segment of the population. Individuals in the middle sector are very ambitious and upwardly mobile, tending to live and plan far beyond their economic means.

In addition to being economically prosperous, the middle sectors are also politically active. Here again, however, they display a lack of common goals and ideals, and members of this stratum are found throughout the political spectrum. The businessmen who thrive on stable economic conditions tend to oppose change. On the other hand, professionals who cannot find work in their own fields may become frustrated politicians and enter the leftist political arena. Often the intellectuals are the leaders in the radical political movements.

The social activities of the middle sector differ in one major aspect from those of the elite. Whereas the latter center much of their activity within the family, the middle sector prefers to participate in clubs and other voluntary associations. Many international social clubs such as the Rotary International, Freemasons, and the International Order of Odd Fellows are popular and do a good deal of philanthropic work within the country. Middle class men also participate in business and professional organizations, many of which voice the political views of their members. Special periodicals and newspapers designed to meet the expanding interests of this sector have appeared.

The most dynamic subclass in the middle sector is the newly rich, the highest social stratum to which most individuals without the proper family pedigree can aspire. Trujillo gave birth to this segment through the expansion of military and bureaucratic positions, and many ambitious members of the lower and middle classes saw this as a viable method of improving their economic position. During his reign, most of the political power was concentrated in the hands of the military but, after his assassination civilians who accrued wealth during his term have used their economic status to bolster their political power as well. The boundaries of the newly rich are still easily crossed; one need only attain a high government or military post or accumulate enough wealth.

The traditional elite resented what they considered to be penetration of their social sphere by the newly rich, who are still perceived as a potential threat to elite status. Of necessity, the two classes have often been paired in the political and economic arenas, but social distance has been stiffly maintained. Although the social patterns of the two groups are similar, any alliance has been temporary and has been easily broken when the goal was attained. This pattern may not continue indefinitely, however, as constant interaction, mutual support, and intermarriage may bring the elite and the newly rich more into line with each other.

The Elite

The elite, generally described by Dominicans as *de primera* (derived from *la clase de primera*—the first class), derives and perpetuates its status through ancestry and intermarriage. One of the main roles of this group is the preservation and dissemination of the traditional Hispanic values and culture. Members of this stratum are of white European descent who are primarily engaged in business, politics, industry, real estate, and in professions such as law, engineering, and medicine. Most elite reside in the large urban centers of Santo Domingo and Santiago de los Caballeros, as only a few have large estates in the countryside.

The Dominican Republic does not have a powerful landed oligarchy as do most Latin American countries. Even though the elite has controlled political affairs during most of the period of independence, various events took place that periodically destroyed their accumulated wealth and interrupted their exercise of power. The Haitian occupation of the mid-nineteenth century forced many of the elite into temporary exile in Cuba, Puerto Rico, and Venezuela. Many of these people returned after the occupation and began to reconsolidate their positions, settling in the Cibao region. A large exodus again took place under the regimes of Ulises Heureaux (1892-99) and Trujillo (1930-61) further undercutting the aristocratic hold on the economy of the country. Trujillo was the last to preempt the elite's economic and political bases of power and to disrupt its cohesiveness; they were able to begin consolidating their forces again only after his assassination.

The geographic center for the elite is still the Cibao region, especially the city of Santiago de los Caballeros. The people of Santiago consider themselves the pinnacle of Dominican society. They are more Castillian or European in origin; their manners are more courtly; and their family traditions are better preserved than in Santo Domingo. Furthermore, the elite in Santiago de los Caballeros has been oriented towards business and property ownership, whereas its counterpart in the capital city is largely professional or political.

The family is the bulwark of the elite and its main mode of self-preservation. Rather than joining social clubs, the upper class centers its social activities around the home. Each family is headed by the patriarch, who serves to unify the members and arbitrate family disputes. In her role as matchmaker, the matriarch serves an equally important function in the preservation of the elite family. Through her skillful manipulation of intermarriage, the elite is able to preserve their closed, exalted position in the society. This group, composed of about 100 families, has aptly been referred to as the *tutumpote* by other Dominicans. (The term comes from "totem pole," implying extreme worship of family and ancestry.) The most prestigious of these families can point to interdependent histories; and a recent marriage between two members of the elite disclosed seven former presidents in the combined parentage of the newlyweds.

Acceptance of outsiders is rare, although some members of lower strata have achieved higher status through marriage into the elite class. One group that resides on the periphery of the elite is composed of individuals largely descended from Italian, Armenian, Syrian, and Lebanese immigrants of seventy years ago who have married into traditional elite families. Many newly rich have tried to gain the acceptance of the *de primera* but have discovered that mere wealth is not sufficient for admittance to their ranks. Even Trujillo and his family, who ruled the Dominican Republic and controlled its economy for thirty years, were never wholly accepted by the Dominican elite.

Wealth is a corollary of elite status, although it is certainly secondary to family background. Some family fortunes originated through the production of rum and tobacco, whereas others based their wealth on landownership or various commercial or industrial endeavors. An elite family may lose part of its wealth and still maintain its high social status, although it may have trouble keeping up with other members of the group. The life-style of the *de primera* is not necessarily ostentatious; but nevertheless money is spent on vacations, jewelry, and education for their children. Popular vacation spots are Puerto Rico, the United States, and Europe, although some prefer to maintain a house in the country in addition to their urban residence. Members of the elite are not oblivious to their poorer countrymen and possess a

61

strong sense of noblesse oblige and philanthropy. Their attitude toward the lower class has been traditionally paternalistic, however, and often their charity serves only to widen the gulf between the two classes.

Education plays an important part in the development and maintenance of the elite. Girls are usually sent to private Roman Catholic schools in the country, whereas boys are educated abroad whenever possible. Schools in France and Spain have been traditionally popular, although emphasis is increasingly toward schools in the United States and Canada. Whereas education plays a large part in the socialization of elite children, the Roman Catholic Church plays a relatively small part. Although they support and encourage similar behavior patterns and have served as historic reinforcements for each other, the church and the elite have not always been aligned politically. Moreover, being a Roman Catholic is something so ingrained in the Dominican personality that it is taken for granted. Church attendance and strict adherence to Roman Catholic practices is limited and few upper class men join the priesthood.

Civilian leadership has traditionally fallen on the shoulders of the elite. Members of the elite are almost always included in important governmental and cabinet positions, if one is not occupying the presidency itself. The Dominican elite are found throughout the political spectrum—from left to right and from liberal to conservative. Moreover, the extensive network of connections and mutual interdependence between the government and the elite has assured the latter of powerful positions despite political upsets. The only period in history when this has not been the case was during the Trujillo dictatorship, when both the political and the familial roles of the elite were seriously—and perhaps irreparably—undermined.

Unlike many Latin American countries, military leadership in the armed forces do not form part of the social elite in the Dominican Republic. The armed forces have been traditionally composed of those of mulatto and middle class origin, like Trujillo, whom the elite regard as uncultured and uneducated. This idea was strikingly reinforced in the mind of the elite during Trujillo's dictatorship; and in the ten years since his assassination, little effort has been made to conciliate the two forces.

FAMILY AND KINSHIP

The family is still the most important social unit. Despite a gradual weakening throughout the Trujillo years, it has remained the focal point for loyalty, love, and leisure for the average Dominican. Although the family may take different forms throughout the society, it is the most cohesive unit for all classes. There are three kinds of marital union—civil, church, and consensual. The first two are found at the upper level, whereas the consensual, or common law, union predominates at the bottom. An important accessory of the extended family is the *compadre,* or godfather, and the *compadrazgo* (coparenthood—see Glossary) system is a vital institution at every level of the society.

Structure and Functions of the Family

The structure and functions of the Dominican family are further reflections of the Spanish colonial and slave heritages of the past. Traditional values of solidarity, honor, and parental authority were brought by early settlers and established as desirable goals in family patterning. Slaves, by contrast, could not hope to follow the Hispanic lead in kinship organization because many times they were not even permitted the rite of marriage. Furthermore, white upper class plantation owners effectively established a pattern of informal unions with black women. The implications of this heritage for lower class Dominicans cannot be overemphasized, and many contemporary domestic structures can be seen as the result of colonial life-styles.

The idealized family structure and the one most emulated by the majority of Dominicans is exemplified by the upper class. It serves to integrate the individual into the closed stratification system, which in turn it supports and perpetuates. Upper class kinship patterns are distinctly oriented along patrilineal lines, and the oldest man is the unquestioned authority in all matters. He is the arbiter of family affairs and is responsible for the welfare of its members and for the maintenance of its honor. Sibling ties are very solid and continue into adult life, providing the focal point for the majority of social activity. Solidarity is stronger among brothers than sisters, partly because in the patrilineal family women are expected to give primary allegiance to the husband's family. Nevertheless, brothers usually continue to look after the welfare of both married and unmarried sisters, as well as that of their mother. The mother's role must not be underestimated in the patrilineal Dominican family; for if the father is the representation of supreme authority and power, the mother represents familial love and unity in every class in the society.

The extended family, consisting of a three-generation kin group, is still the strongest and most cohesive unit for the Dominican elite, and all other forms of social organization are considered secondary. There is some evidence this kinship structure was appreciably weakened, however, during the thirty years of the Trujillo dictatorship. Families were split both ideologically and geographically as old taboos against intrafamily dissent gave way under political pressure. Since Trujillo's assassination, many families have been reunited, but the concept of the family as an impenetrable fortress no longer exists to the degree it did in pre-Trujillo days. Increasing social change and industrialization have also introduced alternative priorities that may conflict with kinship loyalties.

Although lower class Dominicans would like to follow the pattern set by the elite family, historical factors and contemporary social and economic pressures work against it. As in other situations where fulfillment of upper class dictums is unworkable, a stretching of values occurs to adjust for discrepancies between the real and the ideal. An understanding of this background helps to explain why many lower class kinship patterns are in apparent opposition to upper class norms. For example, the ruling elite historically demanded formal marital unions among themselves, while condoning informal consensual unions at the lower levels of society. Because there have been few sanctions against common law marriages and because both civil and religious ceremonies are expensive, complicated procedures, many poor people view the consensual union as a viable alternative to marriage.

The pervasiveness and instability of these informal sexual relationships further explains lower class family structure. This kind of domestic organization weakens the combined authority of both parents while seriously circumscribing the role of the father. Poverty and low status are conducive to common law unions, which in turn generate male and female role models quite different from those of the elite. For the family as a whole this means the mother or eldest woman, rather than the eldest man, may be the dominant and stable family figure. Such a household is sometimes characterized by the absence of adult men living permanently in the family dwelling. It is in this situation that the mother may take over traditional male responsibilities, becoming the main economic provider and stable authority figure for her children.

If this situation persists for several generations, the result is the so-called grandmother family—the extended matrilineal family. The composition of such a household or grouping consists of the matriarch, her unmarried children, her married daughters, and the children of these unions. She may become the stable parent figure for her grandchildren, especially if the mother is working and the father is absent from the family. She has a great deal of influence over her sons' behavior, whether or not they are married, and is considered the unquestioned source of emotional support and moral suasion. In contrast to the patrilineal upper class family, lower class adults tend to plan their social interaction around the grandmother. Sisters maintain a stronger bond with one another after reaching adulthood, and strong ties of trust, affection, and mutual help are even found among half-brothers having the same mother.

The lower class family may appear to be noncohesive and disorganized to the outsider, and in some respects it is a weaker institution than the elite family. Nevertheless, it does perform some vital functions for its members. For the poor Dominican, one of the most important of these is economic. Mutual financial help is a necessity in a society that cannot provide enough employment or social welfare to meet the needs of its population.

The Role of Children and Childraising

The number of children in the Dominican family varies inversely with class status—the higher the position on the social ladder, the fewer the number of children. It is rare for an elite or middle class family to have more than four children. It is equally rare for a lower class household to have fewer than four. The value and role of the children are also determined by sex and social class, but at all levels they are a vital part of the domestic structure. Male children have a higher value than female, especially the first born. Many male children are seen as a reflection of the father's virility. If a couple is unable to have children, it is considered a serious failure on the part of the woman. An equal amount of damage is done to the man, however, as the lack of offspring casts doubt on his masculinity. Childless unions are considered unsatisfactory and are easily dissolved, particularly, if the two people are not formally married.

With increasing social and economic development, new attitudes toward children are forming among the upwardly mobile segments of the lower classes. The rural poor have traditionally maintained large families, having as many children "as God sends." In the past, there has also existed an anti-Haitian sentiment that encouraged Dominicans to fill up their country, thus circumventing the pressure of immigration from their neighbors to the west. Finally, the larger the family, the greater the degree of security for the parents in their old age. This pattern appears to be slowly changing, however, due to a combination of governmental and socioeconomic pressures to reduce family size. Upwardly mobile Dominicans especially feel the desire to limit the number of children and to alter their life-style. It is these individuals and their offspring who are becoming the core of the middle class and the most likely perpetrators of social change.

Because over half of the marriage unions are initiated without civil or religious ceremony, a high percentage of births is illegitimate. Very little social stigma is attached to illegitimacy. In the past, illegitimate natural children could become legitimate through subsequent marriage of the child's parents. Formal recognition was encouraged by Trujillo and involved completion of simple forms and a RD$1 fee. It meant the child would be his parents' full, legitimate heir under the law. Thus, although illegitimate natural children are not ostracized, especially in the lower echelons of society, legitimacy is perceived as a positive value and it is encouraged as a desirable goal.

The adoption of children is more common than official figures show. A high adoption rate results from the high incidence of nonlegal adoption among middle class and lower class households and is perpetrated, in turn, by the expensive and complicated legal procedures attached to formal adoption. Sometimes a child is taken into a household to provide a regular and inexpensive servant or to balance the ratio of male and female children in the family. In other cases, however, the child may be a relative who has been taken in because of the precarious financial situation of his parents. When formal adoption does occur, the child receives legal status and inheritance rights.

Compadrazgo

The Roman Catholic custom of selecting godparents for one's children is still a common practice at all levels of Dominican society and is formalized at the infant's baptism. The baptism is an important social event because it gives formal church sanction to these ritual kinship rites. The tradition of *compadrazgo* represents a moral, social, and emotional bond between the parents and *compadres* (godparents). To be selected as *compadre* is both an honor and a responsibility, and is invested with the same trust, mutual esteem, and importance that characterizes blood kinship.

The selection of the *compadres* is done with great care because the act hopefully represents an on-going relationship, not a mere symbolic gesture. In the majority of cases, blood relatives are chosen, further cementing intrafamily ties. For the lower classes however, *compadrazgo* can mean potential security and financial aid for the newborn. Parents may try to choose godparents who will be able to help provide the child with food, clothes, or schooling.

The relationship between the parents, the child, and his godparent is indelible; open quarreling among them is as serious an offense as public arguments between blood relatives. Trujillo used the *compadrazgo* system as a ploy to bolster his own political power. Because it is treasonous to conspire against one's *compadre*, Trujillo held mass baptisms where he became the godfather of thousands of peasants' children. Such a baptism was also desirable to the peasant because his *compadre* was the president of the country, and in the early years of his regime, Trujillo gave a RD$100 bill to the parents of each of his godchildren. President Balaguer has followed this lead, although he has not carried it to the extremes employed by Trujillo.

Marriage and Consensual Union

The legal, Christian, and monogamous marriage is universally accepted as the most respected manner of consummating a relationship. There are two classes of marriage recognized by law—civil marriage, which is performed in accordance with civil law, and religious marriage, as prescribed by canon law. A couple may choose either form of marriage ceremony, and the elite and newly rich classes commonly celebrate both. As this is a double expense, however, many middle class and lower class parents cannot afford both forms in the same day.

The common law union is the most prevalent form of marital union among the Dominican lower classes. It involves neither legal nor religious procedure, merely the consent of the individuals involved and their parents. Although aspiring toward marriage, the average girl has little chance of a formalized marriage. Many young women must settle for the consensual union because of their low socioeconomic position and consequent lack of bargaining power in the marriage market. Often a girl is only fourteen or fifteen when she sets up housekeeping for the first time, and more often than not she is pregnant or already a mother. A young man may avoid formal marriage, initially because his obligations to wife and children are therefore increased, whereas abilities as a free agent are decreased. He may experience more than one common law marriage while waiting for a "better" woman (one of lighter color or higher status) to come along. Consequently, the decision to marry may come at middle age and after the birth of several children.

RELIGIOUS LIFE

Although the Dominican Republic is a strongly Roman Catholic country in terms of believers and traditions, there is evidence that the influence of the church outside the realm of spiritual values and observance of holidays is not strong. Of the 2 percent who do not consider themselves Roman Catholic, the majority are Protestant. There is also belief in the Haitian-based religion, voodoo, but both of these religious influences are negligible. The position and strength of the Roman Catholic Church fluctuated throughout its history, experiencing serious setbacks at the beginning of this century. Trujillo's timely election and rise to power bolstered the church by giving it a semblance of secular power during most of his regime. The vacillation and divisiveness demonstrated by the clergy during and after the last of his years in office is an indication of the lack of cohesiveness that affected the Roman Catholic Church in 1972.

During the early years of the colony the Roman Catholic Church was the prime agent in the transfer of Spanish culture to the island (see ch. 3). The early clergy was considered the fount of intellectual and humanitarian endeavor, and many of their polemical arguments over the spiritual nature of the Indians reached the court in Spain.

The church reached the apex of its power by the mid-sixteenth century. After this early period of strength, however, it experienced a decline that paralleled the economic decline of the seventeenth century. A short revival was curtailed by the Haitian occupation (1822–44). During the nineteenth century many foreign influences were felt in the Dominican Republic, including those of Haitian voodoo and Protestantism. The Haitians ruled the church with the same iron hand with which they ruled the country, and they did more to circumscribe Roman Catholicism than any other force.

The strength of the Roman Catholic Church continued to fluctuate throughout the century, and the church's hold on the society weakened. The numbers of clergy or churches remained stable, and ideological rifts developed between the Vatican and the Dominican branch of the church. A controversy over the ownership of church lands began during the Haitian regime and continued into the twentieth century. The culmination of the dispute came in 1929 when the Supreme Court of Justice declared that the church had no legal personality and submitted a measure to Congress for the liquidation of all church property. Trujillo took power at this point and had the measure defeated.

During the Trujillo years the church and state achieved a degree of mutual support second only to that experienced during the early colonial period. The dictator openly favored the church, and it, in turn, upheld his regime. Under his influence, the church grew in power, wealth, and influence, and he became known as the Benefactor of the Church. Some of the measures enacted to strengthen the Roman Catholic position included the construction of new churches, the institution of the religious marriage ceremony and religious education in the schools, and the restoration of the juridical personality of the church. The Concordat of 1954 recognized Roman Catholicism as the official religion of the state and incorporated the aforementioned measures. After the concordat dozens of new priests came from Spain and Canada and millions of dollars were spent on new religious institutions.

This harmony and mutual admiration began to erode during the final years of Trujillo's dictatorship, and the church openly severed ties during his last two years in power. It began challenging his control by removing his authority in administrative matters in the 1950s. Changes were also reflected in the personnel and leadership, particularly in the highest levels. The most important of these changes was reflected in the office of the archbishop of Santo Domingo. Octavio Beras, a fifty-four-year-old Dominican-born priest of liberal leanings replaced Archbishop Pettini, an eighty-year-old Italian-born ultraconservative.

With the rumblings of discontent getting louder and more threatening, Trujillo replied with a new wave of terrorism. He jailed many leading citizens, and for the first time Roman Catholic priests were among the prisoners. This resurgence of terror, the jailing of churchmen, and the change in the orientation of the Roman Catholic clergy resulted in a pastoral letter forecasting the final break with the government. Trujillo reacted in a conciliatory manner, and the church thereafter refrained from attacking him officially. Although the official position was ambiguous, individual clergy continued to criticize the regime publicly. The oppressed upper and middle classes found among these members of the clergy the support they needed to overthrow Trujillo.

The dozen years after Trujillo's death were marked by further vacillation on the part of the church and by continued discord among the clergy. After his assassination, religious leaders joined the anti-Trujillo movement, and the church was brought even closer to a reversal of its previous policy. Following this wave of democratic sentiment, the religious hierarchy declared itself in favor of social, economic, and political reform and encouraged the formation of political parties. Nevertheless, as the 1962 elections drew near, some priests began to fear the consequences of electing Juan Bosch to the presidency. They expressed their trepidation publicly and tried to dissuade Dominicans from voting for him on the pretext that he had communist leanings.

After his election, Bosch made no attempt to allay the fears of the church. His new constitution was particularly annoying to devout Roman Catholics and the church because it sanctioned divorce, common law marriage, and state inspection of religious schools, and extended state protection to illegitimate children. The pious viewed this legislation as an attack on the traditional Roman Catholic norms ruling marriage and family and feared the result would be the abolition of religious instruction in the schools. Some equated the new president's actions with pro-Castro and procommunist tendencies, and these clergymen began to coalesce with dissatisfied elements of the military and elite in their opposition to Bosch. Although the Roman Catholic Church and its hierarchy maintained an officially neutral stance concerning the Bosch regime, it was evident that they breathed a sigh of relief after his overthrow.

Thus far the Roman Catholic Church had demonstrated that it could act as a barometer for public sentiment and political discontent, and it proved it would support political and social change—up to a point. Its ambivalent position after the Bosch overthrow, and especially during the 1965 crisis, has brought it under criticism, nevertheless. Church efforts to maintain the status quo were viewed as obstructionist, and intense antichurch sentiment was the result. In response to this criticism and in the face of the increasingly liberal orientation of the Vatican, the Roman Catholic Church has begun to play a more constructive role in the process of social change.

Contemporary Religions and Practices

Roman Catholicism

The Roman Catholic Church hierarchy is organized with the archbishop of Santo Domingo at the top of the pyramid; immediately under him are four bishops whose jurisdiction extends over their specific geographic regions. In 1969 there was a total of 446 priests. There were 324 regular priests, that is, those belonging to an order such as the Jesuit or Franciscan; 122 were secular priests, that is, under the jurisdiction of a bishop of a diocese. Despite the fact that the increase in parishes and priests between 1950 and 1960 (during the Trujillo years) was greater than in any other Latin American country for the same period, the Dominican Republic still exhibits one of the lowest ratios of priests to inhabitants. In 1969 there was one priest for every 8,945 Dominicans. Only Cuba and Haiti had fewer priests per inhabitant.

69

The overwhelming majority of the Roman Catholic clergy is engaged in parish work and education. Education is still an important function of the church, along with the operation of hospitals and other charitable institutions. In the past the church has run thirty-seven schools, seven hospitals, and many relief stations, social centers, and cooperatives. Catholic Relief Services—or CARITAS, as it is known in the majority of Latin American countries—is an agency that handles refugee and relief problems and works closely with the rural poor. Often Roman Catholic priests are not only the spiritual leaders of the community but also provide leadership in social, economic, and political affairs. They have promoted labor seminars and consumers' cooperatives in the countryside, while establishing means to help the urban migrant as well.

The Roman Catholic Church in the Dominican Republic is not as large or as extensive an institution as it is in other Latin American countries. Furthermore, it is often torn from within over various social or political issues. Finally, it is not a very wealthy institution as it possesses no large land holdings or industrial interests. There were many problems facing the church in 1972, and there was some evidence that its influence is decreasing in the modern sector, especially in the urban areas. Devout Dominicans feel the decline in the church's power may be the result of several problems: the lack of nationals in religious vocations; the absence of effective collaboration between foreign religious communities; the need for greater Roman Catholic influence in the schools; and the need for more effective dissemination of current Roman Catholic thought through modern communication media.

In spite of these apparent weaknesses, the church continues to form the base for the Dominican cultural pyramid while functioning as an influential organization in several spheres. It may openly express its opinion through Sunday sermons, church-owned radio stations, or pastoral letters. It may use its influence in a more covert manner through social services, lay organizations, and labor groups that draw their inspiration from Roman Catholic principles. Important government functions usually have a church official in attendance to give the appearance of official church sanction to the event. Finally, at the lower and more basic levels of the society, the village priest may still be the most educated man in the community, and his opinion will be respected in both sacred and secular matters.

Protestantism

Two percent of the Dominicans are not Roman Catholic, and the majority of these are Protestants, called *evangélicos* by the Dominicans. Despite its small size, the Protestant community has grown in influence, respect, and effectiveness since the first missionary arrived in 1889. In 1972 there were more than twenty Protestant denominations. The marked increase in their numbers since 1935 appears to be an internal phenomenon that is more evident in rural rather than in urban areas and among women rather than among men.

70

In general, Protestants are not persecuted, and Freemasonry is tolerated. Immediately after the signing of the Concordat of 1954, Protestant missions and congregations in the interior of the country temporarily suffered increased intimidation. In 1957 Trujillo expelled missionaries of the Jehovah's Witnesses. In recent years, however, relationships between the Roman Catholic Church and Protestant sects have been very cordial, and interdenominational study groups have been formed to promote the ecumenical spirit of Christianity.

The largest Protestant sects include: Seventh-Day Adventists; the Dominican Evangelical Church; the Assembly of God; and the Protestant Episcopal Church. The congregations, following the historic pattern, are largely drawn from the poorer, darker segments of Dominican society. One of the most important of these sects is the Dominican Evangelical Church, which was founded in 1960 through the merger of several Protestant groups already established. It is the only major denomination that can claim indigenous status, and the ministers and leading laymen are all Dominicans. In addition to evangelism, the Dominican Evangelical Church carries out educational, cultural, and welfare activities. It has organized clinics for babies in several cities and has become involved in family planning and birth control through one of its women's groups. Other activities include establishing cooperatives, housing projects, playgrounds, sewing centers, and literacy and sports programs.

Voodoo

Among the various cults in the rural areas are the Liborista cult and the Brotherhood of the Congo. The most prevalent, however, is voodoo, which was brought into the country by the Haitians. The word *voodoo* is Dahomean and is probably best translated as "god." It is a general term for all deities. In Haiti voodoo presents a well-knit, organized system of theology and ceremonialism that includes several categories: one concerned with the great gods; a second consisting of a series of familial deities associated with the kindred and the gods of the ancestral cult; a third, which is a group of personal forces that includes the deities of the divining cult and the souls of men; and a fourth, which is magic. Special priests and priestesses attend the needs of the believers, as well as performing certain rites in the unique so-called languages of their cults.

In 1972 voodoo practices are still most often encountered among Haitian immigrants or their descendants who have settled along the border or in other predominantly rural areas. Nevertheless, as these rural people migrate to the city they carry their beliefs and practices with them. This explains why, in the market in Santo Domingo, one may encounter prayer cards to semi-Christian deities in which reference is made to black magic practices. The government and most Dominicans consider voodoo to be African, barbaric, and anti-Catholic. As a result, the practice of voodoo is secret, and the nature and extent of these practices and the number of its adherents is not known or even estimated.

Religious Shrines and Practices

With the exception of the voodoo ceremonies, the majority of religious practices and customs are firmly rooted in the Roman Catholic tradition. During the early part of the colonial period the island's patron saint was Our Lady of Mercy (Nuestra Señora de la Merced), and the most important shrine in the country is dedicated to this Spanish madonna. According to the traditional story, Columbus and his men were surprised by an Indian attack one night and were almost defeated, when suddenly a vision of the Virgin Mary appeared on the Cross. The Indians were awed and frightened, allowing the Spaniards to repel the attack. Thousands of Dominicans visit this shrine every year, and soil from the spot where the cross originally stood is accredited with many miraculous cures.

This Spanish madonna was later replaced in popularity by a native Dominican patron, La Altagracia (the Virgin of the Highest Grace). The traditional story is told that a very old and mysterious pilgrim— reputedly one of the apostles—came to a small village in the eastern part of the country and asked the father of an ailing daughter for food and shelter. When the pilgrim departed, he gave a small picture of the Virgin Mary to the father and, upon looking at the picture, the child was healed. Ever since, this particular madonna has been venerated by Dominicans, who attribute miraculous cures to her. She is still the most popular intercessor among Dominicans, and studies of Santo Domingo indicate that 40 percent of the people questioned prayed directly to her. She has been the country's official patroness since 1922.

A very common religious practice in the Dominican Republic is the *rosario* or religious procession. Such processions are often organized to ask for rain or to ask for intercession in a common problem. An image of a saint or madonna is carried at the head of a procession followed by the person who leads the singing and carries a large rosary made of wood. Behind the lead singer come the musicians and then the other members of the procession. *Rosarios* may go to a church or stop at a home by special request, but members cannot leave the procession until it returns to its starting place. There are many religious holidays, but by far the most popular is Christmas. It is the most joyful celebration of the year. Preparation begins in early December and continues throughout the month.

In the lower segments of society, Roman Catholicism sometimes becomes interlaced with local superstitions and practices that are believed to guard possessions and well-being. Among these practices are *formularios* and *oraciones*, which are similar to incantations and are probably closely tied with voodoo or other magical practices and superstitions. The incantations may be used to ward off the evil eye or bring good luck and usually carry a tone of supplication. They are sold in the marketplaces of the rural areas, as well as in the poorer markets of the capital city itself.

SOCIAL VALUES

Traditional behavior patterns in the Dominican Republic were adopted from Spanish culture and emphasized the values of paternalism, the cult of the individual, and male supremacy. Trujillo's efforts to impose new values and life-styles plus the impact of the industrial and technological revolutions have affected some traditional values. Within the classes there is increasing dissension and differentiation as societal changes increase the possibilities for social mobility. Peasants moving to the cities in ever-increasing numbers come into contact with a growing middle class. The accelerated pace of events in the second half of the twentieth century is continuing to offset and alter the social fabric.

The Individual

The concept of individuality is at the core of the male-oriented Hispanic tradition and is present in all the strata of the society. The correlated complex of attitudes and actions that emphasizes individual qualities and interpersonal trust is aptly referred to as *personalismo*. It stresses the uniqueness of each human being, valuing personal integrity over abstract rights and institutions, and individual dignity and honor above group responsibility. Idealism is also an important corollary of *personalismo*, and utopian ideals of an absolute and unattainable quality are glorified. Compromise has little value, if any. More often than not, compromise is considered a slur upon one's sense of pride and dignity, for it casts doubts upon the purity of one's ideals. The consequences of this behavioral patterning for societal and political interaction are immeasurable.

Personalismo determines the very quality of Dominican social life and helps to explain the overt warmth and friendliness that characterizes interpersonal relationships at all levels. Among family and friends this is demonstrated through a great deal of affection and intimate mutual concern. Even the most casual encounters are invested with a marked degree of politeness and cordiality, because individual honor is extremely sensitive to praise, insult, or slight. Consequently, rather than perceiving each other in the impersonal light of status or occupational roles—customer-clerk, employer-employee, governmental official-constituent—social interaction among Dominicans is couched in terms of the personalities involved.

Closely interwoven in the fabric of *personalismo* are values and attitudes that characterize political behavior. This is most clearly manifested in the notion that individual men shape the destiny of the country. In the past at least, this idea has been a self-fulfilling prophecy, for nowhere in the hemisphere has *personalismo* at the government level been more persistent than in the Dominican Republic. In a society where ideological content is minimized, political parties and social action groups mobilize around the individual. The politician, in turn, tries to present himself as a dramatic personality and dynamic leader rather than as the synthesis of the opinion of the public.

Along with the Hispanic heritage of *personalismo* is another ethic that was further reinforced under the plantation system—that of the *patrón*. This colonial system was influenced by many personal face-to-face relationships between masters and their slaves, and it served to emphasize the symbolic father role played by the plantation owner in opposition to the child role played by those serving him. Although the *patrón* phenomenon would appear to occur in the countryside only, it is actually extremely pervasive at all levels of Dominican society. The idea of the *patrón* has come to be equated with the concept of paternalism and has come to represent the leader, the teacher, and the father. The *patrón* is expected to be kind, demanding, and fair and can expect unquestioning loyalty in return for his paternal devotion. Obviously, the role of the *patrón* is filled in most families by the father or the grandfather. On the societal level, it is the obligation of the elite, the political and labor leaders, wealthy industrialists, and the clergy—or anyone in a position of authority—to play the role of the *patrón*.

Male Role Model

The complex of behavior and attitudes that defines the male role in the traditional Hispanic manner is called *machismo* (literally, maleness), and it is integral to the most basic understanding of Dominican culture. *Machismo* accompanies the concepts of *personalismo* and the *patrón*, and all of these behavioral values are mutually reinforcing. The degree of maleness is perceived in terms of virility, daring, forcefulness, and competitiveness, characteristics that are enhanced by a love of the dramatic and concurrent senses of fatalism and humor. The more effectively a man displays these qualities, the greater his degree of *machismo*. This behavior pattern is characterized by undertones of heroism, sexual prowess, and leadership potential and plays a major part in the political and social spectrums of the society.

Machismo is also closely tied to the historic image of the *caballero*, the gentleman-knight of medieval Spain. This image stressed the values of good breeding, learning, generosity, and disinterest in material gains. The *caballero* scorned manual labor in favor of a gracious and cultured existence enhanced by artistic or intellectual endeavor. Even today the most popular professions are not necessarily the most lucrative but are usually the most humanitarian and cultured: law, architecture, and medicine. Ideally, the male's main concerns should be the arts, politics, and philosophy. This mode of behavior is very prevalent among the elite and, because so much positive value is attached to *machismo* and the characteristics of the *caballero*, all male Dominicans attempt to model their behavior along these lines.

74

Machismo for the lower class male is as desirable a behavior pattern as for his social superiors. Nevertheless, the *macho-caballero* ethic presents some special problems for him. He cannot hope to engage in intellectualism or expect to lead a leisurely and cultured life because he may have to spend the majority of his waking hours looking for work or food. His pride suffers because he is never on the giving end of the *patrón* system but always at the receiving end. Finally, unless he becomes the leader of a group of his peers, it is unlikely that he will ever be the head of anything—even his own family. Consequently, the lower class male tends to emphasize those elements of *machismo* that he can fulfill, namely physical and sexual prowess; demonstrated success in these areas may even make him a leader among his peers.

At all levels of society the male is encouraged to prove himself and demonstrate his *machismo* through the conquest of females. A lower class male may maintain more than one family and, although this is not accepted at the higher levels of the society, the maintenance of a mistress is considered a natural outlet for the healthy Dominican male. Sexual prowess invariably provides a source of amused and admiring gossip.

There is little evidence that the basic complex of behaviors exalting the male, the individual, and the paternal overseer is changing. The specific activities of the gentleman or *caballero*, however, have been modified by social and economic changes. The rise of the middle class as well as the development of a powerful industrial and commercial group have resulted in a more receptive attitude toward working for money, and the increasing availability of education has allowed lower class Dominicans to participate in so-called gentlemanly activities to a degree never before possible.

Female Role Model

The Dominican woman has traditionally derived her position in the society from her male counterpart, and to a great extent she continues to do so. The image of ideal womanhood is exactly opposite to *machismo*, although there is no concomitant term to capsulize her behavior pattern. She should display passivity, gentleness, and a willingness to derive her public status from that of her husband. Ideally, her role is to dedicate herself to the domestic scene, making a comfortable and gracious home for her husband and devoting her life to the welfare of her children.

At all levels of society the woman is expected to center her life around her home, but the orientation differs appreciably among the classes. Among the upper classes the woman patterns her life-style after the lady-of-leisure image of the past, rarely pursuing a career outside the home after marriage. Her education is usually in the humanities, and her education is perceived as an end in itself and is not expected to lead to a lifetime career. Abnegation and self-sacrifice are expected of women in their domestic roles, and the husband is considered the final authority and arbiter of family affairs. Despite all this show of apparent weakness and docility, the woman actually has almost complete responsibility in the domestic sphere. The building, managing, and perpetuation of the aristocratic extended family falls squarely on her shoulders and, considering the importance of the family, this is no small task.

The activities of the elite woman are traditionally those befitting a lady of her rank. She is encouraged to value charm more than efficiency and beauty more than excessive toil. Her husband will attempt to have as many servants to aid his wife as his means will allow. A wealthy woman is expected to devote the leisure time this allows her to being attractive and well dressed for her husband, and she will spend hours on her appearance. This is not to imply an ethic of laziness, however. Ideally, the upper class woman devotes much of her time to charity and to cultural affairs, in addition to attending social functions and mass as the family's representative before the society and the Roman Catholic Church. The cohesiveness of kin groups is reinforced by constant visiting among female relatives, and family rituals such as mourning are attended predominantly by the female members.

The difference in role behavior that exists between upper and lower class males also occurs among women, but to a lesser degree. The role of the lower class woman in the family may be extended, especially if she is deserted by the male and is forced to be the provider as well as the moral backbone of the family. Contrary to the lady-of-leisure ethic, she may have to spend most of her life working outside the home. Physical attractiveness, however, is just as valued among the lower as the upper classes, and poor women use as much make-up as they can afford.

As in most Latin American countries, there is a double standard in sexual relations. Not only is it unthinkable for the woman to be unfaithful, but she is socialized to expect her husband's digressions and to accept them with dignity and resignation. The woman of every class is expected to give unswerving loyalty to her man, whether or not she is formally married to him. Dominicans are as scandalized by an unfaithful woman as they are accustomed to the infidelity of her spouse.

The role and the image of the woman in the Dominican Republic has changed to a notable degree. The liberalization of the feminine role began with the extension of political rights and educational and employment opportunities, and it has certainly been advanced by increasing diversity in the society in general. Her behavior is less restricted and prescribed, and consequently she plays a greater role in the economic and political sectors than ever before. There are few sanctions remaining on women who choose to pursue a career after marriage, although the great majority would prefer to be supported entirely by their husbands. Nevertheless, the high cost of living and low salaries of the middle class may make it more desirable for the married woman to retain her job. Upper class women are also working alongside the men in increasingly large numbers, and many hold very prestigious positions in the government. There are women in the professions and in both houses of Congress. President Balaguer has also increased the relative power of a number of women by appointing them as provincial governors both in 1966 and in 1970 and by appointing a woman as the acting secretary of foreign relations in 1972.

Interpersonal Relations and the Social Order

Personalismo, paternalism, the *patrón* ethic, and the idealized male and female role models help to shape interpersonal relationships. Primary loyalty is given to kinsmen and close friends, and primary relationships are based on the family rather than on an occupational or interest organization. In the past this ethic has led to nepotism at governmental levels—an attitude that is not only accepted, but condoned. Ritual kinship, or *compadrazgo*, is the most popular way of initiating a friend into the family scheme, thus permitting the persons involved to deal with one another as family members. The importance of the *compadrazgo* system for interpersonal relations is emphasized by the popular usage of the terminology itself. Dominicans will commonly refer to each other and especially to their intimate friends as *compadre*. This is an indication of the deep affection and respect between the two individuals.

The relationship between the Dominican and his leaders is also defined in terms of the individual and the *patrón*. In Hispanic society, where privilege and power were largely hereditary, both peasant and noble recognized and accepted the difference in their status while respecting the personal dignity of each individual. Associated with the notion of hierarchy is the conviction that the privilege of high status and leadership brings concomitant responsibilities. The social tradition stressed not only a rigid hierarchy of power and status but also a centralized authority, which allowed little leeway for local initiative and collective decisionmaking. The traditional concept of the leader is quite different from that envisioned in democratic theory. Thus, although professing adherence to the notions of political democracy, many of the deeply ingrained values and norms work against it.

Ex-President Trujillo had more effect on Dominican interpersonal relationships than any other single influence before or after his thirty-year regime. He exhibited a dynamic blend of *machismo, personalismo*, and the *patrón* ethos and was brought to power as much by his personality as by his qualifications. Dominicans were attracted by his physical appearance, his martial bearing and dignity, and his magnetic aura of force and authority. He simultaneously gave the impression of being a wise and knowledgeable man, although he had no formal education, and of being a doer and a builder—a veritable dynamo of a man. He was admired for his prowess with women as well, and this

77

brought him much respect. Once in office, he retained his strong sense of individuality, jealously guarding his power and delegating very little of it. At the peak of his career, he had both the capital city and the highest mountain renamed for him. He cultivated an extremely paternalistic attitude towards the Dominican poor, and this was most clearly manifested in the mass baptisms where he became the godfather to hundreds of children at a time (see ch. 7).

Although astutely employing certain features of the Dominican behavioral complex, Trujillo severely circumscribed other important aspects, especially those involving family and trust. He demanded unswerving loyalty and was quick to punish an erring offender. He purposely planted the seeds of distrust and insecurity at the familial level and waited for this discord to bear fruit. He did not have long to wait. Suspicion and mistrust began to replace the open friendliness that had characterized the Dominican personality for so long. Friendships became calculated affairs, and there were even frequent refusals to recognize kinship obligations. These consequences were devastating to a society that was poorly integrated to start with. Many Dominicans blame Trujillo for the brittleness of social relationships and consider fragmentation and polarization his legacy to the Dominican people.

CHAPTER 5

LIVING CONDITIONS

The pattern of living conditions in the Dominican Republic differs from that in a majority of the Latin American countries in the sense that there is no remaining indigenous population that lives in a fashion significantly different from that of the population having Hispanic or other external origins.

The quality of Dominican living depends principally upon level of income and, secondarily, urban-rural locality. To some extent it depends also on skin pigmentation and the social values and other considerations that this pigmentation entails. In varying degrees, to all social groups the quality of life is more varied and, for the most part, more rewarding in the capital city and in the Cibao Valley, where the most prosperous agricultural land and the old city of Santiago de los Caballeros are located.

During the long period of the regime of Rafael Leónidas Trujillo Molina, the dynamic factors that might ordinarily have affected living conditions were in large measure suppressed. In particular, the movement of people from the traditional life in the countryside to a new life in town was actively discouraged.

After the collapse of the remnants of the regime, in 1962 pent-up urban migration flooded into the cities, and agencies in socially important fields, such as welfare, housing, and health, were established or expanded. These innovative movements were badly dislocated by the 1965 and 1966 civil disturbances, and during the following years the administrators of social services, such as welfare, housing, medical care, and environmental sanitation, found it difficult to keep pace with a combination of rapid urbanization and one of the fastest population growth rates in Latin America.

NUTRITION AND DIET

The average Dominican diet is deficient both in quantitative and qualitative terms. For the years 1964 and 1965 it was estimated by an international organization that the average per capita daily food intake was made up of 2,230 calories, fifty-three grams of protein (including twenty-two grams of animal origin), and fifty-three grams of fats and oils. In each category, the amounts were slightly more than those that had been estimated for 1959, but the levels remained well under the 2,654 calories, sixty-eight grams of protein, and sixty-three grams of fats and oils estimated by the same international agency as representing the average for seventeen Latin American countries during the 1960s. A national nutrition survey reported by the government in 1970 indicated that the average caloric intake in communities studied was 79 percent, and the protein intake was 82 percent of standard normal needs. The consumption of calcium was 62.5 percent of standard normal needs; iron, 79.2 percent; vitamin A, 57 percent; thiamin, 86 percent; riboflavin, 55 percent; niacin, 94 percent; pyridoxine, 54 percent; and folic acid, 37 percent.

The deficiencies in diet probably varied radically by income distribution and between urban and rural areas, but the overall incidence has been sufficiently serious for the government to create several public entities to deal with deficiency problems. The Nutrition Department, established in the National Public Health Laboratory with assistance of the United States-based William Waterman Fund, studies possibilities of diet enrichment through better food selection. In 1969 a national nutrition survey, conducted with the assistance of the Institute of Nutritional Sciences of Columbia University, led to the recommendation that a national nutrition council be established, and the Nutrition Division was subsequently added to the Ministry of Public Health and Social Welfare.

During 1970 the government conducted a supplementary feeding program for mothers and children that reached some 137,000 persons, and several projects involving training in nutrition were carried out. Coordination was maintained with public and private foreign and international organizations. The government also operated the first of what was designed to become a series of *comedores económicos* (low-cost dining rooms) to be established in all parts of the country. The pilot dining room, located in a working-class suburb of Santo Domingo, featured complete meals at a cost of RD$0.25 (1 peso equals US$1—see Glossary). The unit was reported to serve 1,500 sitdown customers daily, and takeout customers were said to purchase one or two meals in order to serve five or six family members.

A 1969 government survey of 552 Santo Domingo families in a wide range of income brackets and believed to be representative of 85 percent of the city's population provided a picture of the general pattern of urban food consumption. Rice was by a wide margin the most important cereal food, followed by wheat flour and wheat products, such as bread and pasta. Starchy root crops, in order of importance, were white potatoes, cassava, sweet potatoes, and taro. Onions were the most popular of the garden vegetables, followed by tomatoes, peas, garlic, and red peppers. In addition to bananas, the most frequently eaten fruit, avocados and plantains most often were important elements in the diet. Citrus fruit consumption was minor, and the consumption of the more exotic tropical fruits, such as papayas and mangoes, was negligible. Most of the standard garden vegetables and a wide variety of tropical fruits are available seasonally in Santo Domingo, but temperate fruits and some vegetables, such as cauliflower and asparagus, are imported and find a good market at high prices.

The survey showed beef to have represented about half of the cost of all meat purchases. Poultry ranked next, and there were limited purchases of pork and of goat meat. Sheep raising is a rarity in the Dominican Republic, and consumption of lamb and veal was too minor to be listed as a cost item. Domestic beef is generally regarded as being of mediocre quality, but the preference for it was so marked that lower income families devoted a larger proportion of their food budgets to it than did families with higher incomes. Fish and seafood consumption was minor, but the proportion of the budget devoted to it tended to increase with the level of income. There was also an appreciable consumption of prepared meats. Among the more important prepared meats are imported tinned items and sausages produced by the German-Jewish colony of Sosúa, which also cures hams and makes butter, cheeses, and sandwich bread for sale in Santo Domingo.

Diets in urban localities in the interior are somewhat less varied than those in the capital city because of difficulties in transporting and storing perishables. Both in rural localities and in working-class urban households, most of the diet consists of rice, kidney beans, starchy root crops, and bananas. Green vegetables other than onions, garlic, and tomatoes are rarely eaten. A piece of meat is sometimes added to the family stewpot, but fish and poultry are rarely served. Although most small farmers keep chickens, few are killed because their eggs can be sold at a good price. Fish consumption is low because seafood cannot be transported without considerable spoilage, and in the Dominican Republic—as in much of Latin America—it is little esteemed as a dietary component.

Most of the milk production is of mediocre quality, and it is consumed principally in the form of cheese. The bacteria count in raw milk is generally high, and even in Santo Domingo—where pasteurized milk is available—the irregularity of the bacterial count indicates the desirability of boiling. Turkey and ham are more expensive than beef and are eaten principally by the urban well-to-do. Most farms raise hogs, however, and such residual pork products as ham hocks provide an important part of the countryside diet. Goats are kept in towns as well as in the countryside for both milk and meat; the real importance of these products probably far exceeds the amounts listed in available statistics.

Although the country exports fruits, vegetables, and meats, in the late 1960s the value of imported edibles represented up to 20 percent of the value of all imports, and the per capita domestic food production was on the decline. The index of food production excluding sugar and cocoa (1957–59 equals 100) declined to 80 in 1967 before recovering to about 90 in 1970. During the early 1970s the principal imports were wheat flour, edible oils, and miscellaneous processed items. Of particular importance among the processed food imports was *bacalao* (salted cod) from Canada and Norway, which may have contributed much more to the protein diet than any kind of fresh fish.

Probably the most frequently prepared meal in the countryside as well as in town is some form of *sancocoho*, a thin catchall stew that is common to all of Latin America. It is made with tubers, some greens, and whatever pieces of meat may be available. A more savory concoction based on similar ingredients is the *sopa criolla dominicana* (native soup), which is fashioned from stew meat, pasta, onions, greens, and seasonings. Another standard is the *pastelón de vegetables* (vegetable pastry), a baked concoction of potatoes and a variety of garden vegetables that have been seasoned and thickened with flour and eggs before being cooked in butter or fat. At its best, Dominican cuisine is filling more than it is innovative or elegant, and the specialties seldom find their place in cookbooks featuring the more exotic Latin American specialties.

DRESS

Clothing in rural areas consists mainly of factory-made cotton dresses or skirts and blouses for the women and trousers and white shirts for men. Very young boys frequently go about without clothing. There is little or no home weaving of cloth, and inexpensive purchased garments are preferred to those made in the home from purchased materials. Shoes, coats, and ties are usually reserved for very formal occasions. They are worn most frequently by persons over the age of fifty, and relatively prosperous people feel a responsibility for wearing these articles of apparel at such occasions as fiestas and weddings as a mark of respect. Among the upper class rural families, dress corresponds to that worn in the city and is generally stylish and of good quality.

The dress of urban working-class people is not markedly different from that in the countryside, except that shoes are generally worn and small boys do not ordinarily run about unclothed. A large proportion of the urban working-class people were themselves raised in the countryside and, in the mid-1960s, their limited income precluded buying many shirts that cost from RD$2 to RD$3 and trousers that cost RD$5. The upper class dress stylishly and with some elegance in subdued colors.

HOUSING

Little recent housing data are available, but in 1969 a Dominican housing expert estimated that in 1967 there had been a deficit of 376,495 units. The expert calculated that the deficit could be eliminated by building 18,825 new units annually during a twenty-year period but that it would be necessary to build another 21,609 annually in order to accommodate the growth in population at the then current rate of growth. He noted that this volume of construction—an annual building rate of about 40,000 units—would exceed all Dominican capabilities. Other estimates indicated that in 1961 about 70 percent of the housing deficit was in rural localities and that 65 percent of all units in the country were substandard.

In 1960 a little over half of the units counted in the census of that year housed five or more people, and about 12 percent housed nine or more. The 1960 data did not include a count of numbers of rooms, but the 1950 census had found that 8.1 percent of the homes consisted of a single room, 44.6 percent had two rooms, 25.1 had three rooms, and 22.2 percent had four rooms or more. In most instances, however, where houses had more than one room, at least one was set aside for purposes other than sleeping. It was estimated in 1967 that some 66 percent of all houses were one-bedroom units.

Other data available only from the 1950 census showed that 70.7 percent of the dwellings were owner occupied, 15 percent were rented, and 14.3 percent were unexplained or occupied under other forms of tenancy.

Rural housing is typically represented by the *bohio*, a rustic dwelling made frequently either of *yagua* (material made from the fronds of the royal palm), used both for the walls and the roof, or of thin sticks loosely woven together with vine, string, or wire and sometimes plastered with mud. Roughly cut board siding is also common, and the gabled roofs are also sometimes made of metal or bark of the royal palm. Floors are almost always earthen; in 1967 it was estimated that floors were made of earth in 70 percent of the units in the country as a whole. The better rural houses are made of cement or concrete blocks and occasionally of shingle or tile. A few have cement or wood floors. Windows are often kept closed because of the belief that drafts and fresh air cause illness, but they are fairly large and numerous and give the dwellings a degree of airy spaciousness unusual in peasant homes elsewhere in the Latin American countryside.

Furnishings are limited to the bare essentials, including homemade chairs, tables, and beds of rude, slatting material. Electricity is seldom available, and indoor water and sanitary provisions are rare. Outdoor latrines are fairly common, and most laundering and bathing take place in nearby streams and springs. Decorations frequently include colored lithographs of the patron saint of the country—the Virgin of Altagracia—and the Sacred Heart of Jesus.

The inhabitants of small towns and hamlets enjoy more luxuries in the way of housing and furnishings. Houses are more substantial, and it is common for a young couple to defer marriage until the man is able to provide a full set of furniture, including a wooden bed, chairs, and a small table, some bed linen, tin cutlery, and a set of cooking pots.

Closets and dressers are beyond the means of most, however, and clothing is kept in suitcases or boxes.

In Santiago de los Caballeros and a few neighborhoods in Santo Domingo there are old Spanish colonial homes of the elite built around open patios. Construction is predominantly of wood, stone, or brick with tiled roofs and terrazzo flooring. In the capital city most of the better residential districts, rebuilt after the 1930 hurricane that leveled much of the city, are characterized by pleasant tree-lined streets and modern tropical-style residences surrounded by attractive landscaping and flowering vegetation.

Housing of the urban working class was increasingly difficult to secure during the 1960s and early 1970s as a consequence of the increasing flow of urban migration. It was only in Santo Domingo, however, that crowded slum districts had become serious problems. Shacks made of scrap materials were numerous in squatter communities in the outskirts of the city. In older sections, bordering on the Ozama River, shopping and commercial districts were mixed with inner-city slums, where many of the lower income people lived in *casas de vecindad*—tenements in which families occupied one or more rooms with access to communal sanitary facilities. An extensive 1967 survey of Santo Domingo families at various income levels found that nearly 35 percent lived in tenements and that only about 2 percent lived in apartments. Apartment and tenement units differed in that the former had kitchens and bathrooms.

According to 1969 estimates by the Pan American Health Organization, 32.1 percent of the population lived in dwellings with inside or easy access piped-water connections, and 12.4 percent lived in ones with sewer connections. Most of the water and all of the sewerage installations were in urban localities. In the early 1960s it was estimated that some 58 percent of all urban homes had electrical connections, but the 1967 survey of Santo Domingo homes found nearly 90 percent of the homes surveyed to have electricity. Rural homes continue to rely principally on kerosine lamps for lighting, but in early 1972 the Inter-American Development Bank extended a US$7.2 million loan from its Canadian fund to provide electricity to 160 rural communities.

Although the housing shortage at the beginning of 1973 remained formidable, the expansion of credit during the years since the collapse of the Trujillo regime was encouraging to new construction, and the public housing program had expanded substantially. In particular, an impressive number of tidy concrete houses dotted the countryside between the airport and the city.

The government's housing program was launched in 1962 with the enactment of laws creating the National Housing Institute, which was to prepare and execute a general housing plan, and the National Housing Bank, intended to promote housing construction and a mortgage market. Other legislation authorized the creation of savings and loan associations. Later, the Aid and Housing Institute and the President's Special Fund were also created. The institute is a housing development entity with particular concern for the interests of public employees. The President's Special Fund is a fiduciary entity that has contributed extensively to public housing costs. During the late 1960s and early 1970s its social importance and high visibility gave public housing first place among the projects sponsored by the administration of President Joaquín Balaguer.

During the 1966-70 period the public sector entities supplied 8,508 families with dwellings. Some 64.9 percent of the units were constructed with assistance from the President's Special Fund; 26.5 percent, by the National Housing Institute; and 8.6 percent, by the Aid and Housing Institute. With the assistance of the well-managed National Housing Bank, some eleven savings and loan associations had been established by the end of 1970. Membership totaled over 40,000, and 5,461 loans with a total value of RD$37 million had been authorized. During the period home loans by development financing institutions and banks increased at a faster rate than loans for any other purpose.

During 1969 about 20,000 units were constructed by public and private sectors combined, a number not quite sufficient to accommodate population growth alone. The reported total probably did not include some informally constructed rural *bohios*, however, and the 1970-74 National Development Plan called for the construction of 27,050 units annually—a number that would make possible some reduction of the shortage.

The prospect of further acceleration of the housing-construction program during the early 1970s was not without its hazards. The social value was evident, and the work would generate additional current employment and income, but the program would contribute only very indirectly to the productive potential of the economy. Moreover, the import content of construction costs in the early 1970s was about 25 percent on low-cost units and higher on more expensive ones. Import content had risen during recent years, at least in part as a consequence of the prohibition of tree felling in 1967 and the closing of the sawmills. It has been suggested that the critical balance-of-payments situation facing the economy in the early 1970s cast doubt on the desirability of acceleration of the building program in the immediate future and that an alternative might involve shifting to low-cost housing rather than the medium and higher cost units that had predominated in the late 1960s.

HEALTH

Medical Facilities and Personnel

Most of the population relies on services provided by the government for curative as well as preventive health care. The Ministry of Public

Health and Social Welfare is responsible for the general public health program; through the National Health Service it directs technical divisions concerned with infant and maternal health, communicable diseases, malaria, tuberculosis, hospitals, environmental sanitation, statistics, health education, pharmacies, and nursing. The National Health Service also directs and coordinates administration of provincial and local public health programs.

A separate medical system for personnel insured under the country's social security program is directed by the Dominican Social Security Institute (Instituto Dominicano de Seguro Social—IDSS), an autonomous public agency under general direction of the Ministry of Public Health and Social Welfare (see Welfare, this ch.). In 1971 the IDSS operated thirteen hospitals—including a 500-bed unit in Santo Domingo—with a total of 1,300 beds, plus forty-two outpatient units operated by doctors and eighty attended by nurses, and maintained sixteen ambulances. It employed 358 doctors and maintained its own corps of graduate and auxiliary nurses. On a reimbursable basis, it also contracted for the use of public and private health facilities and personnel. In 1970 some 35,000 hospital cases, including 6,000 maternity cases, were attended under the IDSS program.

In 1971 there were reported to be 11,340 hospital beds in the country, about 2.7 beds per 10,000 of the population. This proportion represented a slight decline from the proportion of 2.8 beds per 10,000 of the population in 1966, but twenty-five new public hospitals were reported to be under construction. About 23 percent of all beds were in private institutions, for the most part small units known as *clinicas* (clinics). Most of the private hospitals were operated on a commercial basis by groups of doctors. Some were operated by sugar plantations; notable among these was a well-equipped forty-bed unit with eight doctors at the big La Romana sugar plantation on the Caribbean Coastal Plain. A scattering of units were operated by religious institutions and missions, but few were maintained by private charitable organizations.

In the mid-1960s it was estimated that over 50 percent of the doctors, nearly all of the graduate nurses, 50 percent of the hospital beds, and over 25 percent of the hospitals were concentrated in Santo Domingo. The bed-patient ratio per 10,000 population was 7.6 in the National District and 1.8 elsewhere in the country. Moreover, outside the National District the facilities tend to be small and inadequately equipped. In the mid-1960s nearly half had limited kitchen facilities or no kitchens, and many were without laundry facilities. Conditions tended to be crowded, and patients found it necessary to wait long hours before receiving treatment. Public health hospitals were free, but in outlying areas many of the smaller hospitals as well as the outpatient facilities did not have doctors attached to them and, as a consequence, were reduced virtually to the status of first aid and vaccination centers.

Most hospitals are handicapped by a shortage of administrative personnel. In smaller units, doctors whose services are badly needed for the treatment of patients often find it necessary to divert most of their time to administrative matters. In cooperation with the Pan American Health Organization the government offers scholarships for public health administration and related activities and conducts some inservice training in the field. Interest, however has been reported to have been limited.

In 1966 some 78.7 percent of the beds were in general hospitals. About 5 percent were in hospitals for pediatrics; 3.3 percent, for maternity; 6.4 percent, for mental cases; and 1.2 percent, for leprosy. In public· health hospitals only, in 1967 the average stay was 8.3 days, and the average rate of occupancy was 72.3 percent. The duration of stay was close to the average for countries of Latin America, and the rate of occupancy was considerably above the average.

Data concerning outpatient facilities are incomplete. In 1972 the only figures available showed that in 1968 there were fifty-three clinics and dispensaries, attended by an unreported number of patients, and ninety-three maternal and infant centers, attended by 171,000 mothers and 183,000 infants.

The number of physicians in the country is reported to have declined from 2,153 in 1964 to 1,935 in 1971. The 1971 figure represented a little less than five per 10,000 of the population, close to the average for the countries of Latin America. The apparent decline may reflect either inconsistency in reporting or a heavy emigration of physicians during the 1960s. The director of a large Santo Domingo hospital estimated that as many as 80 percent of the 1969 medical graduates of the Autonomous University of Santo Domingo (Universidad Autónomo de Santo Domingo—UASD) were practicing in the United States in 1971. At about the same time the professional journal *El Médico Dominicano* estimated that at least 30 percent of the country's medical graduates during recent years—the exact timespan was not stated—were in practice in the United States.

Some of the doctors are engaged on a full-time basis by the Ministry of Public Health and Social Welfare or by the IDSS. Others work three or four hours daily and devote the remainder of the day to a more lucrative private practice. Despite the apparently high emigration rate of doctors, the medical profession enjoys considerable social prestige, and enrollment in medical studies at the UASD during the 1960s was consistently one of the highest in the institution, exceeding even that in law, perennially the most popular in most Latin American universities.

During the 1960s the number of medical students graduated from the UASD varied radically from year to year but averaged about 100. Medicine was also taught at the Pedro Henríquez Ureña National University, which opened its doors in the capital city in 1966. The course of study lasts six years and is followed by a year either of internship or of service in one of the rural public health facilities.

Some 550 dentists were in practice in 1971, as compared with 479 in 1964. A majority were in private practice. The dentist-patient ratio per 10,000 of the population in 1971 was 1.4—well above the average for Middle America but far below the average for South American countries. Dentists are trained in five-year courses of study at both of the universities offering medical training. Dentists do not enjoy the prestige enjoyed by doctors, and their services are used principally for extractions. In 1970 IDSS dentists performed 56,957 extractions as compared with 6,268 fillings.

A shortage of nurses is one of the principal impediments to improved health services. In 1971 there were 220 graduate nurses, and in 1968 there were 2,172 nursing auxiliaries. The number of midwives is believed to be substantial, but a majority have received no formal instruction. Graduate nurses are trained in three-year courses at the National School of Nursing and at the School of Nursing of the Madre y Maestra Catholic University in Santiago de los Caballeros. In 1969 each of the two schools had an enrollment of seventy-eight, and the National School of Nursing graduated eighteen. No graduation data were given for the second school, but the total output was clearly insufficient to affect the nursing shortage.

Health Hazards and Preventive Medicine

Neither cause of death nor incidence of disease is fully or accurately reported to public health statisticians. In 1966 the Inter-American Development Bank speculated that at least 20 percent of all deaths were not reported, and in 1968 almost half of the reported deaths were attributed to "senility, ill-defined, and unknown causes."

During the four-year period from 1965 through 1968 the principal cause of mortality was gastroenteritis and related diseases of the digestive tract, which accounted for nearly 18 percent of all reported deaths. Diseases of early infancy were second in reported importance, and the greater likelihood that infant mortality might go unrecorded suggests that diseases of infancy could have been first in incidence. Cancer was next, and other diseases causing 600 or more deaths a year were nutritional deficiency, heart disease, tetanus, and pneumonia. When combined with bronchitis and other diseases of the respiratory system, pneumonia accounted for well over 1,000 deaths each year.

Among the communicable diseases most frequently reported are influenza, malaria, venereal disease, whooping cough, measles, trachoma, and tuberculosis. Malaria, which in 1945 affected one out of three persons in the country, has been drastically reduced through a concerted program. In 1970 more than 600,000 blood-smear slides were examined, but only 161 positive cases were reported, as compared with over 16,000 in 1961. A preventive program conducted with assistance of the United Nations Children's Fund and the Pan American

Health Organization was established in 1952; by 1970 more than 93 percent of the population lived in areas where the campaign had progressed from the attack to either the maintenance or the consolidation stage. None of the 116 new cases in 1970 were reported in these areas.

Tuberculosis is particularly serious in Santo Domingo, where urban crowding creates conditions favorable to the spread of the disease. Reported cases declined from more than 1,000 in 1961 to 435 in 1967 before rising to 893 in 1969. In 1970 the government signed an agreement with the Pan American Health Organization to institute a national control program.

No cases of yellow fever have been reported since the early 1900s, but in the early 1970s the *Aedes egypti* mosquito was still present in a few localities. Another mosquito-borne disease, filariasis, was endemic to the country but was most prevalent in the Negro population of coastal areas.

Diseases of the digestive tract were least susceptible to elimination through health campaigns. Impure food and water and generally unsanitary living conditions made gastroenteritis and dysentery endemic to the entire country. In the early 1970s a large proportion of the population was afflicted by some type of intestinal parasite. Whooping cough was common but was being combatted by routine immunization of schoolchildren. In 1969 there were over 1,600 leprosy cases in the active register, a majority were in the southern coastal region. Some 7 percent of the cases were hospitalized, and 97 percent were under surveillance. No smallpox was reported in the 1960s, but a limited preventive campaign was continued; vaccinations administered annually varied from nearly 109,000 in 1967 to 9,000 in 1968. To combat fairly high rates of venereal disease, during the late 1960s control posts were maintained in fifteen health centers and hospitals. Other diseases with high rates of incidence included measles, typhoid and paratyphoid, and diseases of the eye and skin.

Attitudes Toward Medical Care

In urban areas overcrowded conditions in the hospitals and outpatient facilities attest to the fact that modern medical treatment is desired. In particular, there is a high degree of acceptance on the part of pregnant women who have observed the effect of prenatal and pediatric care on maternal and infant mortality. Curative rather than preventive medicine occupies first place in the demand for urban health services, however, and in many cases a doctor's care is sought only when the patient becomes seriously ill.

In rural areas the situation is different. In the peasant's mind diseases are caused by misfortune, bad air, or mysterious circumstances. In many areas the principal contact with modern medical services is through the generally effective preventive programs against diseases such as malaria. Births in rural places are often attended only by an untrained midwife, and a doctor or nurse is sought only if complications occur. In some rural localities, particularly in those close to the Haitian frontier, the assistance of a folk practitioner called a *curiosita* is engaged. Belief in folk practices is lessening, but in more remote areas the application of medicinally valuable herbal remedies is accompanied by the use of symbols and incantations.

Environmental Sanitation

Most of the serious illness in the country is directly or indirectly related to unsanitary living conditions. Although the population is extraordinarily clean in homes, clothing, public buildings, and streets, sanitary water supply and waste disposal facilities are seriously deficient, and at least half of the houses are so constructed as to provide favorable breeding grounds for insects, rodents, and other disease carriers.

The water supply in Santo Domingo comes from two tributaries of the Ozama River that converge a little to the northwest of the city. Water samples are checked daily, and treatment includes sand filtration and the addition of purifying elements. In 1970, however, it was reported that the city water was often contaminated with surface seepage and sediment after heavy rains and should be boiled. Santiago de los Caballeros has a good water supply system; several other cities have basically satisfactory systems, but checks for bacteriological contamination were reported to be inadequate in the mid-1960s.

The public Santo Domingo sewage disposal system served nearly half of the city in 1960, and there were several small private systems. At that time, the public sewer lines were being extended to the poorer sections of the city, but urban growth of the late 1960s and early 1970s was at a rate probably in excess of the rate of sewer extension. In 1965 Santiago de los Caballeros and some 10 percent of the other cities with populations in excess of 10,000 also had sewerage service. The remaining urban centers and all rural localities continued to rely on septic tanks and latrines.

The public agency charged with provision of sanitary services is the National Water Supply and Sewerage Institute. As part of a plan for the 1969–72 period the institute planned to integrate some 40 percent of the systems previously maintained by municipalities. The program's goals included the provision of water facilities to 62 percent of the urban and 25 percent of the rural population and sewerage facilities to 14 percent of the population in urban centers. In addition, nearly 1,400 latrines were installed in 1970, and an operational plan for the construction of 30,000 such units over a period of four years was completed.

Garbage and refuse are collected daily in Santo Domingo, and in other major urban centers there are collections several times a week.

Even in Santo Domingo, however, poor garbage collection in some districts and the tropical climate combine to encourage infestation by insects and rats.

The Division of Environmental Sanitation of the Ministry of Public Health and Social Welfare is charged with the inspection of slaughterhouses; milk, sausage, and other food-processing plants; and restaurants. It is also responsible for pest control. Manpower available for this duty in 1965, however, included only three veterinarians and about 300 largely untrained health inspectors, who in many instances had other primary responsibilities. The milk produced by the country's one pasteurization plant in Santo Domingo was reported of uncertain purity in 1970 as a consequence of the frequently high bacterial count in the milk as it is received at the plant.

In 1970 the municipal slaughterhouse in Santo Domingo had modern equipment, and the meat processed was considered sanitary. Modern supermarkets had improved their refrigeration and handling practices, and their sanitation standards were relatively high. The more than 100 slaughterhouses elsewhere in the country functioned without regular meat inspection, however, and unsanitary practices in storage and handling of food in local markets is common throughout the country.

WELFARE

The government's social security programs provide old-age, disability, sickness and maternity, survivor, and work accident and occupational disease coverage. The programs are administered by the Dominican Social Security Institute (Instituto Dominicano de Seguro Social—IDSS), which maintained twenty-eight regional offices during the late 1960s. The social security system had been established in 1948, but during the Trujillo era there had been few beneficiaries, and in 1962 it was extensively restructured.

The IDSS system is a unitary one that does not make the distinction between blue-collar manual workers and white-collar employees that is made in the programs of many Latin American countries. Compulsory or optional coverage is extended in theory to most of the economically active population between the ages of fourteen and sixty employed in the private sector. The scope of mandatory coverage includes regularly employed wage and salary earners in industry and services, farmworkers, sharecroppers, temporary workers, some apprentices and unpaid family workers, and manual workers in enterprises owned or operated by the government. Optional enrollment is available to the self-employed.

Salaried personnel employed by the government are covered by separate noncontributory systems paid out of the national treasury. In the late 1960s persons in the private sector earning more than RD$46 a week, persons employed by their spouses, minors under the age of fourteen, disability pensioners, domestic servants, and apprentices earning less than RD$3 a week were excluded. In late 1971, however, it was reported that extension of coverage to higher paid workers and employees was being studied.

The system is financed by contributions from the insured person, the employer, and the government. The amounts are computed on the basis of the averages at the rate of 4 percent of the basic wage from each person insured, 7 percent from each employer, and 2.5 percent from the government. Persons covered at their own option contribute 7.5 percent.

In 1967 about 140,000 persons (12 percent of the labor force) had sickness-maternity, disability, and old-age coverage. More than 161,000 persons were covered for work accidents and occupational illness.

Old-age beneficiaries must have made at least 800 weekly contributions and must have retired from an occupation covered by the program. The monthly stipend, payable at the age of sixty to both men and women, amounts to 70 percent of the average earnings during the last four years of employment. Reduced payments are made to pensioners having between 400 and 799 covered weeks of employment, and contributions plus interest at the annual rate of 5 percent are returnable to workers having fewer than 400 covered weeks. The number of old-age annuitants increased from 883 in 1964 to 4,060 in 1970; the average amount paid during 1970 was RD$365.

Disability pensions are payable to beneficiaries whose earning capacity has been reduced by at least two-thirds. The full pension is payable to those who have made at least 250 weekly contributions and amounts to 40 percent of average earnings for the last two years of employment plus 2 percent for every 100 weeks of contribution beyond 200. A reduced pension is available for persons having less than 250 weeks of covered employment, and supplemental benefits are payable for dependents. Between 1964 and 1970 the number of disability pensioners increased from 1,038 to 1,432. During the latter year the average disability pension paid was RD$356.

Dependent survivors of insured personnel are entitled to a lump-sum payment amounting to one-third of the insured person's earnings during his last year of work. In addition, a funeral grant is paid, based on wage class of the deceased.

Sickness benefits include medical services and cash payments. A single week's contribution is necessary to qualify for medical services, and six weeks are required for establishment of eligibility for cash payments. Medical services include hospitalization for a maximum of twenty-six weeks. The cash benefits are payable for a maximum of twenty-six weeks after a six-day waiting period. They amount to 50 percent of average earnings if the beneficiary is ambulatory or 25 percent if he is hospitalized. Maternity benefits are comparable in amount and scope to those for sickness. Wives of insured workers are eligible, and the benefits include free pediatric service for the first eight months of the infant's life.

Private social insurance programs maintained by business firms consist principally of supplementary payments in the contingencies covered by the IDSS schedule. The most widespread is paid leave for the six-day waiting period in connection with illness. Some enterprises supplement the IDSS old-age pension with a lump sum or additional small periodic payments, provide small grants to survivors, or contribute to payment of insurance premiums. These programs exist principally in large enterprises and are usually secured by collective contract.

During most of the country's history private welfare was largely an interest of the Roman Catholic Church, but programs were limited and for the most part were concerned with education and individual charitable works by parish priests. In the 1950s the church began to play a more important role, and by the mid-1960s the church operated twelve small hospitals and fifteen other charitable institutions, such as homes for orphans and the aged. Catholic lay groups, such as Catholic Action and the Daughters of Mary, were engaged in advancing self-help programs.

The Catholic Relief Services of the National Catholic Welfare Conference of the United States became active during the 1960s. By the middle of the decade this program was providing food for more than 250,000 persons through various local outlets and drugs and equipment to hospitals and clinics. The Sisters of Saint Dominic, a North American order, worked with the needy near the Haitian border in teaching food preparation and personal hygiene. The Redemptionist Fathers, also a North American order, maintained a community development project in the San Juan area.

Protestant welfare programs, local as well as overseas, are operated largely through the Church World Service, a part of the Christian Rural Overseas Program with headquarters in New York. Projects include training in agricultural practices, distribution of donated food, training in health and hygiene, and supplementary feeding for schoolchildren.

The United States economic assistance program and the Peace Corps have been active in various welfare undertakings, and activities of the Cooperative for American Relief Everywhere (CARE) have frequently been carried out by members of the Peace Corps. The Federal Republic of Germany (West Germany) and Israel have contributed to development of cooperatives and programs designed to raise the living standards of workers.

Upper class women engage in a variety of charitable undertakings, a majority of them sponsored by the Roman Catholic Church. Welfare-connected activities of voluntary groups, such as local rotary clubs and chambers of commerce, are also of significant importance, and the Dominican Red Cross provides important welfare services in emergencies.

PATTERNS OF LIVING AND LEISURE

Holidays and Working Hours

Sunday is a day of rest, and the workweek must terminate by noon on Saturday except in certain establishments that have been granted exemptions by the Ministry of Labor. Legislation enacted in 1967 reduced from twenty-two to nine the number of legal holidays, which were increased in number to ten in 1968. These holidays are New Year's Day (January 1), Altagracia Day (January 21), Duarte Day (January 26), Independence Day (February 27), Good Friday, Labor Day (May 1), Corpus Christi, Restoration Day (August 16), Crowning of Our Lady of Mercedes (September 14), and Christmas (December 25). The executive power may also declare national days of mourning, which become legal holidays for the year in which they are declared.

The working day in Santo Domingo starts early. Most business firms works from 8:00 A.M. to noon and from 2:00 to 5:00 P.M. Monday through Friday. Government offices have a thirty-hour workweek in order to enable public employees to hold outside jobs; a unitary day (*jornada único*), a fairly common practice in tropical Latin America, is observed from 7:30 A.M. to 1:30 P.M. Retail stores are usually open from 9:00 A.M. to noon and from 3:00 to 6:30 P.M. from Monday through Friday; on Saturday their hours are from 8:00 or 9:00 A.M. until noon. Hours are generally similar in other urban centers. They tend to be somewhat less regular, however, and the practice of a midday break long enough to permit a siesta is more frequently the case.

Consumption Patterns

A survey conducted by the Dominican government during 1969 involved 552 Santo Domingo families with monthly incomes in five income brackets ranging from RD$50 to RD$100 and from RD$400 to RD$600. The survey found that food was the most important purchase item in proportions that were in inverse ratio to income. The lowest income bracket spent 50.3 percent, and the highest spent 35.3 percent on food. Proportions spent on housing and furnishings ranged downward from 27.1 percent for the lowest income bracket to 20.8 percent in the RD$300 to RD$400 bracket. For the families in the bracket receiving RD$400 to RD$600 monthly the proportion expended rose to 25 percent, probably because it was in this income level that a considerable number of the families were able to afford domestic servants. Costs of wearing apparel and accessories also ranged upward from 5.7 percent in the lowest category to 12.5 percent of the families with incomes from RD$300 to RD$400 before declining to 8.7 percent in the RD$400 to RD$600 income group.

Proportions of expendable income remaining for miscellaneous spending ranged upward from 16.9 percent in the lowest bracket to 31 percent in the highest. Within this category the principal item was for taxes and gifts; from the lowest to highest bracket it ranged from 1.1 percent to 7 percent of the total. Medical expenses ranged irregularly from 2.8 to 5.4 percent. Costs of personal care items were remarkably consistent at between 2.5 and 2.9 percent. Expenditures for education ranged irregularly from 1.3 to 2.7 percent. Costs of transportation were progressively higher—from 2.1 percent for the lowest bracket to 6.8 percent for the highest, where the families were presumably able to afford taxis and some owned automobiles.

The Santo Domingo survey did not include data on savings. A 1966 survey of 175 families in Santiago de los Caballeros, however, furnished information on the urban savings pattern. In order of preference, money saved was placed in banks, in a rotating credit program, on reinvestment in the family business, in stocks, in real estate, in hoarded cash, and in bonds. The principal savings goals were purchase of a home and accumulation of funds for emergency needs. Next in order were education of children, trips, and purchase of durable consumer goods.

The cash income of most farm families is limited to wages earned at harvesttime on larger farms or to proceeds from the sale of occasional surplus produce of the family farm. With so little to spend, the subsistence farmer remains virtually outside the market economy. Living quarters are constructed almost entirely from materials at hand, and most of the food is produced at home. Cash expenditures are limited to such items as clothing or yard goods, salt, kerosine for lamps, cigarettes, beverages, and occasional supplementary food purchases.

Consumer costs experienced only slight rises during the late 1960s, but a small decline in 1970 was followed by a substantial increase in 1971, and the upward trend continued during 1972. During the late 1960s a rise in food costs, the principal budget item for most families, was partially offset by a decline in costs of clothing and housing. A more important factor affecting consumption patterns—and one with more important long-term implications—was the growing demand for imported luxury goods, particularly those from North America. In the freer atmosphere that followed the collapse of the Trujillo regime, the well-to-do were becoming accustomed to a way of life that involved a demand for these imports, which was increasing to an extent that the country could not well afford.

Recreation

Dominicans may be the world's most ardent baseball fans. Teams play in both national and international leagues, and the game is played before enthusiastic audiences in hamlets with improvised equipment as well as in Santo Domingo. The country has contributed outstanding players to teams in the United States major leagues, the standings of which are reported regularly in the press. Two Dominican players participated in the World Series in 1972, and plans were being made for developing a complex of leagues made up of 500 teams in the towns and villages of the interior to provide recreation and hopefully to develop additional player material for the major leagues. It has only half jokingly been observed that there has never been a revolution during the baseball season. Volleyball and basketball are popular, and soccer is played occasionally, but no other sport rivals baseball.

For the well-to-do in Santo Domingo the available sports include swimming, water skiing, sailing and motorboating, riding, polo, tennis, bird hunting, and freshwater fishing and surf casting. An eighteen-hole golf course is located on the outskirts of Santo Domingo, and another has been installed at the new tourist resort complex at La Romana.

Gambling is popular, and the weekly National Lottery is an extraordinarily intricate one in which prizes range from the RD$60,000 first award to a return of the purchase cost to holders of tickets having the same last number as that of the winner. Substantial homes (valued at RD$9,000 to RD$12,000) can also be won. Four are awarded each week, and by the end of 1971 some 500 homes had been won in the Barrio de la Lotería, a suburb of Santo Domingo. Lottery tickets are sold throughout the country and are at a premium in New York City. There are three gambling casinos in Santo Domingo, and wagers are legal on cockfights held in pits throughout the country. Card playing is popular among all classes, but dominoes is probably the most popular game.

Almost every small town has at least one motion picture theater, but the average per capita attendance of two performances a year during the early 1960s was far below the average for Latin America. The prices of admission—ranging from RD$0.50 to RD$1.50 in Santo Domingo—caused motion pictures to be prohibitively expensive for many families, although those with automobiles could attend one of the several well-patronized drive-in theaters that charged a flat rate per vehicle regardless of the number of occupants. New and old United States films with original sound tracks and Spanish subtitles predominated. The Palace of Fine Arts (Palacio de Bellas Artes) in Santo Domingo is the scene of regular symphony concerts and occasional recitals by solo artists, plays and ballets by visiting groups, and operas and plays performed by students and faculties of local educational institutions.

In many of the towns, concerts are given by municipal bands in the central plazas several nights a week, events that provide the opportunity to meet friends and converse as well as to enjoy the music. Among the surviving traditional forms of entertainment is the evening promenade enjoyed by young people of all classes. During the early evenings and on Sundays after mass, young men walk about the plaza to exchange glances and occasional conversation with young women strolling in pairs. This traditional practice is diminishing to some extent, but even in Santo Domingo it was reported still occurring on the

Malecón, the broad, palm-lined avenue along the Caribbean waterfront.

Recreational outlets are more varied in Santo Domingo than in the rest of the country, and society tends to be more open and cosmopolitan. The well-to-do are less clannish than in many other Latin American capitals and more ready to entertain foreigners as well as business acquaintances in their clubs and homes. In the interior of the country, society is more traditional. In Santiago de los Caballeros, in particular, the elite tend to restrict entertaining in their homes to gatherings with family members and a small circle of peers.

Urban women enjoy visiting one another during the day. The beauty parlors are a favorite gathering spot. Men often meet in coffeehouses in midmorning and late afternoon. The collapse of the Trujillo regime was followed by a noticeable increase in traveling, both within the country and abroad, particularly to Puerto Rico.

Music and dancing to the *merengue*, the most popular dance-music form, are popular everywhere and are indispensable elements of fiestas. In many small communities there is a center for dancing with a board or concrete floor and a roof of palm fronds or corrugated metal. Births, baptisms, name days, the building of houses, and the clearing of fields are all occasions calling for fiestas, which sometimes last all night and are accompanied by the consumption of much food and drink as well as by music and dancing. Weddings are festive times of particular importance in which bride and groom wear elaborate and colorful garments, and they and their parents give ceremonial dance performances. Even funerals are festive to the extent that singing and dancing to small bands, as well as prayers and lamentations, are part of the ceremony.

There are fewer community fiestas honoring the patron saint of the locality or observing some local secular occasion than in most Latin American countries. Carnival is widely celebrated during the three-day period that precedes the beginning of Lent, however, and Independence Day is marked by carnival-like activities. Holy Week is the occasion for numerous processions and the burning in effigy of Judas Iscariot. In Santo Domingo, Epiphany was formerly celebrated with costumed parades and fireworks, and Columbus Day on October 12 was celebrated with impressive ceremonies. Both these dates, however, were removed from the calendar of national holidays in 1967.

In all parts of the country, Christmas is the most joyous festival of the year. Early in December, elaborate decorations are assembled in homes and shopwindows, and street bands similar to troops of Christmas carolers in other countries begin to appear. On Christmas Eve, attendance at mass is followed by elaborate dinners in the homes. Celebrations continue through the following week, and on December 31 the old year is ushered out to the accompaniment of street dancing, music, and fireworks.

CHAPTER 6

EDUCATION, CULTURAL LIFE, AND

PUBLIC INFORMATION

During the early 1970s the educational system was experiencing fundamental change as well as phenomenal growth. Substantial increases in enrollment had also occurred annually during the 1960s, but the programs of study had undergone little change since the early 1950s and bore little relation to the country's needs. Teachers and classrooms had been in increasingly short supply, particularly in the countryside, where little schooling of any sort was available beyond the first few grades of primary school and much of the population remained illiterate. At all levels, a high proportion of the students dropped out of school or repeated grades. The shortcomings of public education were reflected in the progressively increasing number of families who sent their children to schools in the small private sector, maintained for the most part by religious orders.

Beginning in the late 1960s substantially increased national education budgets were reflected in a corresponding increase in the rate of school construction. Primary and secondary enrollment maintained its fast rate of growth, and university matriculations soared. A particularly heavy rate of increase in the several university schools of education gave promise of an improved future supply of secondary teachers, but the overall pace of growth at the public university in Santo Domingo, where a large majority of all postsecondary students was enrolled, was such that the government was concerned. Its growth placed increasing demands on the national budget, and many in the swollen student body appeared to be more concerned with political activism than with learning a profession.

In 1971 the Ministry of Education and Fine Arts commenced implementation of a change that its architects hoped would correct the most evident deficiencies in the educational system and make the program more responsive to the country's needs. The secondary-level reform was designed to alleviate the critical shortage of primary teachers by improvement and expansion of the secondary schools for training of primary-level teachers; to bring about a massive increase in secondary enrollments in the largely neglected prevocational fields; and to improve the preparation of university matriculants by broadening and modernizing the content of the academic secondary-school program.

Under terms of a concordat signed in 1954 by the Dominican Republic and the Holy See, education provided by the state in public schools is guided by the principles of Roman Catholic doctrine, and religious instruction is generally mandatory at both primary and secondary levels. The state guarantees to the Roman Catholic Church full liberty to establish and maintain schools of all types and levels under ecclesiastical authority, and certificates awarded by primary and secondary institutions of this kind—which make up the bulk of the schools in the private sector—have the same validity as those awarded by the corresponding state institutions.

Although traces of French and North American influences may be found in the country's literature, graphic arts, and formal music and African influence is evident in its folk music, Dominican culture is basically Spanish in origin. The value attached to *hispanidad* (Spanishness) was greatly reinforced as a reaction to subjection to Haitian rule in the early nineteenth century.

Known as the "cradle of America" in the early colonial period, the colony was the center from which European civilization spread to the new world. It had the first schools and convents in America, and literature, theater, architecture, and other arts flourished. By the middle of the sixteenth century, however, the quality and quantity of literary and artistic work had begun to decline, never fully to recover.

The political pattern of swinging from anarchy to tyranny, with interludes of foreign intervention and occupation, has not provided fertile ground for the development of intellectual and creative activities. Nevertheless, in the late nineteenth and early twentieth centuries, a number of Dominican literary figures, responding to international trends—first romanticism and later modernism—produced outstanding works. Also, a new musical form emerged with the incorporation of the popular *merengue* into serious compositions.

During the long, harsh rule of Rafael Leónidas Trujillo Molina cultural life experienced a serious setback. Few of the writers and artists who stayed in the country were able to rise above the officially prescribed themes, which generally lauded the accomplishments of Trujillo. A new literature of social protest was initiated, however, by persons writing from exile—most notably Juan Bosch.

The reemergence of scholarship and the arts after the assassination of Trujillo was halting and, like other aspects of national life, was retarded by the civil war of 1965. Since the late 1960s, however, there has been an attempt, especially on the part of the young, to arrive at a unique form of national self-expression. Writers and artists have hoped that this movement, known as *"la nueva ola"* (the new wave), would begin to provide the cultural cohesion sorely needed to integrate the society. More nearly defined by mood than by uniformity of style or content, the movement has found expression in cultivation of folklore, political irony and statire, and paintings and murals inspired by the civil war.

In 1972 people throughout the country listened to radio broadcasts—the most influential of all mass media in the republic. More than ninety originating radio stations broadcast programs of music, news bulletins, cultural subjects, sports news, and drama. Most of these stations were profit-making enterprises and would sell time to political groups or parties. Television broadcasts influenced a limited number of viewers, who generally watched newscasts and a few special shows. A large proportion of the television program material originated in the United States.

The literate population was served by a number of independent daily newspapers published in Santo Domingo and in Santiago de los Caballeros; the total circulation of these dailies was estimated at more than 115,000. All of these newspapers subscribed to at least one United States wire service, and two carried United States columnists. The most widely read periodical was a weekly news magazine, *Ahora*, whose circulation was estimated at about 12,000.

Although most of the people listened to radio broadcasts and urban middle and upper class people were influenced by newspapers, citizens of all classes in 1972 continued to value personal contact and rumor as sources of information and ideas. News was often introduced into villages by travelers and itinerant merchants. Men picked up information at work, during the evening stroll, or in coffeehouses and bars; women exchanged gossip in the marketplace or after Sunday mass. The family structure also constituted an important network of communication.

EDUCATION

Administration and Finance

As organized under the 1951 Organic Law of Education, the school program in 1972 was directed by the Ministry of Education and Fine Arts through undersecretaries for administrative and technical services. Through the undersecretary for technical services, the instructional program was carried out by directorates for primary, secondary, technical, and adult education. An administrative reform in 1961 had combined the previously separate directorates for rural and urban primary schooling.

For administrative purposes, the national territory was divided into fifteen educational departments which, in turn, were divided into a total of 125 school districts. A corps of inspectors performed their functions at the district level. Although the pattern of organization was a decentralized one, regional and district authorities were concerned principally with day-to-day administration and making recommendations on such matters as teacher appointments. Administrative decisionmaking was centralized at the ministerial level.

The ministry was responsible for the administration of all public schools, formulation of policy and initiation of legislation, appointment of teachers, approval of curricula, syllabi, and textbooks, and conduct of final examinations. Aided or semiprivate schools at both primary and secondary levels were also under direction of the ministry; institutions in this category were privately operated but received public subsidies. Private schools dependent on tuition fees and other nonpublic sources of income controlled their own staffs but were required to conform to the public standards with respect to curriculum, syllabus, and examination. A few vocational schools and training centers were administered by the ministries of public health and social welfare, labor, agriculture, and defense. The country's universities, private as well as public, received public financial support but were operated autonomously. The National Council for Education, which had wide representation from the educational system, other ministries, the teaching profession, and the public, was the highest organ of educational policy determination and was headed by the president of the republic.

The cost of public education is borne by the central government. Expenditures totaled 6.6 percent of the national budget in 1961, but they rose rapidly after the end of the Trujillo regime and reached 14.7 percent of the total in 1966. In compliance with the national austerity program, expenditure rates were almost frozen through 1968; but the following year the allocation of public funds increased substantially, and in 1970 the proportion rose to 17.4 percent of all public expenditures. In 1971 the proportion was estimated to have risen still further to 20.4 percent (see ch. 8). In 1970 some 40 percent of the funds appropriated were marked for the primary system; and 19 percent, for the secondary system. Nineteen percent was received by the universities, 4 percent was in the form of subsidies to private institutions, 7 percent was for miscellaneous purposes, and 11 percent was for general administration.

During the 1966–69 period capital expenditures averaged 4.5 percent of all government investment. The proportion rose progressively during the period, and budget appropriations for 1970 were more than 7.4 percent of the total. Most of the funds expended during the 1966–69 period were for school construction, minimal amounts remaining for furniture and equipment. Investment by the private sector was also considerable.

Primary Schools

During 1970 some 726,000 children—virtually equal numbers of boys and girls—were enrolled in the primary schools. Enrollment during the previous five years had grown at a rate of about 7 percent annually, considerably greater than the rate of growth of the school-age population. About one-third of the students enrolled were in urban localities, but almost nineteen out of twenty of the public schools were located in the countryside. Many of the rural units were one-room schools in which a single teacher presided over all classes. All but six of the 342 private primary schools were in cities and towns. Private schools, including those receiving government subsidies, represented less than 9 percent of the primary-school population, but during the 1960s private enrollment had increased at a rate six times that of the public units. The extraordinary rise in private enrollments reflected increasingly crowded conditions in public classrooms combined with a rising level of family income and an accelerated migration from the countryside to urban localities, where all but a few of the private schools were located.

Primary schooling is free in the public system and is compulsory for children between the ages of seven and fourteen, or until the six-year primary cycle is completed. The absence of nearby schools in many rural localities prevents enforcement of this rule, however, and in 1969 some 19.8 percent of the children between the ages of seven and twelve had had no schooling.

Standards are low, particularly in the rural areas. In 1970 only 17 percent of rural schools had all six primary grades, and 57 percent had three grades or fewer. Some urban schools are incomplete. The dropout rate in both rural and urban sectors is high. In addition, grade repetition is regarded as excessive by country authorities, particularly in the lower grades. As a consequence of lower grade repetitions and early dropouts, in 1970 about 75 percent of the total primary school enrollment was in the first three grades (38 percent in the first grade), and fewer than 6 percent were in the sixth grade. Primary students graduating in 1970 represented 17.1 percent of the number that had entered six years earlier. In general, girls had a somewhat better record than boys for staying in school and for being promoted.

Kindergartens had a 1969 enrollment of a little more than 6,000 children, mostly in urban private schools. Dominican children as a rule, however, begin their education with the first grade. The primary-cycle curriculum includes reading, writing, and arithmetic, introductions to science and nature study, health, and sports. Urban and rural curricula in the early 1970s were similar and had not been substantially changed since the 1950s. Rural schools, however, also offered practical training in agriculture for boys and domestic science for girls.

During the middle and late 1960s a number of schoolbooks were published in accordance with syllabi drawn up by specialists of the Alliance for Progress program. First graders were given a series of four basic texts for Spanish America, and their teachers were issued complementary manuals of instruction. Other manuals were distributed to instructors on the teaching of language arts, natural science and mathematics, and hygiene and techniques for grouping students for instruction. Fifth- and sixth-grade students received booklets on the human body and health.

Textbooks as a rule, however, are not free at any school level, and their cost represents a serious problem for low-income families. At a 1972 press conference, President Joaquín Balaguer asserted that the state should distribute free textbooks only to those absolutely too poor to afford their purchase. He further stated that it should encourage competition among publishers to lower prices to the moderate price of RD$0.50 (1 peso equals US$1—see Glossary) at which some standard texts were already being sold.

The shortage of primary teachers was equaled or overmatched by a shortage of schools and classrooms, which in some instances made it necessary for instructors to preside over classes of up to 100 students of widely differing ages in several grades. An accelerated building program during the early 1970s was directed primarily toward rural schools; under the country's agricultural reform program, 50 percent of the new construction in the 1970-74 period was allotted to key rural areas. Also, additional rural classrooms were to be installed to make possible the extension of incomplete schools to the full six primary grades.

Secondary Schools

Preliminary data for the school year ending in 1970 indicated an enrollment in the six-year secondary system of 112,286 in schools of all kinds. Between 1965 and 1969 enrollments increased by an average of 14.7 percent annually, reaching a total of 91,300 in 1969. During the 1965-67 period about 76 percent of the primary school graduates matriculated at the secondary level, and the students who completed their courses of study represented about half the number that had entered the system six years earlier. Half of the students, however, were over-age or repeaters. Girl students slightly exceeded boys in number. In 1969 the median age of secondary students was about seventeen years, and about 10 percent were twenty years or older. Some 27 percent of the total school enrollment was in private and semiprivate institutions. These units were smaller than those of the public schools, but during the 1960s their enrollments increased at a considerably faster rate. Most were church operated, but their faster growth was based—as in the case of the private primary schools—on excessive public school crowding, the generally better education offered, the heavy migration from the countryside to urban centers where nearly all of the schools were located, and the progressively greater ability of parents to pay tuition rather than on religious considerations.

Under the existing program, which was being revised during the early 1970s, secondary education consisted of a two-year intermediate cycle for all students, followed by a four-year upper or secondary cycle designed primarily as a preparation for university entrance. In 1970 more than 52 percent of the secondary students were in the intermediate grades; 45 percent were in the general or academic secondary cycle; a little more than 2 percent were in technical or vocational courses; and less than 1 percent were in the normal schools at the secondary level, which prepared teachers for the primary system. Enrollments continued to reflect the precept, traditional in much of Latin America, that secondary schooling was an upper class prerequisite designed for university preparation.

Students successfully completing general secondary school received baccalaureate (*bachillerato*) diplomas leading to university admission. As a result of reforms instituted in 1961, two vocational schools were authorized to give baccalaureate diplomas in order to encourage enrollments in the poorly attended units in the vocational system. In rural localities there were few schools, and young people had relatively little access to schooling at the secondary level. In 1969 about 17 percent of the population between thirteen and eighteen was engaged in secondary studies; in rural localities only intermediate-level schools were available, however, and these accounted for only 8 percent of the nationwide total in the intermediate grades.

At the two-year intermediate level, subjects studied in primary school were reviewed, and new courses in history, geography, civics, and English were added. At the four-year general secondary level, study during the first three years was made up of general courses. During the fourth year students specialized in philosophy and letters, natural science, or physics and mathematics. Other specialized courses and additional foreign languages were added. Portuguese was among the languages offered; the Dominican Republic was the only country in Latin America to schedule Portuguese as a regular elective part of its secondary foreign-language curriculum.

Incomplete figures for the technical and vocational secondary schools show 1970 enrollments of 924 in commercial, 668 in agricultural, and 526 in industrial courses. Because several of the institutions in this sector offered schooling at both the secondary and postsecondary levels, enrollment data are imprecise.

During the late 1960s and early 1970s four agricultural schools offered courses combining general education, theoretical and practical agriculture, and management programs. Their workshops were reportedly well equipped, their practice farms were adequate, and their staffs were competent. Industrial education was provided by the well-run Loyola Polytechnic Institute (Instituto Politécnico Loyola) in San Cristóbal and the Salesian School of Arts and Crafts (Escuela Salesiana de Artes y Oficios) in Santo Domingo. It was also available in the public National School of Arts and Crafts (Escuela Nacional de Artes y Oficios) in Santo Domingo. The Madre y Maestra Catholic University inaugurated a secondary-level industrial program late in the 1960s.

Business and commercial programs of widely varying quality were offered by some eighty private schools not considered part of the regular secondary system. In addition, complete commercial programs were offered by two commercial schools at the secondary level. The Polytechnic School for Girls (Politécnicos Femininos) offered a broad spectrum of studies, including home economics and commercial courses. The program ranged from primary schooling to academic and technical courses at secondary and higher levels. The schools, administered by a religious order, were well equipped and staffed.

Enrollment in five, small secondary-level normal schools for the training of primary teachers increased irregularly from 319 in 1960 to 531 in 1970. Interest in primary school teaching as a profession remained limited, however, and even with the increased enrollments the units in 1970 were operating at less than capacity. Schools in Santo Domingo and Santiago trained teachers for urban schools, and schools in San Pedro de Macorís, San Cristóbal, and Licey al Medio trained personnel for the rural system. In the rural units, training in agriculture for men and home economics for women was part of the regular course of study. The three-year course of study in both urban and rural programs corresponded to grades ten through twelve, and graduates became eligible either for appointment as primary school teachers or for matriculation at one of the universities.

Deficiencies in the predominant academic track of the secondary system were underlined by the action taken in 1964 by the Autonomous University of Santo Domingo (Universidad Autónomo de Santo Domingo—UASD) in opening a preparatory course of study for entering students who had received inadequate schooling at the secondary level. Secondary-level normal schools had a curriculum that was heavily academic and theoretical in content, having little relevance to the capabilities of the students or to the teaching program for which they were being prepared. Vocational secondary schools had made some progress during the 1960s in developing useful courses of study. Vocational enrollments in 1970 were outnumbered by enrollments in the general-studies cycle by a ratio of nearly nineteen to one, however, and students completing or dropping out of vocational schools were poorly prepared for most jobs in the sectors of production. Employers were becoming more sophisticated and expected applicants to have prevocational experience upon which to build on-the-job training.

To meet these multiple deficiencies in secondary education and to relieve the critical quantitative and qualitative shortage of primary school teachers, the government at the end of 1968 issued a decree calling for the complete restructuring of the secondary system. Plans for the project were drawn up with the assistance of the United Nations Educational, Scientific and Cultural Organization (UNESCO), and the government in 1970 requested financial assistance from the International Development Association (IDA), a member of the World Bank Group (see Glossary). Early in 1971 the IDA extended a credit to cover half of the project's anticipated initial cost of the equivalent of approximately US$8 million in United States and Dominican currencies.

Under the reform program, the two-year intermediate cycle was gradually to be replaced by a lower secondary cycle of general studies, which would have a duration of three years for prevocational and four years for academic students. Increased emphasis would be placed on mathematics and science, and an introduction would be given to industrial arts, commerce, and agriculture in an effort to direct more students toward vocational studies in the upper secondary cycle. The upper cycle, consisting of two or three years of study, would be offered in multilateral or diversified schools having multiple vocational and academic schedules. The program was introduced in several schools in a modified form during the school year ending in 1972, and a curriculum-development committee undertook the rewriting of syllabuses and the provision of introduction guides for teachers. The secondary-level normal school schedules were to be converted into two-year programs for students who had completed four years of lower secondary school, and the curriculum was to represent a better balance between general education and professional training and make provision for practice teaching.

As planned in 1970, the project called initially for establishment of three new lower-secondary units and provision of equipment for three existing schools. All six institutions would be coeducational and would have a combined enrollment of 3,360 students. They would be located in the fast-growing cities of Santo Domingo, Barahona, Bonao, Santiago de los Caballeros, La Romana, and Puerto Plata.

A corresponding number of coeducational multilateral secondary schools would be established in the same cities but would attract students in areas extending well beyond their metropolitan areas. In accordance with the reform proposals, they would be model institutions with a strong prevocational orientation, and the nature of the curriculum would be such that graduates would be readily employable. All units would include two industrial, two commercial, and one division of home economics and nursing training. Each would be composed of 120 students. The course of study would have a duration of three years beginning with grade ten and would include general as well as practical subjects. There would also be two academic streams, also with 120 students in each. The academic program would be two years in duration, beginning with grade eleven, and would consist of a common program supplemented by electives.

The phase of the program for training primary school teachers would involve establishment of a new unit at San Juan, expansion of the units in San Cristóbal, San Pedro de Macorís, and Licey al Medio, and relocation and expansion of the one in Santo Domingo. Each school would enroll 400 students in a two-year course beginning with the eleventh grade and was expected ultimately to graduate about 190 teachers annually. Beginning in 1975, when the project schools were to reach full operation, they were expected to satisfy some 85 percent of the annual needs for primary teaching personnel.

Higher Education

During the school year ending in 1970 the country's university enrollment totaled more than 15,000 students; 549 were graduated from courses of study ranging in length from two years for special programs to six years. About 40 percent of the students were women. Between 1967 and 1970 the number of university students had tripled, and newspaper reports indicated that by the end of 1972 the total may have reached or surpassed 30,000.

The largest and oldest of the country's institutions of higher education, the Autonomous University of Santo Domingo (Universidad Autónomo de Santo Domingo—UASD), in 1970 had an enrollment that made up more than 80 percent of the total. Until the 1960s it had been the country's only university but in 1962 was joined by the Madre y Maestra Catholic University, a private institution in Santiago de los Caballeros. The Roman Catholic institution had received RD$200,000 from the government for building costs, and in the early 1970s it continued to receive annual public operating subsidies. It maintained faculties of philosophy and education, law, business administration, and mechanical and electrical engineering and had a 1970 enrollment of 1,500 students. Another private institution of higher education that received government subsidies was the Pedro Henríquez Ureña National University. Established in Santo Domingo in 1966, the university had a 1970 enrollment of about 1,000. Late in 1970 the Eastern Central University opened its doors at San Pedro de Macorís as a public institution specializing in technical subjects and agronomy.

During the early 1970s ten other institutions provided postsecondary schooling equivalent to one or two years of university education. For a majority, these postsecondary years marked the conclusion of courses that began at the secondary level. All ten were privately operated, but all received government operating subsidies. Of particular note among these is the Higher Institute of Agriculture in Santiago de los Caballeros, which was opened in 1962. Also, the Institute of Higher Studies, opened in 1965 in Santo Domingo with help from the United States assistance program, is a two-year school at the postsecondary level for training in business administration and related fields, including the teaching of commercial subjects.

During the 1970 school year most of the students in the three universities then in operation were engaged in the study of medicine, social sciences, and humanities, and a little more than one-fourth were studying science and technical subjects. The faculties of education, with 13 percent of the total, ranked first in enrollment. Next in order were medicine, with 12 percent; civil and other fields of engineering, 9 percent; humanities, 8 percent; commerce and finance, 7 percent; law, with 4 percent; and agronomy, a little less than 4 percent. About 28 percent of all university students, however, were enrolled in the University College for General Studies, which provided a one-year preparatory cycle established at the UASD in order to give further preparation to secondary-level graduates in scientific and technical subjects insufficiently covered at the secondary level.

The UASD, a large institution, has nine faculties (*facultades*), academic units similar to the departments of North American institutions but generally offering complete courses of study in minor as well as in major subjects. The faculties in existence in the early 1970s were those of law, engineering and architecture, medicine, pharmacy and chemistry, dentistry, philosophy and education, agronomy, and veterinary medicine. Courses of undergraduate study range from two years in some special programs, to three years in regular programs in education and social work, and to six years in medicine. The regular undergraduate degree is the degree of licentiate (*licenciatura*). There was no master's degree program, but a doctoral degree was awarded in some faculties after additional study and presentation of a thesis. Most Dominican students seeking graduate study, however, looked for it abroad. In 1972 it was estimated that about 100 Dominican graduate students were studying in the United States. Graduate study was facilitated by the Educational Credit Fund, a semiprivate organization that made graduate study loans available at an annual rate of 4 percent.

The newer universities offer more restricted choices in courses of study. Both of the private institutions, however, also have courses of varying duration and content in education for teachers in the secondary-school system; these courses are open to graduates of normal and general secondary schools. The training in this field is regarded as being of such urgency that the 1970–74 National Development Plan listed secondary teachers as constituting 70 percent of the minimum of 3,300 university graduates needed by the country during the 1970–75 period. Economists and public and private administrators were listed in second place at 9 percent; and agronomists, third at 7 percent.

The UASD and the two private institutions offer general training for teachers. The Pedro Henríquez Ureña National University specializes in inservice upgrading courses, and the Madre y Maestra Catholic University provides specialized training for educational administrators and guidance personnel.

During the early 1970s the absence of programs of study to train teachers of technical and vocational studies at the secondary level was conspicuous. The program for reform of secondary education, however, included the recommendation that such a program be added to the curriculum of one of the higher educational faculties and that vice principals for technical education be named in the new multilateral upper secondary schools and be given a year's specialized study abroad.

Claims are occasionally made on behalf of the UASD, the country's only mass-education institution of higher education, that it is the oldest university in the western hemisphere; this claim is based on the belief that it is the lineal descendant of a university founded in Santo Domingo in 1538. The lineage is tenuous, however, and the UASD in its present form was not organized until 1937. It has been government supported since 1944, and in 1947 it moved to its present campus at University City.

During the Trujillo years its academic standards were low, and freedom of expression by its teachers and students was severely limited. In 1962, however, legislation was enacted granting the entity autonomy and assigning to it 5 percent of the annual revenue of the central government. The institution's organic statute, approved the same year, authorized student representation on all of its administrative boards.

Under terms of the organic statute, the administration of the university is the responsibility of its rector, assisted by the University Council, which is composed of representatives elected by professors, students, and alumni. A larger student-professor council called the Cloister (Claustro) is concerned with day-to-day administration, and within each faculty similar student-professor councils exercise control over intrafaculty matters. The UASD pattern of student participation in administration is not emulated elsewhere; in particular, students of the Madre y Maestra Catholic University have no voice in the operation of the school.

Such a large proportion of the student body of the UASD, an urban institution, is employed full time or part time that most of the classes are held in the late afternoon or evening. In this kind of atmosphere, students progress from one grade to another at irregular rates, so rates of those leaving school or repeating grades cannot be quoted. There is, however, a heavy concentration in the lower grades.

During the 1960s and early 1970s UASD enrollments soared. Student leaders loudly defended the continuance of an open-admissions policy, but by 1970 the government had begun to question its advisability and to express concern over the cost entailed. In 1962 legislation had been enacted assigning the university 5 percent of the central government's revenue, but during the next four years its receipts never approached that proportion, and by 1966 the government was reported in arrears in its payments by about RD$30 million. By 1970 government subsidies of 5 percent or more were being paid; but between 1962 and 1970 the enrollment had tripled, and by 1972 it was reported at a level six times that of 1962.

Such factors as higher family incomes, the migration of many young people from the countryside to Santo Domingo, where the university was located, and a progressively increasing number of secondary-school graduates during the 1960s contributed to the extraordinary growth of UASD enrollments during a decade in which the demand for post-secondary education was so great that two new universities were established and a third was preparing to open its doors. Another contributing factor was the more open political and social atmosphere that prevailed after the collapse of the Trujillo regime. During the Trujillo period, education had been used by the government as an instrument for control of the people and for propaganda. All expression of dissent had been stifled, and the university had offered little that was attractive to talented young people. During more recent years, more liberal government attitudes toward the university have encouraged increasing numbers of secondary-school graduates to seek university matriculation. Some have evidently been less interested in studies than in the opportunity to engage in political activism, but others have been attracted to the university by the opportunity for education and intellectual growth, which had existed only to a minimal extent under Trujillo.

At a press conference called in mid-1972, President Balaguer stated that great popular pressure was being exerted for drastic action with respect to the status of the university on grounds that it had become one of the most politicized institutions in the country and less a center for studies than a focal point for subversion. Noting the remarkable rate of enrollment growth, he asserted that the number enrolled should be reduced and that acceptance quotas should be imposed at levels in keeping with the needs of the country. He asserted also that many of the students were not of a caliber for professional studies and that many others who were enjoying free education could very well pay tuition to an institution that should be free only for the deserving poor.

Later in the same year, the University Council announced that students would be dropped from the university rolls if they received marks lower than sixty points in the preparatory course or seventy in the faculties. The daily press quoted radical student leaders as stating that no buildings in University City would be left standing if the new rule were to be applied.

Literacy and Adult Education

Data based on census findings show the rate of adult literacy (population aged fifteen years and over) to have risen from 42.9 percent in 1950, to 64.5 percent in 1960, and to 67.2 percent in 1970. Various estimates made during the late 1960s and early 1970s by international and foreign national entities and by individual authorities indicated, however, that literate persons might still represent 50 percent or less of the adult population. The discrepancy between the census data and the consensus of estimates may be in terms of the probably large proportion of people in the countryside who had learned a minimum of reading and writing without ever attaining full functional literacy or who had become marginally literate but had dropped back into illiteracy because of failure to use acquired reading and writing skills. In 1960 the population aged twenty-five and over had an average of barely two years of formal schooling, but three or even four years of classroom attendance are customarily considered to represent the minimum time needed for attainment of functional literacy.

Data refined from 1960 census figures indicate that literacy was highest, at 82.6 percent of the total, in the fifteen-to-nineteen age bracket and that it declined progressively in older brackets to a low of 26.8 percent among those aged sixty-five and over. Rates for men and women were 66.8 percent and 62.5 percent, respectively. The 1960 census did not show comparative rates for urban and rural populations, but other data indicate the rate in urban localities to have been at least twice that in the countryside.

Adult education during the Trujillo years consisted principally of forced attendance at literacy classes, in accordance with the Compulsory Literacy Training for Adults Act of 1951, under threat of severe penalties for nonattendance. Recorded literacy rates did improve markedly, but the harsh nature of the program left a general distaste for education so profound that it had an adverse effect on school attendance during subsequent years.

After the collapse of the Trujillo regime, the public adult-education program was expanded to include primary and intermediate courses for adults as well as literacy classes and basic courses in geography, history, principles of cooperatives, and the use of leisure time. Inservice training of teachers gained in importance, particularly for the numerous unqualified personnel in the public primary school system. Vocational courses were also organized, but most of the adult vocational training offered during the 1960s was the product of private foundations, international organizations, and religious orders. Their efforts, with government cooperation, were effective but suffered from the failure of the regular school system to provide the prevocational training needed as a foundation for adult training.

By the mid-1960s more than 100,000 persons were enrolled in adult courses of various kinds; a large majority was in rural localities. The focus remained, however, on literacy training. The compulsory literacy training law of 1951 remained at least technically in force, and efforts were concentrated on young adults between the ages of fifteen and thirty years. In 1968 the adult education and literacy program was reorganized with the advisory services of a technical mission from the Venezuelan Ministry of Education. Initial goals of the revised program included literacy training for 100,000 persons by volunteer workers and provision of primary schooling for 35,000 persons, including 5,000 to be trained through correspondence courses.

Early in the 1960s instructional classes by radio for adults had been introduced on a limited basis. In 1971 the government inaugurated a half-hour evening radio program, carried by all of the country's radio stations, that was designed to make literacy training available to another 100,000 people. In 1972 a television channel devoted to radio-visual education was inaugurated.

The Teaching Profession

The shortage of teachers has been such that the use of an increasingly high proportion of unqualified personnel was necessary during the 1960s. A major part of the program for the reform of secondary education during the 1970s was the expansion and improvement of the normal school system at the secondary level for the preparation of primary instructional personnel.

At the primary level in 1969 the ratio of students to teachers was forty-seven to one in urban areas and sixty-two to one in rural localities. It was somewhat lower in private than in public schools, at both the primary and the secondary levels. The output of the normal schools, however, remained almost constant in the face of a 33-percent increase in primary school enrollment between 1965 and 1969; this imbalance made necessary the employment of additional unqualified personnel. At the end of the period less than 20 percent of the teaching staff were normal school graduates, and in rural schools some 70 percent had completed eight years of schooling or less. The lack of demand for admission in the secondary-level normal school system, which made the schools operate at less than capacity during the late 1960s, represented a serious challenge to the expanded capacities envisioned in connection with the secondary school reform program initiated in 1971.

An undetermined, but probably very high, proportion of overage students in primary classes during the late 1960s led school administrators to predict hopefully that the growth in enrollments would slow during the 1970s, even if all children in the seven-to-twelve age bracket were brought into the schoolrooms. A decline of as much as 50 percent in the annual enrollment growth rate during the late 1960s, however, would mean that 7,000 new teachers would be needed by 1980 to supplement the 12,200 that were on the rolls during 1969.

Primary and secondary school teachers in the public system come most frequently from the middle or lower middle classes, and the attitude of the community toward them varies according to the region in which they are employed. In the countryside and in small towns they are generally esteemed and respected, but the prestige enjoyed varies in inverse ratio to the size of the community, and urban society in the early 1970s was not yet fully prepared to accept teaching as a true profession. The status of secondary school personnel was higher than that of primary, but it was more likely to derive from a university background than from being a part of the secondary school system. In general, moreover, a study in the late 1960s found that 27 percent of the students completing teacher training instruction never engaged in the teaching profession.

The fact that women make up a large majority of the teaching staff at the primary and a small majority at the secondary level—about 70 percent of the combined total in the late 1960s and early 1970s—has probably contributed to the reluctance to recognize teaching as a real profession. The proportion of women in the country's labor force is one of the lowest in Latin America, and a relatively small number of upper class women engage in any kind of remunerative employment. In addition, the prestige of the teaching profession suffered badly during the Trujillo era, when its members were forced to become instruments of

113

propaganda and to follow the official line in order to keep their positions. A decade after the regime's collapse, the damage had not entirely been repaired, and teaching personnel remained subject to political pressure in the sense that appointments were made by executive authorities on the basis of slates of candidates submitted by regional administrators.

Several steps were taken by the government during the late 1960s to improve the status of teaching personnel, particularly in the field of salaries. These had been much lower than those in other professions, but in 1972 it was possible for President Balaguer to point out in a press conference that the basic salary of RD$256 monthly received by a teacher in one of the new diversified secondary schools was the same as that of a justice of the peace and more than that of a hospital intern. Primary school personnel salaries had also improved. By 1970 qualified primary school teachers received modest but competitive salaries beginning at RD$1,625 annually, about five times the per capita national income.

In 1969 the ratio of students to teachers in general secondary courses was about twenty-six to one. It was about nineteen to one in vocational and technical classes and a little more than eight to one in normal schools. Instructors for secondary-level institutions are prepared in three-year courses at the university level, and the very rapid increase in university faculties of education during the 1960s gave promise of an improved supply of teachers during the 1970s. Most of the secondary teaching corps in 1969 had completed secondary school, but less than one-third of the staffs in general schools and less than half in the normal schools held diplomas in education or in any other field. Data on vocational and technical teachers are not available, but the absence of any university programs designed for these personnel suggests a generally low level of preparation.

Some of the teachers in the secondary system are professional people who devote a few hours a week to teaching, but the country has a higher proportion of full-time personnel than in most of Latin America, where part-time teaching at the secondary level is common practice. In the rapidly growing private system a large proportion of the personnel are members of religious orders.

University professors—predominantly male—are customarily professional people who teach a few hours a week to gain additional prestige and income but who have little interest in the life of the university, and they are seldom available to students outside the classroom. An essential part of the reform program initiated after the downfall of the Trujillo regime has been the recruitment of a larger proportion of full-time professors. The Madre y Maestra Catholic University in Santiago de los Caballeros opened its doors in 1962 with a teaching staff composed entirely of part-time personnel, and in the mid-1960s fewer than 10 percent of UASD personnel taught full time. The prestige of the university system is of the first order, however, and salary for full-time personnel compares favorably with that in other professional fields.

Procedures for appointments and promotions differ somewhat among institutions. At the UASD new appointees are selected by the University Council on the basis of recommendation of the faculty council concerned. The selections are made from applications received pursuant to widely advertised announcements. Teaching personnel are usually appointed as assistant professors and must have university undergraduate degrees. After three years of service and if a graduate degree is held, they become eligible for associate professorships. After another three years of service, they become eligible for promotion to the rank of titular professor, which carries with it life tenure.

ARTISTIC AND INTELLECTUAL EXPRESSION

The Pre-Columbian and Colonial Eras

Because of the early obliteration of the Indian population that occupied Hispaniola when the Spaniards arrived and failure of the early explorers and settlers to investigate thoroughly the Indian society and develop trustworthy or comprehensive records, knowledge of the country's pre-Columbian culture is extremely sketchy. The Taino Indian culture seems to have found its richest possibilities of expression in the ceramic and sculptural arts. Most of the surviving works are small and, from their totemic combination of man and beast, appear to have ritual significance. The greater part of the stone and hardwood carvings and objects in terra-cotta and other ceramic material depict some aspect of life but are symbolic rather than naturalistic. They have an abstract, geometric quality and a classical perfection of proportion that demonstrate preoccupation with and mastery of concepts of pure form.

There are a few surviving specimens of another, more utilitarian, genre of work in the form of low seats or stools known as *duhos*. These are made of carved, dense black wood and, in several instances, are ornamented with insets of gold leaf. The best comprehensive collection of Taino art is reputed to be that on display in the National Museum of Santo Domingo.

There is little precise knowledge of the aboriginal music and instruments that were means of expression for the Tainos. Early observers described the music and dancing of these people as exemplified in the *areíto*, a festival dance. The dancers formed a line, one behind the other, each with his hands on the shoulders of the dancer in front of him. Their feet measured an intricate pattern in unison and in time to a chant, consisting of antiphonal phrases or group responses to a leader. The women danced in a separate column. Chanting was accompanied by reed fifes and percussion or other rhythm-making instruments, some of which seem to have been the forerunners of such instruments as the maracas and *güiros* found in the Antilles today.

115

Santo Domingo's prominence as the seat of the first Spanish vice-royalty in the New World was of short duration, and the entire colony suffered an economic decline after the Spaniards made secure their conquest on the mainland. Nevertheless, the city maintained its importance as the cultural and ecclesiastical capital of the eastern Caribbean region for over 200 years.

The city's early builders worked with skill and imagination, and Santo Domingo had an imposing cathedral and other public and religious buildings and dwellings long before such structures appeared on the American mainland. The outstanding figure among the architects and builders of the early period was Rodrigo Gil de Liendo, who created the Church of Our Lady of Mercy and part of the cathedral. The style of these and other early structures is a combination of late Gothic and early Renaissance.

Many other outstanding monuments of colonial architecture demonstrate the vitality and eclectic taste of the builders of the period. Forms of medieval Gothic, Italian Renaissance, and classical Greek and Roman, together with the richly ornamented Spanish and Moorish architecture, were reproduced or adapted in the city. Of particular significance are the Cathedral of Santa María, with its columns and Gothic vaulting, elaborately decorated high altar, and ornate marble shrine of Christopher Columbus; the Alcázar, or castle-fortress of Diego Columbus, which was the first palace in America, built in 1510 in Renaissance style with accents of the Isabelline Gothic; and the church and monastery of Santo Domingo, in which the ancient University of Santo Tomás de Aquino was founded in 1538. By the seventeenth century, however, architecture was not flourishing in Santo Domingo as it was in the more wealthy colonies on the mainland, and little use was made of the rococo decoration characteristic of the later Spanish baroque.

Dominican culture owes a debt to the churchmen who were the spiritual governors of the colony. They were the teachers, scholars, and patrons of music who molded the artistic and intellectual life of the community. The celebrated friar of the Dominican order, Bartolomé de Las Casas, began to write his *Apologética Historia de las Indias* (Historical Apologia of the Indies) in the monastery at Puerto Plata. He is considered the spiritual father of the more modern trend known as Indianism (*indigenismo*). A canon of the Cathedral of Santa María, Luis Jerónimo de Alcocer, was one of the principal historical writers of the early colonial period whose works have survived, at least in part. During the last century of the colonial era Antonio Sánchez de Valverde, a lawyer and cathedral functionary, achieved distinction as a geographer. His main work is entitled *Idea del Valor de la Isla Española* (Idea of the Worth of Hispaniola). An annotated version of this work was republished in 1947.

The early adventurers brought with them an acquaintance with and love for the heroic and romantic verse of Spain. Juan de Castellanos, an early chronicler, wrote that it was customary to circulate topical and generally satirical verses criticizing public officials and events anonymously, and that there were so many writers engaged in this activity that it was often impossible to determine who was the author of any particular piece.

Poetry in a more elegant vein was an avocation of the upper class. One of the most important local poets of the seventeenth century was a canon of the cathedral, Don Cristóbal de Llerena. Women were also versemakers. Leonor de Ovando, mother superior of the Dominican sisters at the Church of the Queen of the Angels, and Doña Elvira de Mendoza, wife of a high civil official, enjoy the acclaim of modern critics in the country.

Secular music had an important place in the daily life of the people during the colonial era. Songs and dances from Spain, such as the bolero and the fandango, were introduced during the eighteenth century. Itinerant musical entertainers using the string and wind instruments of Europe were in demand. Spanish and European tradition was followed not only in popular music but also in the music of the church.

The Beginnings of National Self-Expression

The wars and racial troubles that convulsed the greater part of the island of Hispaniola beginning at the end of the eighteenth century opened up a period of vicissitudes that brought Dominican arts and letters to a low ebb. Because of Haitian incursions, many of the upper class families left the country. The country not only lost a large number of men and women of wealth and culture but also was denied the potential gifts of many individuals who later gained prominence elsewhere as creative thinkers and writers.

The Haitian occupation, which lasted over twenty years, was a desolate period during which freedom of expression was ruthlessly repressed, the university was closed, and even the use of the Spanish language was frowned upon. The influence of French literary styles became evident. Under Juan Pablo Duarte, however, a new group of the younger people resisted the oppression and maintained the Hispanic tradition. The same young men who formed La Trinitaria, a secret society, for political purposes founded a cultural association, the Philharmonic (La Filarmónica), devoted to literary activity (see ch. 3). The history of a truly Dominican literature, embodying an indigenous variety of Spanish culture, began with this group, one that was nourished by the drive for independence from Haiti.

The leader was Félix María del Monte, who had come to be known as the father of independent Dominican literature. A man of many activities, del Monte is best known as a poet. He was also a writer of elegant, clear prose, the founder of two literary reviews, a member of Congress, and a teacher. His extant works are patriotic, strongly descriptive of the local scene, and couched in colorful language. He produced some popular works for the theater, but by far his best known work is the patriotic legend in verse form, *Las Vírgenes de Galindo* (The Virgins of Galindo), written in reaction to the threat of Haitian aggression. Others wrote narrative poems descriptive of rural life and tinged with concern for social betterment. Nicolás Ureña Mendoza, born in 1822, was the progenitor of a line of important literary personalities that reached down to the 1960s.

Many of the great figures of Dominican letters belong to the period that opened with restoration of independence in 1865. It was a time of renewed faith in progress and in human ideals and in its earlier years was marked by a strong spirit of romanticism and by the development of the theme of the indigenous Indian life (*indigenismo*—a literary genre that spread throughout Latin America) as a significant formative influence. An important inspirational leader who exemplified the broad interests of the men of letters of the period was Federico Henríquez y Carvajal, educator, historian, poet, journalist, and statesman, who died in 1951 at the age of 103. The intellectuals of the period have been characterized as fighters and builders—men for whom a literary calling was often part of their public service.

The theme of Indianism was an outgrowth of the War of National Restoration fought against Spain during the early 1860s. It was not enough to fight the forces of Spain with arms in hand. It was necessary to oppose them on the field of historical criticism and expose the errors and cruelties of the conquest. Thus the long-vanished Indians of the country were remembered not only with deep sympathy but also with patriotic exaltation. Writers depicted the world of the Indians before the conquest as a sort of idyllic golden age. The Spanish were depicted as cruel and treacherous, lusting for power and wealth.

The classic Dominican work concerned with the Indian is *Enriquillo*, an historical novel by Manuel de Jesús Galván, which tells the story of a young chief who led his people in revolt against the early Spanish settlers. Considered by many to be the greatest work in Dominican letters, the novel depicts the tragedy of the Indian in a style that is faithful to the spirit and events of the period depicted.

A literature of *criollismo*, based on the life, customs, and atmosphere of local regions in the country, came into being toward the end of the nineteenth century. Since that time most of the novels and short stories written in the country have portrayed realistic, contemporary Dominican scenes, and a few have been written in the Creole patois (see ch. 4). The statesman and poet Francisco Billini is credited with originating *criollismo* and with popularizing folklore and tales of rural life. *El Montero* (The Hunter), written by Pedro Francisco Bono y Mejiá in 1856, is one of the earliest outstanding novels in this vein. A new edition of the novel, with a thirty-page introduction by the historian Emilio Rodríguez Demorizi, appeared in 1968.

The period produced a number of accomplished historians, chief of whom was José Gabriel García, initiator of modern (postcolonial) Dominican history. His definitive *Historia de Santo Domingo* (History of Santo Domingo) was published in 1900. Salomé Ureña de Henríquez was another of the great literary personalities of the time. Her compositions reflect a deep love of country and concern for family harmony and social betterment. Among her best known works are *La Gloria de Progreso* (The Glory of Progress) and *La Fé en el Porvenir* (Faith in the Future). During the 1880s she was instrumental in establishing the first institution of higher learning for women in the country.

In music the colonial tradition of dependence on Europe persisted well after the breakdown of colonial rule. The sacred music of European composers was heard in the churches and served as models·for local composers. By the middle of the nineteenth century the country had the Philharmonic Society, and a chamber orchestra was giving regular performances at the cathedral in Santo Domingo in the early 1860s. Municipal and military bands reached widening audiences; reception was aided by the climate, which made outdoor evening concerts enjoyable.

Over the course of several centuries folk and popular music had been growing and developing a national character. Some of the instruments used by the Taino Indians appear to have survived, but their forms of music had little, if any, permanent influence. On the other hand, the Negroes imported as slaves and those who entered the country from Haiti made a substantial contribution to the growth of a Dominican musical idiom.

One of the earliest distinctive forms to emerge was the sentimental serenade known as the *barcarola criolla.* Musical dance forms, based on the early *contradanza* imported from Spain, evolved under local influences to take shape as the *tumba dominicana* or *contradanza criolla* and then the *merengue.* The *merengue,* which in its pure form consists of an introduction followed by an eight-measure slow melody and a fast section of the same length, became popular about the middle of the nineteenth century; with little change in its original style, it is recognized today as the national dance. By the time the *merengue* appeared, the popular domestic forms of music were exerting a strong influence in the country's serious musical circles.

The leader in the fusion of musical forms that began to take place at this time was Juan Bautista Alfonseca, who has come to be known as the father of the national school. Born in 1810, he was director of the regimental band and of the chamber orchestra sponsored by the cathedral in Santo Domingo. He was a composer of masses and other liturgical music and also wrote *merengues* and a great many band pieces based on themes taken from Dominican folk music.

Transition to Modernism

The modernist movement that swept over the literary world of

Spanish America toward the close of the nineteenth century and continued its formative course until the 1920s was a logical extension of the feeling that artistic and intellectual independence had been achieved in large measure. In the Dominican Republic the movement was marked by an eagerness to cast off the formalities and restraints of earlier days and to seek out and emulate the best in the new tendencies of the modern world. There was a desire to experiment with whatever was new and fresh but at the same time to adapt the old to the new within a basic fabric of nationalism.

In prose the modernists attempted to rid themselves of a slow and involved solemnity of style and, in its place, achieve simplicity and brevity. They sought a new elegance and freedom of movement. Most of the prose—and the best of it—took the form of essays, articles, and criticism. In short stories the goal was introspection, and the writers of novels aimed at realism. Trends in poetry showed the influence of French symbolism. Writers built on the sheer music of words, abandoning classicism and the strenuous romantic style. New verse forms emerged, and some very old ones were revived, but free verse did not appear until the 1920s.

Realism was particularly well developed in the historical novel. Among the most outstanding works in this category are books describing the tyranny of Ulises Heureaux and the political turmoil of the post-Heureaux period.

Américo Lugo excelled as a historian, and one of the ablest essayists and literary critics of the period was Rafael Alfredo Deligne. Most influential, however, was his brother, Gaston Gernando Deligne, who, as a disciple of the great Nicaraguan, Rubén Darío, wrote excellent poetry and has been called the Dominican Republic's national poet. One of Deligne's better known associates was Fabio Fiallo, who wrote exquisite love lyrics as well as bitter denunciations of the United States occupation.

Something akin to the modernist movement in literature began to take place in music late in the nineteenth century. Composers made greater use of indigenous themes as the basis for musical forms in the classical tradition while attempting to attain greater stylistic freedom. Best known of a small group that took the lead in the modernizing movement and served as a link between earlier romanticism and the new music that was to emerge was José de Jesús Ravelo. Many of his works are liturgical, composed with simplicity and directness. He wrote several oratorios as well as band music and pieces for the piano and organ. Early in the twentieth century he organized and became the first director of the Music School (Liceo Musical), a government-sponsored musical conservatory.

Contemporary music owes immediate inspiration and a sense of direction to Juan Francisco García and Estéban Peña-Morell. Both made use in their compositions of material taken from native songs, dances, and legends as foundations for serious modern music. García composed three symphonies, which are often performed in the Dominican Republic, large works for bands and string quartets, and much dance music. He originated a new dance form, the *sambumbia*, in order to make more effective use of the various kinds of native music.

The Contemporary Scene

Literature

In the late 1920s Domingo Moreno Jiménez was the leader in formulating the concepts of *postumismo*, a school of writing that aims at casting off the restraints of tradition. Early in 1966 he founded a literary review, *El Día Estético*, to be an outlet for the movement. Prominent among his associates were Rafael Andrés Brenes, poet and novelist, and Héctor Incháustegui Cabral, whose free forms of verse, daring use of metaphor, and great variety of imagery place him in the vanguard of *postumismo*.

Poesía negra, the poetry based on Negro life and themes that appeared in the Caribbean toward the end of the 1920s, had an important Dominican exponent in Manuel Cabral. Among his best works is a collection of poems entitled *Negro de América* (Negroes of America). Although known for his *poesía negra*, Cabral did not confine himself entirely to this genre of verse. His *Ocho Gritos* (Eight Cries) deals with social injustice; other poems are lyrical interpretations of the Antillean landscape; and still others evoke the feeling of the French symbolists.

Two women stand out prominently as contemporary Dominican poets. Camila Henríquez Ureña is in the tradition of the great Chilean, Gabriela Mistral. Steeped in an exalted sort of Romanticism, she ignored the traditional restraints surrounding the life of women in countries of Hispanic culture. Flérida de Nolasco wrote first-rate poetry but also produced a number of excellent studies on literary and musical matters.

Contemporary novelists and short story writers have dealt mainly with Dominican themes and the everyday life and customs of the countryside. *Cañas y Bueyes* (Sugarcane and Oxen), by Francisco Eugenio Moscoso Puello, is a story of the sugar industry and its place in the life of the country. Sócrates Nolasco has written novels and shorter pieces based on folklore and history. Juan Bosch achieved a reputation in literary circles with his short stories and has written several larger works of fiction, including *La Mañosa* (The Clever One), a novel published in 1936 that described a revolution. Since he has spent the greater part of his adult life in exile, most of his works have been published outside the country.

Bosch is generally considered the father of the country's modern social-protest literature. *The Unfinished Experiment: Democracy in the Dominican Republic*, published in English in 1965, expresses his hopes and frustrations after a short-lived presidency and several years of attempting to lead a popular political movement. Two of his short

121

stories appear along with contributions by ten other writers in an anthology, *Narradores Dominicanos* (Dominican Storytellers), published in 1969. Compiled by Aída Cartagena, the anthology consists primarily of stories dealing with political repression and social misery.

An annual short story competition, initiated in 1966 by the Cultural Movement "The Mask" (Movimiento Cultural "La Máscara") has offered incentive to unknown writers. Rules for the initial contest required a Dominican setting and excluded political themes, but such restrictions were lifted thereafter. Popular themes and approaches have included existentialism, psychoanalysis, fantasy, and satire. Each year the prize-winning and honorable-mention stories have been published by "The Mask," and works by the first-prize winners for the first three years—Miguel Alfonseca, Armando Almanzar, and René del Risco Bermúdez—were included in the anthology by Cartagena.

Other novelists and short story writers who have adopted the social protest theme include Ramón Marrero Aristy, who wrote of the sordidness of the life of the seasonal sugarcane cutter; Horacio Read, who has dealt with United States intervention and occupation; and Andrés Francisco Requena, who described the problems of rural workers transplanted in the cities and the prevalence of caudillo rule in the country's political life.

The leading contemporary literary critic is Max Henríquez Ureña, a member of the distinguished family in Dominican letters. His *Panorama Histórico de la Literatura Dominicana* (Historical Panorama of Dominican Literature) and *Breve Historia del Modernismo* (Brief History of Modernism) have become standard works of reference for students of Dominican literature. His brother, the late educator and scholar Pedro Henríquez Ureña, gained a reputation throughout the hemisphere as a result of his literary studies. Joaquín Balaguer, in addition to achieving prominence as a political leader, has published twenty major works, including a comprehensive overview of Dominican literature. Recent literary criticism has included sociopolitical interpretation of the development of the short story since 1916, including the effects of the Trujillo era and the United States interventions in 1916 and 1965.

Science and the Humanities

One of the leading scientists of the contemporary period has been Rafael María Moscoso, who published a definitive study of the country's plantlife. Fernando Alberto Defilló is a biologist of repute. Among the professors and scholars of the university, Patín Maceo is an authority on philology; Froilán Tavares and Manuel A. Peña Batlle gained reputations for publications on law and politics; and German-born Erwin Walter Palm has become the leading authority on colonial architecture and the antiquities of the country.

Emilio Rodríguez Demorizi is noted as a historian who managed to escape the intellectual dogmatism of the Trujillo era. His major contribution to the national literature is the three-volume series *Historia de la República Dominicana* (History of the Dominican Republic), published between 1944 and 1959. Historical revision has been undertaken by Emilio Cordero Michel. *La Revolución Haïtiana y Santo Domingo* (The Haitian Revolution and Santo Domingo), published in 1968, attempts to correct the anti-Haitian racial bias of Dominican writings on the Haitian independence movement. Other recent historical works include Carlos Larrazabal Blanco's *Los Negros y la Esclavitud en Santo Domingo* (Negroes and Slavery in Santo Domingo) and *Estudios de Historia Política Dominicana* (Studies on Dominican Political History) by Pedro Troncoso Sánchez.

The Dominican government has lent its support to efforts to stimulate scholarly and creative endeavors. Representatives from editorial houses all over the world were invited to enter exhibits in Expomundial, an international exhibition and cultural festival featuring books, periodicals, theater, ballet, paintings, and other art forms, which took place in Santo Domingo in 1970.

Music

The government-supported National Symphony Orchestra was organized in 1941; together with the National Conservatory of Music and Speech, which grew out of the Ravelo School (Liceo de Ravelo), it has become the center of musical activity in the country. The Spanish-born musician and composer, Enrique Casal Chapí, was the first conductor of the symphony. He encouraged the younger local composers by adding a number of their works to the orchestra's regular repertory. A stimulating and innovative teacher, he has had considerable influence in developing a trend away from the more traditional styles and forms of music among the more serious composers and performers.

Manuel Simó, one of Casal's most talented students, is a composer of symphonies, piano music, and a cantata—*A la Patria* (To the Fatherland). He became conductor of the National Symphony Orchestra in 1964 and continued to hold that position in 1972. Another of Casal's prominent students, Niñon de Broüer Lapeiretta, is a leading composer of music in the modern idiom and president of the Musical Society for the Arts (Sociedad Musical Pro Arte). Luis Frías Sandoval is well known in musical circles as a composer of choral works and as the leader of the National Chorus.

Enrique de Marchena is one of a number of composers who achieved success during the first half of the twentieth century. His music is colored by an impressionism suggestive of the early works of Claude Debussy. He has written extensively on musical subjects. Among the country's performers who have achieved international recognition is the violinist and conductor Carlos Piantini.

An important musical event in 1972 was the Inter-American Musical Festival, which took place in Santo Domingo in March. Sponsored by the Organization of American States, the governments of the Dominican Republic and the Commonwealth of Puerto Rico, and a number of private foundations, the festival featured the internationally known composer and cellist Pablo Casals and the symphony orchestras of the Dominican Republic and Puerto Rico. Among the composers whose works were performed was Margarita Luna de Espaillat of the Dominican Republic.

Indian music disappeared as the indigenous population died off. Survivals of the African dances are also rapidly disappearing, although a few may still be found in remote rural areas. There was no serious attempt to collect and study the country's folk music until the 1960s, when folkloric groups, such as that of René Carrasco, began to perform. An outstanding promoter of this trend is Edna Garrido, who published a volume of Dominican versions of traditional Spanish ballads. Most folk music, however, is regional; there is no nationally recognized folk tradition.

The Graphic Arts

Much of the contemporary painting and sculpture exhibit the same experimental trends as are found in modern circles in Europe and the United States. A tendency toward blending the abstract with Indian designs and the use of African primitivism, as well as a daring use of colors, suggests the type of work done by such masters as Pablo Picasso and Georges Braque. The more advanced works have been inspired, in part at least, by Spanish-born artists who became Dominican citizens, such as José Vela Zanetti, muralist and teacher in the National School of Fine Arts. Of the younger painters, Clara Ledesma is an outstanding portraitist and landscape artist. She is one of a limited number of the country's artists who have shown their work abroad.

Jaime Colson and Darío Suro have experimented with various international trends. Colson passed through a period of fascination with cubism and has done a number of pieces reminiscent of the sculptural stage of Picasso. Regardless of differences in style, his works, often depicting nudes, have a highly sensual quality. Suro has been influenced at one time or another by the Mexican revolutionary school, by surrealism, and by United States expressionism. He is particularly noted for collages charged with social content. Critics have observed something peculiarly Dominican—an Afro-Latin symbiosis—in the work of both men.

Swirling and gliding combinations of fine and heavy pen strokes distinguish the drawing style of Ada Balcácer. Many of her drawings, such as *La Gorda* (the Fat Woman), have a sculptural form suggestive of the work of Henry Moore. Jorge Severino excels in the difficult medium of watercolor. His images, with poignant facial expressions, border on folk art. The work of Mario Cruz, generally described as primitive, is characterized by weighty, rounded forms. Guillo Pérez paints with disorderly explosive strokes, whereas the work of Fernando

Peña Defillo is noted for its geometric order. Aquiles Antonio Azar García complements cleanness of brush stroke with richness of color and texture.

Sculptor Domingo Liz works primarily in wood. One critic has said that his work is always monumental, regardless of its size. His abstract piece known as *Origin II* has a robust, sprouting quality. The Museum of Fine Arts in the capital houses a collection of representative Dominican art.

PUBLIC INFORMATION

Freedom of Expression

Although guaranteed by the constitution, freedom of expression during the Trujillo regime was virtually nonexistent. During the first two years after his assumption of power in 1932, Trujillo brought under his control all sources of public information by using a combination of political, economic, and social pressures in which coercion played a prominent part. Later, after he had gained control of the media, he attempted to formalize his procedures through legislation. The basic statute around which restrictive legislation centered was the communications law of 1938.

A law promulgated in 1944 required submission of printed matter to the secretary of state for interior and police. Shop machinery was liable to confiscation as payment of fines imposed for violation of government regulations, and penalties of correctional imprisonment were established for violators. In 1949 a law created the National Commission of Public Spectacles and empowered it to formulate regulations affecting motion pictures, drama, radio, and television broadcasting. All performances considered offensive to good customs or critical of the government were prohibited. Under a law promulgated early in 1961, vendors of radio and television receiving sets were required to submit to the director general of telecommunications the names of all purchasers.

The Constitution of 1962, framed after the assassination of Trujillo, reaffirmed the principle of freedom of expression, but a law promulgated in December 1962 repeated the Trujillo statutory regulations relating to communications media and made those media carrying appeals for civil disobedience liable to prosecution. The Constitution of 1963, enacted during the presidency of Juan Bosch, stated that the press might not be subjected to "any type of coercion or censorship"; after President Bosch was overthrown, however, the government returned to the Constitution of 1962. Dissemination of all forms of communist propaganda was prohibited, and owners and managers of broadcasting stations and publishing concerns who carried material originating with proscribed organizations were declared guilty of misdemeanors.

In 1964 the government established a censorship committee to enforce a ban on all political broadcasts. During the late 1960s, however, steps were taken to eliminate the legacy of the Trujillo dictatorship, and the government relaxed its controls.

Radio, Television, and Motion Pictures

During the 1950s and 1960s the number of licensed radio transmitters in the republic increased dramatically, as did the number of radio listeners. The importation of inexpensive battery-operated transistor receiving sets during the 1960s launched a communications revolution.

In 1972 there were approximately ninety-six originating radio stations. Approximately seven of these broadcast on shortwave frequencies only; about twenty-one broadcast on both mediumwave and shortwave; and the remainder transmitted on mediumwave only. Thirty-two had permission to operate on frequency modulation (FM) frequencies. There were thirty-three radio stations in Santo Domingo and fifteen in Santiago de los Caballeros. Under normal conditions only about nine of the Santo Domingo stations could be heard in the interior.

The number of receivers in the country was estimated at 2.5 million. About 700,000 of the total number could receive shortwave broadcasts. Because of the difficult terrain FM transmission was used principally to link studios with standard transmitters. Most of the stations in Santo Domingo and Santiago de los Caballeros, as well as a number of other stations, were well equipped and used modern cartridge tape recorders for music and commercials. Four of the more powerful stations subscribed to a United States wire service, and four stations broadcast daily news programs, which were rebroadcast by twenty-eight stations in the interior.

With the exception of a government-owned station, no radio station was identified with any particular philosophy or political party. Among the more important stations broadcasting from Santo Domingo in 1972 were Radio Universal, Radio Mil, the government-owned Radio Quisqueya Internacional, and Broadcasting Nacional. Popular stations broadcasting from Santiago de los Caballeros included Radio Santiago and Radio Hit Musical. Radio Quisqueya Internacional, with a fifty-kilowatt transmitter, was the most powerful station in the country. A number of stations had a ten-kilowatt capacity; several operated on five kilowatts; and a large number used one kilowatt.

In 1972 about 75 percent of the people lived within the primary reception area for the country's four television channels, but only an estimated 25 percent of the population watched television—on approximately 250,000 receiving sets. All four channels originated in Santo Domingo.

Radio Televisión Dominicana, government owned, operated on channel 4; it had one relay station (channel 5) in the interior. Color Visión, a private station, operated on channel 9 in Santo Domingo and had a relay station (channel 2) in Santiago de los Caballeros. Rehintel, also a private station, operated on channel 7 in the capital city and had a relay station (channel 11) in the interior. The fourth channel, Tele Inde (channel 30), officially opened in August 1972, broadcast using ultrahigh frequencies and introduced a new system of audiovisual education.

Each television station broadcast approximately nine hours. Along with newscasts, the stations' program material consisted of drama series, cartoons, and old films. A large proportion of this material originated in the United States.

In 1972 there were more than 100 motion picture theaters in the country with a total seating capacity of about 50,000. The majority of the films shown were originated in the United States and were subtitled in Spanish, but films from Spanish-speaking countries, particularly Mexico, and from certain European countries were also exhibited.

There were two basic kinds of motion picture theaters. First-class theaters showed United States and certain other foreign films. These were found only in the two major cities, and the price of admission limited attendance generally to foreigners and middle class and upper class Dominicans. Most Dominicans, however, could afford to attend the cheaper, less comfortable theaters, which showed older or poorer quality films. The people tended to regard motion pictures solely as a medium of entertainment.

Newspapers, Periodicals, and Books

In the past, the lifespans of newspapers in the Dominican Republic have been ephemeral. *El Telégrafo Constitucional de Santo Domingo*, the first newspaper printed in the capital city, appeared only briefly in 1821. *El Dominicano*, the first newspaper published after independence, appeared in 1845, but soon ceased publication because it assumed an antigovernment position. The *Listín Diario*, founded in 1889, established a reputation for being one of the most independent newspapers in Latin America, and in 1972 it maintained its position as a leading daily. During the Trujillo regime all publications were subjected to strict government controls, but after the assassination of the dictator the press was generally free.

In 1972 there were seven independent daily newspapers in the republic—five in Santo Domingo and two in Santiago. One of the two more important dailies was *El Caribe*, founded in 1948; it was a morning paper published in Santo Domingo. In its advertising it stated that it was read by "members of households having the highest incomes as well as leaders of industry, business, government, and professional groups." It had a reputation for being moderate and nationalist, and its circulation was estimated at more than 30,000. It carried United States columnists. The other leading daily, *Listín Diario*, had a reputation for being moderate and reform-minded and energetically promoting economic progress. *Listín Diario* carried United States bylines and had an estimated circulation of over 30,000.

Other Santo Domingo newspapers were *El Tiempo, El Nacional de Ahora,* and *Ultima Hora. El Tiempo,* with an estimated circulation of 6,000, was rightist, anticommunist, and promilitary. *El Nacional de Ahora,* an afternoon tabloid with a circulation of approximately 25,000, was strongly nationalistic and sensationalist. The other tabloid published in Santo Domingo was *Ultima Hora,* with an estimated circulation of 9,000. *Ultima Hora* was established by *Listín Diario* in 1970 in order to challenge *El Nacional de Ahora.*

The two dailies published in Santiago de los Caballeros were *La Información* (circulation about 10,000) and *El Sol* (circulation approximately 15,000). *La Información,* an afternoon paper, was conservative. *El Sol,* a morning paper, appeared initially in January 1971 and was the country's newest daily. Its policy was regarded as moderate.

Among the press services used by leading Santo Domingo newspapers in 1972 were the official news agencies of Spain and France and the Associated Press, United Press International, King Features Syndicate, Copley News Service, Los Angeles Times Service, Washington Post News Service, Newsweek Features Service, and New York Times Service. Copies of the *New York Times* and the *Miami Herald* could be obtained in Santo Domingo on the date of publication.

Probably the most influential of the nine magazines published in the country in 1972 was the weekly news magazine, *Ahora,* with a circulation of about 12,000. This publication subscribed to a number of feature services and to United Press International wire services. A substantial portion of its material originated locally, and it provided good coverage of political and cultural developments. The magazine was the parent organization of a publishing and broadcasting complex. Other magazines were *Horizontes de América* (circulation about 6,000); *Dominicana* (circulation approximately 4,000); *Amigo del Hogar* (circulation about 10,000); and *Economía Dominicana* (circulation about 6,000).

In 1972 about a dozen firms classified as publishers had an estimated output of less than 200 books, many of which pertained to the social sciences. Approximately six importers-exporters of books handled volumes published in the United States, Spain, Argentina, Mexico, and other Latin American countries.

The people were served by more than 100 public libraries. All towns of 10,000 had at least one library containing works by both Dominican and foreign authors.

Foreign Government Activities

In 1972 small scholarship programs were supported by the United Nations, the Organization of American States, Belgium, Brazil, Spain, France, the Federal Republic of Germany (West Germany), Israel, Great Britain, Italy, and the United States. Informational and educational activities were conducted in the Dominican Republic by cultural groups representing France, Japan, Italy, West Germany, the Republic of China, Venezuela, Lebanon, and Spain.

There were organizations of the French Alliance (Alliance Française) in Santo Domingo and in three interior cities. The Dominican-Japanese Cultural Association and a Dante Alighieri Cultural Association, sponsored by the Italian embassy, were established in the capital city. The United States Information Service distributed radio and television programs, motion pictures, and press releases to all media. It also maintained a reading room and a binational center in Santo Domingo and smaller binational centers in Santiago de los Caballeros and San Francisco de Macorís. The Santo Domingo and Santiago de los Caballeros centers featured lectures, exhibits, films, forums, and libraries. Radio Havana and Radio Moscow beamed broadcasts that could be received throughout the country.

SECTION II. POLITICAL

CHAPTER 7

GOVERNMENT, POLITICAL DYNAMICS,

AND FOREIGN RELATIONS

The Constitution of 1966, which was in effect in 1972, described the government as "essentially civil, republican, democratic, and representative." Twenty-five constitutions had been enacted in the Dominican Republic between 1844 and 1966. All guaranteed human rights, prescribed a tripartite—executive, legislative, and judicial—division of governmental power, and provided for popular sovereignty. In actuality, however, none of these documents effectively protected civil liberties, established the independence of the legislative and judicial branches of government from the executive, or made public officials significantly responsible to the people. The country's constitutions have generally been symbolic, rather than operating legal documents.

The legacy of thirty-one years of authoritarian rule (1930-61) under Rafael Leónidas Trujillo Molina and of an arrested civil war (1965) marked the political system in 1972. The government of Juan Bosch and the Dominican Revolutionary Party (Partido Revolucionario Dominicano—PRD), the first after the assassination of Trujillo that came to power through elections and attempted to rule in accordance with the constitution, lasted only six months before being toppled by the armed forces in alliance with civilians who saw their economic interests threatened. A clash between the same groups—the Constitutionalists (embracing urban poor, organized labor, students, and the intelligentsia, and elements of the military) demanding the return of the Bosch government and the implementation of its proposed reforms, and the Loyalists, opposing Bosch and his proposed reforms—led to the fall of the military-backed so-called Triumvirate government, civil war, and intervention by the United States and the Organization of American States (OAS).

Joaquín Balaguer, who was serving as president when Trujillo was assassinated, established the Reformist Party (Partido Reformista—PR) and was elected to the presidency in 1966. He has attempted to build upon the clientele system developed under Trujillo in the rural areas and to consolidate the forces to the right of Center in the political spectrum. He has, however, been compelled to deal with a major split

131

in his own party, with the rise of a new party on the far Right, and with a military conspiracy, which he exposed in 1971.

The Balaguer government, reelected in 1970, had seen a proliferation of organizations that, with considerable foreign assistance, was promoting economic development and was presiding over a trend toward economic recovery. Differences over the urgency and direction of change and over the redistribution of both goods and political power, which had sparked the civil strife in 1965, however, had not been resolved.

Groups that had assumed leadership in the Constitutionalist movement had been greatly weakened by losses sustained in fighting the Loyalist military faction and the Inter-American Peace Force, by frequent political violence that occurred during much of 1970 and 1971, and by the schisms that have been characteristic of Dominican parties and other politically oriented institutions. Student activists had been particularly vulnerable to military and police operations. The labor movement, initially the strongest base of Bosch's government, had been sharply divided since his overthrow; and, although the unions were strongly represented among the Constitutionalist supporters, the labor movement had been unable to regain its former organizational strength. The PRD, which, appealing to a coalition of the idealistic and the powerless, had swept the popular vote in 1962, was presumed to have remained the strongest opposition party; but, as Bosch and other leaders had alleged that elections were not free, its strength had not been tested at the polls since 1966.

Among the politically articulate the polarization of the system— between the spokesmen of those who fear socioeconomic change and the spokesmen of those who demand it—remained pronounced in the early 1970s. It was evident not only in the alienation of educated youth, the frequent confrontations between economic sectors, and the persistence of seemingly arbitrary violence but also in disintegrative tendencies within the country's social institutions. The characteristically personalistic alignment, based on loyalty to individuals rather than ideological or programmatic cohesion, and the fragmented party system had not succeeded in aggregating popular demands and channeling them through the relatively new institutions for the resolution of political competition.

Virtually the only issue on which groups of widely varying ideologies could unite was opposition to *continuismo*, or self-perpetuation in the seat of power, as practiced by Trujillo. It was on this issue that parties and groups who had engaged each other in open combat only a few years earlier sought to present a united front against President Balaguer.

Domestic political competition has always been inextricably intertwined with the country's links with the international arena. Nationalism has been undermined by the requisites of national or factional self-preservation. Attempts have been made on various occasions throughout Dominican history to exchange national sovereignty for security under the flag of Colombia, France, Spain, England, or the United States. Like "democracy," however, national independence has become a highly valued ideal, to such an extent that even those who profited from the United States intervention in 1965 have felt compelled to criticize it, and foreign companies with large-scale investments attempt to maintain a low profile.

Aside from the intermittent friction in the country's relations with Haiti, which dates back to the early nineteenth century, the Dominican role in international affairs in the twentieth century has been a function of its ties with the United States and of the nature of its government. The authoritarian government of Trujillo maintained close ties with other authoritarian governments. The Bosch government cultivated ties with governments whose leaders had been chosen in free elections. While eschewing diplomatic ties with socialist countries, the Balaguer government has tended not to differentiate in its relations between authoritarian and democratic governments under capitalist systems.

CONSTITUTIONAL FRAMEWORK

The constitution, promulgated on November 28, 1966, has many of the features of the Institutional Act of August 31, 1965, which, in turn, incorporated certain sections of the constitutions of 1962 and 1963. The constitution may be amended, but it may never be suspended or annulled, and no amendment may be made changing the form of government.

The first three titles of the constitution define the country's territory; individual, social, and political rights; and nationality, citizenship, and the duties of citizens. There is no death penalty, but this punishment may be instituted in time of war for cases of treason. No person may be deprived of his liberty for more than forty-eight hours without being brought before a competent judge. The home is inviolable, and entry may not be made except in cases prescribed by law.

Freedom of expression, association, and worship, subject to respect for public order and good customs, is assured. Union organization of labor is unrestricted, and the right of workers to strike and of employers to a lockout, in private enterprise, is acknowledged, provided it is exercised in accordance with the law and is used to settle labor disputes. Marriage is recognized as the legal basis of the family. Elementary education is compulsory, and both elementary and secondary education are free.

The constitution may be amended if the proposal for amendment is presented in Congress—comprised of the Senate and the Chamber of Deputies—with the support of one-third of the members of either chamber or if it is submitted by the president. The second step in the process is the passage of a law requiring a meeting of both chambers to consider the amendment. This law may not be vetoed by the president and must specify the purpose of the amendment and the article or articles of the constitution that will be affected. The joint session then meets within fifteen days after the passage of the law, with at least more than half of the members of both chambers present. If the joint session approves the amendment, the constitution is published in its entirety, incorporating the amended text where applicable.

THE CENTRAL GOVERNMENT

The Executive

The constitution vests executive authority in the president of the republic, elected to a four-year term by direct vote. No provision precludes the president from succeeding himself. The president is required to be Dominican by birth, at least thirty years of age, and in possession of full civil and political rights. A vice president, who is required to meet the same qualifications, is elected in the same manner to a concurrent term.

The vice president is authorized to fulfill the term of an incapacitated president. If the vice president in turn should be incapacitated, the president of the Supreme Court of Justice assumes executive power until a new president can be elected by the joint session of Congress, which must be convoked within fifteen days after the assumption of power by the president of the Supreme Court of Justice. The president of the republic may not leave the country for more than fifteen days without the permission of both houses of Congress, and neither the president nor the vice president may resign except before the joint session of Congress.

Historically, the special emergency powers devolving upon the president have been the basis of executive supremacy over the legislative and judicial branches of government. Like previous documents, the Constitution of 1966 empowers Congress to declare a state of siege or of national emergency, thereby authorizing the president to take all actions necessary to defend the nation and to suspend all personal rights other than inviolability of life. The president can declare a state of siege or of national emergency on his own initiative when Congress is not in session.

As chief executive, the president is charged with publishing and executing the laws and is empowered to issue administrative regulations and decrees. He is required to report annually to Congress on his administration. As chief of state, the president receives the representatives of foreign governments, directs diplomatic negotiations, and concludes treaties, which are subject to congressional approval. The president regulates the custom service and port authorities, and he issues navigation licenses and administers maritime, river, and military zones. He also has authority to grant or refuse permission for Dominicans to accept employment or decorations offered by foreign governments.

As head of public administration the president appoints and removes cabinet ministers, provincial governors, and all other public officials whose appointment is not vested in any other branch or agency of government. His appointments to the diplomatic corps are subject to approval by the Senate. When Congress is recessed, the president can temporarily fill vacancies in the courts at all levels or on the Accounting Commission, the five-member agency responsible for the general and special accounts of the republic. In addition, he can fill municipal vacancies if the panel of elected alternates has been exhausted or the municipality has proved incapable of filling the positions.

According to Article 55 of the Constitution of 1966, the president of the republic, as head of public administration, may appoint and revoke the appointments of the members of his cabinet, who are called secretaries of state. In order to be a member of the cabinet an individual must be a Dominican citizen in possession of full civil rights and at least twenty-five years of age. Naturalized persons may not become secretaries or undersecretaries of state until ten years after they have acquired Dominican nationality.

In 1972 there were twelve secretaries of state: the technical secretary of state for the presidency; the administrative secretary of state for the presidency; and the ten secretaries of state supervising the ministries of interior and police, armed forces, foreign relations, finance, education and fine arts, public health and social welfare, labor, agriculture, public works and communications, and industry and commerce. Of equal rank but not actually a member of the cabinet was the attorney general, who supervised the functioning of the judicial branch. In 1972 the secretary of state for industry and commerce was a woman, and in September of that year she was appointed interim secretary of state for foreign relations, the first woman to occupy that post. In addition to the twelve secretaries of state, there were fourteen autonomous and eleven semiautonomous agencies, also under the supervision of the executive branch (see ch. 8).

The Legislature

Legislative power is exercised by Congress, which consists of the Senate and the Chamber of Deputies. These individuals are elected by direct vote for four-year terms; while serving in Congress they may not hold any other government position. The members of both chambers enjoy penal immunity for the opinions they express in sessions of Congress, and no senator or deputy may be deprived of his freedom during the legislative session without authorization from the chamber to which he belongs, except in the case of apprehension in the act of committing a crime.

The Senate

One senator is elected from each of the country's twenty-six provinces, and one, from the National District, the territory in which the capital is located. In order to be a senator an individual must be a Dominican possessing full civil and political rights, at least twenty-five years old, and a native of the province from which he is elected or he must have resided there for at least five years. Naturalized persons may be elected ten years after acquiring naturalization if they have resided for five consecutive years preceding the election in the jurisdiction in which the election is held.

Among the exclusive powers allocated to the Senate by the constitution are: the election of judges to the Supreme Court of Justice and all lower courts; the election of the president and members of the Central Electoral Board and their alternates; the election of the members of the Accounting Commission; approval or rejection of diplomatic appointments submitted by the executive branch; and the trial of impeachment cases preferred by the Chamber of Deputies against public officials.

The Chamber of Deputies

The members of the Chamber of Deputies are elected by the people of the provinces and the National District in the proportion of one deputy for every 50,000 inhabitants or fraction thereof greater than 25,000, but in no case shall a province have less than two deputies. The requirements to be a deputy are the same as for a senator, and the same naturalization rules apply. It is the exclusive right of the Chamber of Deputies to present impeachments of public officials before the Senate, but only by a vote of three-fourths of the total membership of the chamber. In 1972 there were seventy-four deputies.

Congress

Congress can legislate on all matters not within the competence of another branch of government. It has explicit powers to levy taxes and determine the method of their collection and expenditure, to approve or reject the statement of collections and expenditures required of the executive, to approve or reject executive requests for special funds, to approve or disapprove loans on the credit of the republic, and to regulate the national debt. Limited by certain constitutional provisions, Congress can acquire or alienate public property.

Congress is empowered to create or abolish provinces, municipalities, or other political divisions of the national territory and to determine their boundaries and organization. It is authorized to determine the number of courts of appeal and to create or abolish other kinds of courts. Congress can also declare the necessity of amending the constitution and proclaim a state of siege or national emergency. It is authorized to legislate on immigration and to approve or reject treaties concluded by the executive. It may also grant authorization to the president of the republic to leave the country, if the absence is to be for more than fifteen days.

Initiation of legislation is the prerogative of senators, deputies, the president of the republic, the Supreme Court of Justice (in judicial matters), and the Central Electoral Board (in election matters). Every bill is subject to two periods of discussion in the chamber in which it originates. Upon approval it is then passed to the other chamber for similar action. Amendments attached in the second chamber are submitted to the first for approval. Bills approved by both chambers go to the president to be promulgated, providing the president offers no objection. A presidential veto causes the bill to be reconsidered during the next session of the chamber in which it originated. If each chamber again passes the bill by a two-thirds majority, it becomes law.

The Judiciary

The country's legal system, in the early nineteenth century, was more directly affected by French law and the Napoleonic Code than were those of other Latin American republics. The Haitians, during their occupation of Santo Domingo, replaced the Spanish legal system established by the Spanish conquest with the laws of Haiti, which had been derived from the Napoleonic Code. Upon withdrawal of the Haitians in 1844, the Dominican National Congress adopted the Napoleonic Code, but this was not officially translated into Spanish until forty years later. The various civil and criminal codes that form the basis of the modern legal system were adopted in 1884.

At the apex of the judicial system is the Supreme Court of Justice, consisting of nine judges appointed by the Senate. The Senate designates one judge to serve as president of the court and substitutes to replace the president in case of his absence or disability. The term of office is not expressly stated in the constitution but is intended to coincide with the five-year constitutional periods for which all elective officials serve. A supreme court justice must be a Dominican by birth, in full exercise of civil and political rights, hold a doctor of laws degree, and have engaged in legal practice for twelve years.

The Supreme Court of Justice has original jurisdiction in all cases involving the president, vice president, cabinet ministers, members of Congress, and judges and prosecutors assigned to the higher courts. It also hears appeals from decisions of the courts of appeal, has disciplinary authority over all members of the judiciary, and can transfer judges from one jurisdiction to another. The court has rarely exercised its prerogative to reopen criminal cases resulting in sentences of imprisonment or interdiction of civil rights, and then only when extraordinary new evidence implying innocence of the person convicted came to light.

Below the Supreme Court of Justice are courts of appeal located in Santo Domingo, San Cristóbal, Santiago, La Vega, San Francisco de Macorís, San Pedro de Macorís, and San Juan. Each court has five judges, including the president. These courts have original jurisdiction over cases involving provincial governors and judges and prosecutors assigned to the lower courts. They hear appeals from decisions rendered by courts of first instance in both criminal and civil matters. Qualifications for judgeships include: Dominican nationality; full exercise of civil and political rights; a degree of doctor of laws; and four years in the practice of law or an equal length of time as judge in a court of first instance.

Each of the twenty-six provinces and the National District form judicial districts, and in each there is a court of first instance. A judge must be a Dominican, in full enjoyment of civil and political rights, have a doctor of laws degree, and have practiced law for at least two years. Generally assigned to each court of first instance is an examining magistrate, whose duties are to investigate and prepare for trial all criminal cases. These courts have general jurisdiction in civil, commercial, and penal cases. In the more populous judicial districts, courts of first instance are composed of separate chambers designed to hear cases involving civil or commercial actions, misdemeanors, and felonies.

The constitution provides for justice of the peace courts to be located in the National District and in each municipality, the number varying with the burden of cases and as created by law. Persons presiding over this lowest court level must have Dominican nationality, be in full enjoyment of civil and political rights, and hold a law degree. The judges of these courts are appointed by the Senate for five-year terms. Appeals from these courts proceed to courts of first instance.

The judicial system includes a series of special courts: land courts, juvenile courts, labor courts, and military courts. Land courts were established by the constitution and given primary jurisdiction over all disputes involving real property. The courts are on the same level as courts of appeal, and each has a presiding judge and two associate judges who must fulfill the same qualifying requirements as judges of the appellate courts.

Juvenile courts, although not provided for in the constitution, were established in 1941 by separate legislation to handle cases of persons under eighteen years of age. A 1950 law authorized the establishment of a juvenile court in the principal city of each judicial district. Labor courts are composed of three judges each, also appointed by the Senate. They may hear disputes in the labor field and have original jurisdiction in conflicts involving strikes. Qualifications for judges are the same as those for judges of courts of first instance.

PROVINCIAL AND LOCAL GOVERNMENT

In 1972 the country was divided for administrative purposes into twenty-six provinces and the National District. Each province is governed by a governor appointed by the president; in 1972 all twenty-six governors were women. In order to be a governor a person must be Dominican, at least twenty-five years of age, and in full possession of civil and political rights. The organization and administration of the provinces, as well as the powers and duties of the governors, are determined by law.

The provinces are divided into seventy-seven municipalities and twenty municipal districts. The National District is governed as a municipality. Municipalities and municipal districts generally consist of a central town, which is the seat of the municipal council, and several outlying villages. The chief executive of the municipality is the mayor; that of the municipal district, the commissioner. The mayor or commissioner is assisted by a municipal council, elected by the people every four years from among the candidates who may be proposed by political parties or by regional, provincial, or municipal political groups. Municipal councils are responsible for the preparation of the municipal budget, and they may impose local taxes provided these do not conflict with national taxes or with the constitution and laws.

The size of a municipal council depends upon the population of the municipality, but it must comprise no fewer than five members. Generally, the councils are concerned with street maintenance, garbage collection, and provision of water and fire protection.

The municipalities are subdivided into sections governed by a first magistrate, and these in turn are divided into wards, each having a second magistrate. The magistrates are nominated by residents of the particular section or ward and are appointed by the mayor with the approval of the provincial governor. Their functions range from investigating infractions of the law and serving as the lowest civil and criminal court to delivering the mail and representing the government at local public events.

THE ELECTORAL SYSTEM

The electoral system was established after the post-Trujillo government in August 1961 asked the Organization of American States (OAS) to send a technical mission to Santo Domingo to aid in setting up a system of free elections. At the top of the hierarchy of election boards is the Central Electoral Board. The board has three members who, under the Constitution of 1966, are elected by the Senate (see ch. 3).

The members of the Central Electoral Board serve twelve-year terms. The board is authorized to name the members of the provincial and municipal election boards, who serve at its pleasure. The board issues regulations to ensure free and honest elections; it directs the distribution of ballots, equipment, and voting materials and supervises the functioning of the other election boards.

The Central Electoral Board is responsible for printing separate, differently colored ballots for each party. The ballots also bear the emblem of the party. Election day is a legal holiday; no liquor may be sold; and the polls are open from 6:00 A.M. to 6:00 P.M.

THE CIVIL SERVICE

In 1972 a career civil service had not been established by law, but funds had been provided by the United Nations in 1971 for a three-year program to develop public administration. Fifteen hundred public officials responsible for key functions in government were to attend training courses, and some officials were to receive fellowships abroad. The National Office of Administration and Personnel (Oficina Nacional de Administración y Personal—ONAP) was responsible for training civil service personnel. This office had charge of studying government administration, training public employees, and preparing the regulations for the establishment of a career civil service, including selection, promotion, retirement, and pensions for personnel.

THE SOCIAL ENVIRONMENT AND POLITICAL ATTITUDES

All of the Dominican constitutions have called for a democratic system of government, and surveys since the assassination of Trujillo have consistently indicated that the term *democracy* has a positive connotation for the Dominican people. Dominican history, however, reveals little experience with democracy or, for that matter, with the implementation of any political ideology. Participation in government has generally been viewed as a means to an end rather than as an end in itself. The majority of the Dominican heads of state have come to power by force, maintained themselves in power by force, and been relieved of that power by force. Intermittent periods between the fall of one caudillo and the rise of the next have been marked by confusion and anarchy.

A survey conducted in April 1962 indicated that the people were oriented toward highly personalistic and paternalistic leadership. Although administrative competency was occasionally mentioned as a desirable trait, the greatest demand was for a benevolent man who would "take care of them." One consequence of this orientation is the extraordinary concentration of power and responsibility in the presidency. There is a tendency for decisions on even the most routine matters to be passed upward in the chain of command until they come to rest on the president's desk. In 1972, for example, a presidential decree was still required for an individual to change his name.

Another consequence is the general weakness of, and lack of legitimacy residing in, institutions. One Dominican commented that, whereas in some of the more highly industrialized countries institutions provided continuity in the face of changes of leadership, in the Dominican Republic institutions change but the leaders often remain the same. The country's political institutions have changed a great deal since the assassination of Trujillo in 1961, but the president in 1972, Balaguer, was the same man who held that title when Trujillo was shot.

The scarcity of new leaders willing to lead and acceptable to large numbers of people is in many respects a consequence of the Trujillo era. Most of the people in the early 1960s who had any political experience had been tainted, at least in the eyes of the urban population, by collaboration with Trujillo, had been in exile and thus to some extent out of touch with the country, or had been so repulsed by the violence and corruption that had been characteristic of the government that they wanted no part of politics.

For the majority of the population the political lessons learned over the years have been that dissent is futile and dangerous and that submissiveness is safe. Nevertheless, the 1962 survey indicated that most of the people had come to believe that their aspirations for relief from poverty and sickness, for acquisition of land and housing, for employment, and for opportunities for their children must be dealt with in the political arena. The election of 1962 and the civil war of 1965 proved that some were willing to exert great effort and take great risks to install a government that would be responsive to their needs.

Political attitudes, however, and inclinations to activism varied greatly between urban and rural areas. Since colonial times residents of the capital have exercised political influence disproportionate to that of the outlying areas. In early 1966 the headquarters of the principal government agencies and of the major interest groups, the most influential newspapers, and the major radio and television stations were situated in Santo Domingo or its vicinity. Residents of this area displayed a high degree of political consciousness. Moreover, they were strategically located to influence decisions of the central government by direct action, and many—largely because of an attenuation of social ties and widespread unemployment—were inclined toward demonstrations. Santo Domingo voted overwhelmingly for Juan Bosch in 1962.

Historically, Santiago, the second-largest city and center of the Cibao region, has been immune from the political turmoil of the capital. Santiago has been the stronghold of the customarily conservative, traditional elite.

In the early 1970s nearly 70 percent of the eligible voters lived in rural areas. Until the Trujillo era political organization in the small towns and villages was rooted in the extended family system, which provided, in degrees varying generally with economic status, collective security and collective responsibility. The concentration of wealth and power that took place during the Trujillo era and the reach of the central government into previously self-contained areas transformed that system. As most families ceased to be able to provide either economic or physical security for their members, individuals with access to the powerful came to serve as brokers for their less fortunate neighbors. This clientele system was temporarily shaken by the mobilization of the peasants and the rise of new leaders that took place in the early 1960s, but since the fall of the Bosch government in 1963, followed by the repression of newly mobilized groups, the clientele system has been reestablished. In general, the rural people have retained their pronounced distrust of political authority and fear of security forces.

EVOLUTION OF THE PARTY SYSTEM

Parties, associational interest groups, and other institutions generally associated with political infrastructure in the more highly industrialized countries are a recent phenomenon in the Dominican Republic. In the nineteenth and early twentieth centuries political parties were small clusters of individuals supporting a particular leader. No tradition of peaceful, democratic change of administrations developed. In 1931 Trujillo founded the Dominican Party (Partido Dominicano—PD), a bureaucratic appendage of his regime which, within a year, claimed the membership of 80 percent of the electorate. To keep up democratic appearances, Trujillo allowed token opposition in 1947; otherwise, PD candidates were unopposed. Trujillo's party disappeared with his rule, and exile groups and the new domestic opposition scurried to fill the vacuum.

Of the groups founded in exile, only Juan Bosch's Dominican Revolutionary Party (Partido Revolucionario Dominicano—PRD), which had a democratic-leftist orientation, won mass support. The Fourteenth of June movement, composed of young revolutionaries who had operated underground since Trujillo's suppression of the Fidel Castro-supported invasion of June 14, 1959, and the National Civic Union (Unión Cívica Nacional—UCN), a movement of business and professional men, were allied in opposition to continued Trujillo influence.

When Balaguer resigned from the presidency in 1962, cooperation between the three groups ended. As the national election scheduled for late 1962 approached, political discussion became widespread, and more than twenty minor parties appeared. Most were small groups designed to promote the leaders who controlled them rather than philosophies or programs. The minor parties established a practice of forming coalitions among themselves and adhering to a major party's national candidates. Of the eight parties that eventually presented candidates, the PRD and the UCN polled 60 percent and 30 percent of the votes, respectively.

The UCN, dominating the Council of State that succeeded Balaguer's government, presided over the election and originally had been expected to win. During the campaign it became popularly identified with the upper class, and its presidential candidate lacked Bosch's appeal. Moreover, the party's single strong issue—exclusion of Trujillo's followers from political life—frightened many people into voting for Bosch. The PRD won the presidency and swept both houses of Congress and most local offices.

Less than a year later the UCN led a coalition of minor parties that supported the overthrow of Bosch by the armed forces and the establishment of the Triumvirate government. The PRD leaders were deported by the Triumvirate, which also banned the declining Fourteenth of June movement, outlawed all communist organizations, and generally repressed political activity. In 1964 and early 1965 demands mounted for restoration of constitutional order and the return of political exiles, principally Bosch and Balaguer. These demands took the form of concerted action when the armed forces, suspecting the civilian head of the Triumvirate, President Donald José Reid Cabral, of attempting to reduce their independence and privileges, deposed him. A polarization within the military itself, reinforcing the polarization of the larger society, resulted in an outburst of violence that lasted several months (see ch. 3).

Acting in alliance, the PRD and the Social Christian Revolutionary Party (Partido Revolucionario Social Cristiano—PRSC) endorsed the Constitutionalist movement, as did the Fourteenth of June movement and two communist parties—the Dominican Communist Party (Partido Comunista Domin :ano—PCD) and the Dominican People's Movement (Movimiento Popular Dominicano—MPD). New national leadership failed to develop during the civil strife, and former presidents Bosch and Balaguer were the leading contenders in the 1966 campaign. Heading a coalition that hoped to hold the balance of power in the event that neither Bosch nor Balaguer won a clear majority was former President Rafael F. Bonnelly.

All major parties held national conventions. Campaigning, which had begun the previous fall, officially opened on March 1, 1966. The general uncertainty and continued threats and incidents of violence were political issues. So, too, were electoral procedures, voter qualifications, and official recognition of parties.

The only functioning party ever to win a national election, the PRD, again nominated Juan Bosch for president. The party sought support among the urban and rural lower class and intellectuals who had previously elected him. Its platform called for revolutionary social and economic change within a framework of political democracy. Candidates were vocal in condemning the intervention by the United States ·and the OAS, in criticizing the Provisional Government and in praising the Constitutionalist movement. They also accused Balaguer of being favored by the United States.

The PRSC supported Bosch's candidacy in accordance with an agreement of February 1965, in which it had joined the PRD in pledging to restore his administration. The PRSC had been founded in exile in mid-1961 by young Christian Socialists. Its leadership became increasingly antimilitary, antiologarchy, and anti-United States and was plagued by factionalism.

The Reformist Party (Partido Reformista—PR) had been founded in July 1963 by Balaguer, who at that time was in exile in New York, and was legally recognized by the Triumvirate government in April 1964. After Balaguer's return to the country on June 28, 1965, it became his vehicle for seeking the presidency. Its platform in that campaign did not differ greatly from that of the PRD, although emphasis was on order and stability rather than reform. It concentrated on winning

143

business support and the relatively conservative rural vote.

The PR has generally been described as a party of the Center-Right, although its members have had little more in common than personal loyalty to Balaguer and, since 1966, an appreciation of the advantages of belonging to the official party. Its lack of a clear programmatic or ideological base has been seen by many as a strategic advantage in a country severely fragmented by competing interests. Organizationally, it has fallen heir, especially in rural areas, to much of the political infrastructure of the Trujillo era.

THE BALAGUER GOVERNMENT AND ITS OPPONENTS

The political system over which President Balaguer presided after the withdrawal of the troops of the Inter-American Peace Force in September 1966 was sharply divided. Nevertheless, the dependence of local government on the central power and the custom of winner take all have lent great importance to supporting the winning presidential candidate, and Balaguer was able to rally to the support of his government numerous factional leaders who had previously opposed him.

The leadership of the PRD and other left-of-Center groups had been depleted through arrests and assassinations since the suppression of the 1965 civil war. Bosch went into self-imposed exile in Europe. The remaining activist element of the PRD was rent by factionalism, and less committed former adherents defected to the Balaguer camp. President Balaguer's attempts to reconcile and bring about consensus among the right-of-Center forces were frustrated, however, in 1967 by the meteoric rise of a new party on the far Right.

The Quisqueyan Democratic Party (Partido Quisqueyano Democrata—PQD), purporting to follow the exiled Loyalist general, Elías Wessín y Wessín, attracted disaffected military officers and many of the former Trujillo collaborators that had not been absorbed by the PR. Within sixty days of its founding it had attained what was estimated to be the third-largest party membership in the country. Once established, however, it responded to the inevitable tendency to schism.

The results of the 1968 municipal elections suggested that the electioneering apparatus of the PR had been firmly established, especially in the rural areas; the refusal of most other parties to enter candidates, however, suggested that a considerable portion of the polity failed to view as legitimate an administration elected to office and inaugurated under the supervision of foreign troops. The PR was successful in sixty-six of the seventy-seven municipalities, receiving 649,765 of the total of 1,028,410 votes cast throughout the country. The PRD, the PQD, the UCN, and most of the other parties boycotted the elections. The PRSC participated, however, and with surprising results. Whereas in 1966 it had received only some 30,000 votes, in 1968 it received 124,719 and won control of two municipalities.

President Balaguer announced in December 1968 that all those who had been exiled for having fought in the 1965 civil war would be permitted to return. General Wessín wasted no time in accepting the invitation, but no word was heard from Colonel Francisco Caamaño Deño, who had commanded the Constitutionalist forces. He had disappeared without a trace from his exile residence a year before, and many feared that he was dead.

Political violence, particularly assassination of party leaders and other political figures of all persuasions, continued throughout the late 1960s. It was intensified at the time of the visit of United States presidential envoy Governor Nelson Rockefeller in 1969 and did not appreciably subside after his departure. This state of affairs led the bishop of Santiago and fifty-three priests to issue a pastoral letter condemning the government for its failure to protect "the right to work or even the right to live." A commission led by a PRD senator charged at the United Nations that the murder of 362 members of the PRD since the end of the civil war was evidence that the government had resorted to political terrorism.

By late 1969 it had become apparent that President Balaguer, without announcing his intentions, was campaigning for reelection. This resulted in a split in his own party, as the country's vice president, Francisco Augusto Lora, with ambitions of his own, left the PR and accepted the candidacy offered by a new splinter party, the Movement for Democratic Integration against Re-election (Movimiento de Integración Democrática Anti-reelección—MIDA).

The mayor of Santo Domingo, who was also chairman of the PR, publicly stated on December 2, 1969, that the prospect of Balaguer's candidacy for reelection was "the greatest obstacle to the Dominican People's choosing their destiny freely." Identical statements were issued simultaneously by spokesmen of the PRD, the PRSC, the MIDA, and a new Center-Right coalition, the Movement for National Conciliation (Movimiento de Conciliación Nacional—MCN). Engulfed by an internal dispute between its own would-be candidates, the PQD did not join the other opposition parties in issuing this statement.

The PRD, expressing doubts that the administration would allow itself to lose, announced its decision to boycott the elections; other left-of-Center parties followed suit. Parties to the right of Center likewise threatened a boycott unless the president relinquished the powers of his office during the campaign. A compromise whereby Balaguer stepped down for one month before the election in favor of Supreme Court President Ramón Ruíz Tejada drew four of the reticent parties into the competition. Opposing Balaguer were Lora of the MIDA, Alfonso Moreno Martínez of the moderately conservative Christian Democratic Party, General Wessín of the PQD, and Héctor García Godoy of the MCN.

Political violence intensified in the months preceding the May 16 elections. As most of the victims were opponents of President Balaguer, opposition parties charged the army and the police with responsibility. The commander in chief of the army had termed Balaguer's reelection a "national necessity." President Balaguer himself attributed the incidents to "uncontrollable forces." Into this highly charged atmosphere Bosch returned on April 16 from his self-imposed exile. Clashes between his supporters and the police at the welcoming demonstrations for him resulted in four deaths, many injuries, and a large number of arrests.

As had been predicted, Balaguer was reelected on May 16, 1970, by a comfortable margin of 55.7 percent, leading his nearest rival, MIDA's Lora, by 305,038 votes. The PR carried all of the voting districts except one—Jarabacoa, the stronghold of General Wessín. The MIDA received 20.7 percent of the vote, deriving much of its strength from Santo Domingo, where it trailed by only 10,155 votes. The PQD's 13.2 percent of the vote came primarily from the rural areas. The PRSC polled 5 percent; and the MCN, whose initial candidate, Héctor García Godoy, died of natural causes two weeks before the election, polled only 4.4 percent. The PR also won sixty of the seventy-four seats in the Chamber of Deputies and all but one of the twenty-seven Senate seats.

All of the opposition parties charged electoral fraud; specific allegations included the waiver of the requirement of voting credentials for women, presumed to be more favorably disposed than men toward Balaguer, and the substitution of prepared ballot boxes for the authentic ones. The allegations were denied by the Central Electoral Board.

The PRD and other leftist parties that were boycotting the election claimed credit for the abstention of some 540,000, mostly urban, voters out of an electorate of approximately 1.7 million. Bosch had appealed to his followers through regular radio programs in Santo Domingo. After the elections President Balaguer, asserting that "a democratic society has to resort to illegal and arbitrary measures if it is threatened by people seeking to bring about chaos," announced on June 12 that censorship of the radio had been introduced. The election was also followed by numerous arrests and dismissals from government service.

The president's hand was strengthened in July 1971 by the discovery of a conspiracy headed by General Wessín. President Balaguer gained political capital by placing General Wessín in front of television cameras and playing a recording of the general's voice announcing the fall of the government. General Wessín was turned over to the three commanders of the armed forces, who sent him into exile in Spain.

By late 1971 the incidence of violence had reached what most observers believed to be the high point since the 1965 civil war. Schools were closed, and Santo Domingo was said to resemble a ghost town as many preferred to stay off the streets. The principal perpetrators of the violence in this case were members of a group known as La Banda (the Band), who had been systematically eliminating persons considered to be opponents of the government. The archbishop protested that the church's pleas for the respect of human rights had gone unheeded, and political leaders of both Right and Left charged that the group was working with the police.

In October 1971 President Balaguer responded to these charges by publicly admonishing the police to shoot only in self-defense and by replacing General Enrique Pérez y Pérez with General Neit Nivar Seijas as commander of the national police. By the end of the year La Banda had reportedly been disbanded, and the wave of violence had subsided.

The topic of primary concern to the politically articulate in 1972 was the prospect of Balaguer's candidacy for a third term. Although the next presidential election was not scheduled until 1974, opposition parties and opponents of President Balaguer within his own party charged that he was already campaigning and taking actions against prospective opponents in preparation for his reelection. Once again the major parties had been discussing the establishment of a common front to boycott the elections if Balaguer offered himself as a candidate. The PRD was hesitant, but in October 1972 it was announced that leaders of the PRD, the PQD, and the MIDA had signed such an agreement. The PRSC had also indicated interest in the boycott plan.

The PRD was still considered to be by far the strongest of the opposition parties, although since 1963 it had suffered a continual depletion of its leaders, through assassination, exile, and imprisonment and, as all other parties, it suffered from internal schisms. Bosch's advocacy, since the 1970 elections, of "dictatorship with popular support" had been rejected by several important party leaders.

The MIDA had essentially the same social base of support as the trunk group of the PR, except that it was stronger in urban than in rural areas; its raison d'être continued to be prevention of the *continuismo* of Balaguer, but it lacked a leader of sufficient popularity to challenge him effectively. The PQD continued to attract military leaders and others whose status had depreciated since the assassination of Trujillo or the fall of the Triumvirate but was handicapped in 1972 by the fact that its leader, General Wessín, was in exile.

Minor parties to the left of the PRD had been greatly weakened through internal security programs since the civil war, and many of the leaders of right-of-Center minor parties that had functioned in the early 1960s had been absorbed by the PR, the MIDA, and the PQD. Groups identifying themselves as parties continued to appear and vanish in rapid succession, but they generally represented the atomization of older parties rather than the mobilization of new groups.

POLITICAL FORCES AND INTEREST GROUPS

The Armed Forces

The principal role of the armed forces has always been within the realm of domestic politics. Before the United States occupation (1916–24) the military consisted of hastily armed and mobilized bands that fought on behalf of competing regional caudillos. The reconstituted gendarmerie that the United States occupation forces left behind became Trujillo's vehicle for attaining control of the government. Once in power, Trujillo used the military to crush opposition and maintain himself in power, but he stripped it of independent political influence.

After the assassination of Trujillo by a group of officers, the military emerged as the strongest institution in the country. The confrontations that followed, however, were not of a clear-cut military versus civilian nature but rather struggles among changing alliances of civilian and military cliques.

During the civil war of 1965 the armed forces nearly disintegrated as an institution. Colonel Caamaño led many younger officers and several whole contingents in support of the Constitutionalist movement. After order was restored, Loyalist leader Wessín (having been promoted to general) and Constitutionalist leader Colonel Caamaño, along with several officers who fought with them, were sent abroad to diplomatic posts. Nevertheless, the move nearly toppled the Provisional Government, and rumors of impending military intervention were heard throughout the 1966 election campaign.

One of the provisions of the Institutional Act, imposed after order was restored, was that the Constitutionalist forces should be reincorporated into the regular army, but that unification did not take place. Those not imprisoned or exiled were isolated in a single base where they have remained.

In the early 1970s, as had been characteristic, the highest-ranking officers were engaged in power struggles among themselves, and a degree of civilian control of the armed forces was maintained through the adroitness of President Balaguer in playing off one faction against another. Reshuffling of the top military commands and positions has been a frequent occurrence. The acceleration of the redistribution of government-owned lands, pledged by Balaguer in 1972, aroused anxieties, however, among some of the officers who had put such land to their own uses and suggested that another crisis of authority was developing. The Agrarian Institute announced on November 1 that the names of all high-ranking officers retaining state lands would be revealed if they did not submit to the institute's land recovery demands.

The Roman Catholic Church

The pastoral letter protesting the mass arrests in January 1960 recovered for the Roman Catholic Church a measure of the popular esteem lost during the years in which it did not publicly criticize Trujillo. The political influence of Roman Catholic leaders, which derived from the religious sentiments of the majority of the people rather than from institutional wealth or legal privilege, became considerable, particularly in rural areas (see ch. 4).

The political emphasis of various Roman Catholic elements differed.

After the end of the Trujillo period the Vatican tried to identify the church with democratic reforms. The peace-keeping and humanitarian efforts of the papal nuncio during the civil strife of 1965 were construed by some of the more conservative clerics and laymen as assistance to the Constitutionalist forces. Demonstrations were organized against him, and the words *Communist Embassy* were painted on the walls of the nunciatura. In both 1962 and 1966 the Dominican hierarchy declined to endorse political candidates. Individual bishops, however, publicly questioned provisions of the 1963 Constitution; most were widely believed to be conservative. A number of individual priests, including Spanish Jesuits previously expelled from Cuba, and prominent laymen campaigned against Bosch in 1962 and subsequently worked for his ouster.

Some of the younger and more liberal clerics, inspired by the emphasis of Pope John XXIII on social and economic justice, had begun in the early 1960s to form peasant cooperatives and to work closely with labor. The PRSC and the labor confederation affiliated with it, with considerable support from liberal clerics, opposed the Triumvirate. They endorsed the Constitutionalist movement and favored Bosch's candidacy.

As with other sectors of the population, the civil war deepened the already existing cleavages within the Roman Catholic Church; the generation gap, in particular, became more pronounced. Changes in the church hierarchy since that upheaval have elevated a number of the younger and more liberal clergymen. The reform-oriented Bishop Hugo Polanco Brito, for example, became administrator of the Santo Domingo Archdiocese, assuming many of the functions of the aging and more conservative archbishop. Such changes were reflected in a pastoral letter issued by the country's bishops in 1968 calling for an equitable distribution of land and in a number of strong statements in the early 1970s on behalf of the church condemning the government for its failure to protect human rights and to improve the standards of living for the majority.

The Economic Elite

The individuals, families, and organizations that occupied the upper strata among landowners, businessmen, and professionals have never constituted a monolithic oligarchy, although in their opposition to Bosch in 1963 they gave the appearance of being a unified group. The Independent Democratic Action (Acción Democrática Independiente— ADI), an ad hoc group formed in 1963 by the merger of business and landowning groups, was particularly visible during that period. It directed the Christian affirmation movement that staged mass rallies against President Bosch just before his government was overthrown.

The so-called "new rich," whose fortunes were made through the industrialization of the Trujillo era, have tended to be more adamantly opposed to reform and more alarmed by the arousal of the political consciousness of the poor than the old aristocratic families, whose wealth had been based on land. Many of the latter group lost both land and many of the perquisites of their social status under Trujillo.

In general, upper class associations—such as the Employers' Association (Asociación Patronal), the Association of Industries (Asociación de Indústrias), the Association of Landowners and Agriculturists (Asociación de Hacendados y Agricultores), and the Chamber of Commerce, Agriculture, and Industry (Camera de Comercio, Agricultura, e Indústria)—remained highly conservative, although no social groups had been immune to the generation gap that was a prominent feature of the political polarization. The 1965 civil war precipitated severe crises and divisions among such professional groups as the lawyers' association and the association of engineers and architects.

Organized Labor

In the early 1960s organized labor emerged as one of the strongest forces competing with the military for the determination of public policy and the sponsorship of policymakers. It was, however, divided into three major groups. On the democratic Left were the Labor Front for Union Autonomy—Labor Center for Dominican Workers (Frente Obrero Pro-Sindicatos Autónomos—Central Sindical de Trabajadores Dominicanos—FOUPSA-CESITRADO), closely associated with the PRD, and the Autonomous Confederation of Christian Unions (Confederación Autónoma de Sindicatos Cristianos—CASC), affiliated with the PRSC. The National Confederation of Free Laborers (Confederación Nacional de Trabajadores Libres—CONATRAL), organized under the auspices of the American Institute for Free Labor Development (AIFLD), emphasized collective bargaining and discouraged the pursuit of social reform through political action. The strategically important teachers and government employees unions tended to look to Castro's interpretation of Marxism. Other communist unions had been organized, but until the civil war was underway their strength was insignificant.

After Bosch's election to the presidency, with the overwhelming support of labor, the PRD initiated a movement to unite all of the labor organizations into a single federation. All of the major groups, with the exception of the CONATRAL, indicated an interest in formal or informal unity in support of Bosch's government. The CONATRAL, however, influenced by the anticommunist orientation of the United States government, business, and labor sponsors of the AIFLD, opposed the creation of a unified labor front and sought to diminish support for the PRD within the labor movement.

Within a few months of the election the labor movement was sharply polarized, as the FOUPSA-CESITRADO continued to call for unity in support of the Bosch government and the CONATRAL criticized that government and called upon the armed forces to defend the country against what it viewed as the communist menace. When Bosch was overthrown on September 25, 1963, the FOUPSA-CESITRADO and CASC bitterly condemned the coup, while the CONATRAL praised the "patriotic gesture" of the armed forces and expressed support for the Triumvirate.

Between the 1963 coup and the outbreak of civil strife in 1965 the officers of the FOUPSA-CESITRADO were periodically imprisoned, and their offices were raided by the police. The CONATRAL, on the other hand, enjoyed a harmonious relationship with the government. The FOUPSA-CESITRADO and CASC were among the first groups to rally to the side of the Constitutionalist forces in 1965. The leadership of the CONATRAL opposed the Constitutionalist revolt but was unable to prevent its members from participating. As a consequence of its position during that struggle, the CONATRAL, which had been the largest single confederation, was discredited among workers and lost control of many of its most important unions.

In the 1966 elections the CONATRAL supported Balaguer, while most other labor organizations supported Bosch. By the early 1970s the CASC had become the strongest of the labor federations and, although some of its leaders maintained their adherence to the PRSC, the organization's strongest ties were with the PRD. The FOUPSA-CESITRADO remained basically aligned with the PRD, although it too had experienced considerable fragmentation, as several of its leaders adhered to parties of the far Left. Although the labor movement had been weakened organizationally, both by repression and by fragmentation, since the early 1960s, observers felt that this loss had been compensated to some extent by gains in political consciousness among the rank and file.

Peasant Movements

Participation by the peasantry in the political processes since the assassination of Trujillo has been sporadic. There were notable efforts to mobilize them in 1962 and 1963, and for a brief period the National Federation of Farmers' Brotherhoods (Federación Nacional de Hermandades Campesinos—FENHERCA), affiliated with the PRD, had a membership of some 300,000. After the fall of the Bosch government, however, peasant organizations were particularly vulnerable to reprisals by the military and the police. The FENHERCA all but disappeared as a mass organization. It reemerged as a skeletal organization in 1965 but played no significant role in the civil strife of that year.

The PRSC also has a peasant arm, but its activities have been extremely limited. A new group, known as Constitutional Action (Acción Constitucional—AC), was established in 1972 largely to discourage illegal land takeovers and to promote the agrarian reform policies of the Balaguer government.

Student Organizations

Since the death of Trujillo students have been among the most persistent and vociferous spokesmen for the economically deprived and politically repressed. All of the major student organizations have been highly nationalistic and anti-United States, and all favor far-reaching socioeconomic change, with differences of degree in their willingness to resort to violence in order to transform the social structure.

Fragua (literally, "forge"), inspired by the Cuban revolution, is the most strongly committed to violent revolution. The Christian Revolutionary University Group (Bloque Revolucionario Universitario Cristiano—BRUC) draws its inspiration from the social Christian movement. It was spawned by the PRSC but has grown far more militant than the party. The Democratic Socialist University Front (Frente Universitario Socialista Democrático—FUSD), formerly known as the Radical Revolutionary University Front (Frente Universitario Radical Revolucionario—FURR), is affiliated with the PRD. Each university organization has had an affiliate at the secondary school level.

In 1964 Fragua replaced the BRUC as the majority group in the nationwide Federation of Dominican Students (Federación de Estudiantes Dominicanos—FED). In student elections that year at the University of Santo Domingo, Fragua candidates won 1,452 votes, followed by 1,157 for the BRUC and sixty-six for the FURR. By 1970 the FUSD had swept university elections and was by far the strongest organization.

Students from all of these groups participated enthusiastically in the Constitutionalist struggle against the Loyalist military faction and the United States forces. Many of them assumed leadership roles, and students as a whole suffered more than most groups from the repression of former rebels after order was restored. Nevertheless, throughout the late 1960s and into the early 1970s student strikes and demonstrations continued to occur frequently. There were indications that many students were alienated from the existing political and social system and pessimistic in regard to the prospects of broadening opportunities for themselves or improvement in the standards of living for the majority.

FOREIGN RELATIONS

Historical Background

Foreign policy during the Trujillo era was determined by the dictator's concern for retaining power and was mostly defensive, but in his later years he was constantly involved in political and paramilitary disputes with neighboring countries. The republic was a party to twelve of the twenty-four disputes considered by the OAS between 1958 and 1960.

Trujillo's major foreign policy goals were maintenance of favorable economic and diplomatic relations with the United States and prevention of foreign invasion. In 1940 he secured an end to the customs convention and in the mid-1940s retired the public debt owed the United States. Trujillo encouraged private United States investment until the mid-1950s and received economic and military aid. He employed United States citizens to publicize within their own country the themes of Dominican political stability, material development, and support of United States foreign policy.

During World War II, Trujillo declared war on the Axis powers and granted naval bases to the United States. When the cold war developed, he severed relations with the Soviet Union and proclaimed himself the world's "Number One Anti-Communist." The Dominican voting record in the United Nations paralleled that of the United States more closely than did the record of any other Latin American government. Whenever criticism of Trujillo's regime threatened to affect United States diplomatic or economic policy adversely, he talked of free elections.

In 1960 Trujillo's foreign policy was failing to gain its objectives. Mass arrests evoked Venezuelan charges of violations of human rights. Allusions to plans for free elections failed to deter the United States from announcing that it would cut off military aid. Venezuela then accused Trujillo of arranging the attempted assassination of President Rómulo Betancourt, and the Sixth Meeting of Consultation of Foreign Ministers of the OAS unanimously declared the republic to be guilty of "acts of aggression and intervention" against Venezuela. The OAS invoked the Inter-American Treaty of Reciprocal Assistance and constrained all member states to break diplomatic relations and to embargo arms and specified commodities. In January 1961 the embargo was expanded.

Relations with the Organization of American States

After Trujillo's death the government adopted measures designed to obtain removal of OAS sanctions. Leaders of the developing political opposition, however, urged the OAS to retain the sanctions. When the Trujillo family fled, the government began to erase the vestiges of Trujilloism, and early in 1962 the OAS removed its sanctions. A technical assistance committee from the OAS helped prepare for the national elections in 1962 that brought Bosch to power as president.

President Bosch did not invite the secretary general of the OAS to attend his inauguration and criticized what he considered to be the shortcomings of the OAS and the Alliance for Progress. A few months later, he called for an emergency OAS meeting in order to protest a Haitian invasion of the Dominican embassy in Port-au-Prince. To settle the affair, he accepted the good offices of the OAS peace commission.

The civil disturbances that ousted the ruling Triumvirate government in April 1965 and the subsequent United States intervention resulted in extensive OAS involvement. On April 30 the OAS Council called for an immediate cease-fire between forces favoring restoration of the Bosch government and the opposing military junta. The Tenth Meeting of Consultation of Foreign Ministers, which convened on May 1 and met throughout 1965 and early 1966, dispatched a peace commission. On May 6 the delegate of the military junta, who had been seated at the insistence of the United States, provided the vote required for OAS adoption of the United States-sponsored resolution creating the Inter-American Peace Force. Chile, Ecuador, Mexico, Peru, and Uruguay voted against it, and Venezuela abstained. Charged with maintaining peace and restoring constitutional government, the Inter-American Peace Force absorbed the United States forces already operating in the country. Under Brazilian command, the peace force was composed mainly of United States troops, with contingents from Brazil, Paraguay, Honduras, Costa Rica, and Nicaragua. After a bloody fight in mid-June, resulting in some 3,000 to 6,000 deaths, both Dominican factions, each for their own reasons, called for the withdrawal of the peace force; it nevertheless continued to function until September 1966 when the last units were withdrawn.

Relations with the United States

In order to secure the withdrawal of United States naval units that stood off Santo Domingo after Trujillo was assassinated, President Joaquín Balaguer announced that he would liberalize the regime. He also declared that no foreign government had been involved in Trujillo's death. By mid-November 1961 Balaguer had secured United States sponsorship of a resolution to lift OAS sanctions. When Trujillo's family attempted a coup d'etat, the United States withdrew this resolution, again dispatched naval units, and announced that troops would land if Balaguer requested them. In early December United States officials directly entered the stalled domestic negotiations, which eventually produced the Council of State as the executive organ for government.

The council was immediately recognized by the United States, which intervened to protect it against several attempted military coups. The council entered into a bilateral agreement favorable to United States enterprises and, after a strong Dominican presentation, the United States adopted a sugar act more favorable to the country than the bills that had been proposed. Alliance for Progress funds, which had been extended previously on an emergency basis, were increased in an announced effort to make the republic a showcase. By the end of 1962 three times the Latin American per capita average in foreign aid funds had been allocated by the United States.

During his visit to Washington in January 1963, President-elect Bosch conferred with President John F. Kennedy, and his inauguration was attended by Vice President Lyndon B. Johnson. In response to

United States as well as domestic criticism of his omission of any reference to the Alliance for Progress or to Castro in his inaugural address, President Bosch denounced communism and denied any intention to resume diplomatic relations with Cuba. He accepted more than US$50 million in United States foreign aid, largely in grants, but he also refused several loan offers.

In 1963, within six hours after Bosch was deposed, the United States severed diplomatic relations with the new Triumvirate government and suspended military and economic aid. Before the coup the United States, through its ambassador in Santo Domingo, warned that no government that deposed Bosch would be recognized and offered the president a show of force to back him up. Nevertheless, leftists and, eventually, officials of Bosch's own political party accused United States personnel of facilitating the coup.

As soon as it agreed to hold elections supervised by the OAS, the Triumvirate was recognized by the Johnson administration, a new United States ambassador arrived in Santo Domingo, and good relations were established. The Triumvirate accepted substantial economic aid and publicly supported United States foreign policies, but the elections did not take place.

The pace of significant developments in the Dominican strife that erupted on April 24, 1965, and of the United States responses to them, was exceedingly swift. The Constitutionalist movement immediately gained supremacy. Initially, the anti-Bosch military officers, with the exception of General Wessín, showed no inclination to challenge the Constitutionalists in battle, but by late afternoon on April 25 they had been persuaded to form a junta and take up arms; this group became known as the Loyalists. By April 27 the Constitutionalists were in control of most of Santo Domingo and appeared to be ready to take Santiago.

The first contingent of United States Marines arrived on April 28. It was announced at that time that President Johnson had authorized the intervention in order to protect American lives. By April 30, when the matter was brought to the attention of the OAS, some 22,000 United States troops had taken up positions in Santo Domingo.

On May 2 President Johnson announced that "what began as a popular democratic revolution, . . . very shortly moved and was taken over and really seized and placed into the hands of a band of communist conspirators." This was alleged to have happened on April 27 when, as a consequence of Bosch's inability to return to the Dominican Republic from Puerto Rico, the leadership of the rebel force passed from Colonel Miguel Angel Ramírez to Colonel Caamaño Deño. John Bartlow Martin, President Johnson's special envoy, had attributed to Caamaño the capability of becoming "his country's Castro." Later the names of fifty-eight Communists allegedly involved in the fighting were released by United States officials to substantiate the claim. By late summer the Constitutionalist rebellion had been subdued; the United States withdrew its support from the military junta and participated in the establishment of a provisional government headed by García Godoy.

The intervention and occupation seemed to leave the United States with few friends in the Dominican Republic. Nevertheless, relations with the government of President Balaguer have been extremely cordial. Some items in the 1963 Constitution were excluded from the 1966 Constitution, and United States investors took advantage of the generous terms offered them. Combined economic and military assistance reached an all-time high of US$111.6 million in fiscal year 1965/66, the fourth-highest sum extended to any Latin American country that year, and some 500 United States officials assumed technical assistance or other duties in the Dominican Republic. The level of assistance had dropped to US$29.7 million in 1971, but it remained fourth highest in the hemisphere.

Relations with Latin America

Trujillo's domestic policies, restrictions on travel, and foreign intrigues tended to isolate the country from general Latin American affairs. This isolation became more formal in 1960 when all the governments that had not previously done so broke diplomatic relations, but it diminished after Trujillo's assassination. Many Dominicans who had developed friendships and personal interests in other Caribbean lands—particularly Puerto Rico, Venezuela, Costa Rica, and Cuba—returned from exile. Post-Trujillo governments expressed interest in joining the Central American Common Market. Domestic uncertainty, however, inhibited diplomatic initiatives, and relations with countries other than those in the Caribbean remained formal. A study of the advantages to be gained from membership in the Caribbean Free Trade Association (CARIFTA) and the Caribbean Development Bank was initiated in 1972.

The policy of alignment with the more authoritarian regimes of Latin America that marked the Trujillo era was reversed by President Bosch, who had been closely associated with leading Latin American liberals during his years in exile. Presidents Rómulo Betancourt, Francisco Orlich, and Ramón Villeda Morales of Venezuela, Costa Rica, and Honduras, respectively, attended his inauguration, as did Puerto Rican Governor Luis Muñoz Marín and former Costa Rican President José Figueres. No representatives were invited from Haiti, Nicaragua, or Paraguay, and only the opposition leaders in Argentina and Peru received invitations. In an unsuccessful attempt to avoid being deposed, Bosch appealed to the liberal leaders.

Venezuela, Costa Rica, El Salvador, Honduras, and Nicaragua jointly urged nonrecognition of the Triumvirate that overthrew President Bosch. A new Honduran government, however, led in establishment of diplomatic relations with the Triumvirate, and by October 1964 only Venezuela, Cuba, and Haiti withheld full recognition. Support for the Constitutionalist faction during the 1965 disturbances was considerable in Venezuela, Chile, Mexico, Uruguay, Peru, and Cuba, but none of these countries went so far as to extend recognition.

The historically friendly relations with the Commonwealth of Puerto Rico were particularly close during the tenure of the Council of State and presidency of Bosch and have again been strengthened under the presidency of Balaguer. Thousands of Dominicans visited the nearby island, with which considerable trade was conducted. Puerto Ricans made up a large part of the advisory missions dispatched under the Alliance for Progress. The only post-Trujillo disputes that involved more than political disapproval occurred with Cuba and Haiti.

The Council of State that succeeded Balaguer accused Castro of attempted subversion, called for OAS sanctions, and threatened to recognize a Cuban government-in-exile. After Bosch was inaugurated, official denunciations of Castro subsided; but diplomatic relations were not resumed, and Cuba continued to accuse the republic of anticommunism and subservience to the United States. The Triumvirate crushed guerrilla activity allegedly sponsored by Castro in November 1963, supported the OAS imposition of sanctions, and denied Cuban accusations that it permitted anti-Castro exiles to use Dominican territory. From the beginning of civil strife in April 1965, Constitutionalist leaders tried to disassociate their movement from Castro's verbal support.

The historic feud with Haiti nearly became war in 1963 when, in addition to bringing charges before the OAS, President Bosch moved troops to the border. Haiti severed relations and called for a meeting of the United Nations Security Council. President Bosch declared that his quarrel was not with the people of Haiti but with their ruler, François Duvalier. He cautioned Dominicans not to molest individual Haitians living in the country. Several Latin American governments complied with his request to break relations with Haiti, and Venezuela offered military assistance, but Bosch recognized no Haitian government-in-exile and withdrew his troops from the border. After Bosch was deposed, the Triumvirate efforts to resume relations with Haiti failed, and border incidents, which resulted in Dominican mobilization and Haitian charges before the United Nations, occurred in 1964. One year later Haiti alleged that the Constitutionalists were preparing a Castroite invasion.

Relations between the two countries improved considerably after the inauguration of President Balaguer. Since the death in 1971 of Duvalier, Haiti's ruler for the previous 13½ years, the Haitian and Dominican governments have entered into agreements to facilitate and expand trade between their countries.

Relations with Other Countries and International Organizations

Except for the Bosch period, relations with the United States and neighboring Caribbean nations have been of primary importance to the Dominican Republic. Partly in an effort to increase his domestic political alternatives, President Bosch tried to intensify relations with Europe. After his election, he visited Europe and conferred with ranking officials in the Federal Republic of Germany (West Germany), Italy, Switzerland, France, Belgium, and Great Britain. Bosch returned to his country to announce that the European countries had promised three times the economic assistance offered by the United States. The Triumvirate canceled the major European arrangements.

Relations with most Asian and African governments have remained perfunctory. Few missions have been established, and trade and consular arrangements have been sketchy. In 1972 the only countries outside the Western Hemisphere and Western Europe in which the Dominican Republic maintained embassies or legations were the Republic of China (Taiwan), Israel, Japan, Turkey, Iran, and Lebanon. Dominican passports expressly prohibit travel to countries ruled by communist parties, but it was announced in 1972 that the establishment of trade relations with such countries was under official consideration.

The republic is signatory to the Charter of the OAS, the Inter-American Treaty of Reciprocal Assistance, the Pact of Bogotá, and all major related conventions. Its relationship to the OAS has generally overshadowed its relationship to the United Nations, of which it is also a member. Dominican governments have invoked United Nations assistance principally when they have failed in an approach to the OAS. For example, after the OAS repeatedly refused to lift the sanctions it had imposed in 1960, the government protested before the United Nations that responsibility for the attempted assassination of President Betancourt rested exclusively with Trujillo, not with the Dominican government.

Originally convened at the request of the Soviet Union, the United Nations Security Council discussed the civil strife and United States and OAS interventions in the spring of 1965. In mid-May the Constitutionalists asked the secretary general to stop the advance of OAS troops beyond an international security zone it had established in the city of Santo Domingo and requested the dispatch of the United Nations Human Rights Commission. The Security Council, which heard delegates from the rival factions, called for a cease-fire and directed the secretary general to send a special observer, who was promptly denounced by the faction opposing the Constitutionalists and by the OAS.

The republic is a member of the United Nations Economic Commission for Latin America (UNECLA), the United Nations Educational, Scientific and Cultural Organization (UNESCO), the International

Labor Organization (ILO), the World Health Organization (WHO), and the International Court of Justice. It has subscribed to the International Monetary Fund (IMF), the International Bank for Reconstruction and Development (IBRD), the International Finance Corporation (IFC), and the International Development Association (IDA). It is a participant in the International Civil Aviation Organization (ICAO), the Universal Postal Union (UPU) and the International Telecommunications Union (ITU). It is also a member of the World Meteorological Organization (WMO), the Postal Union of the Americas and Spain, and the International Atomic Energy Agency (IAEA).

SECTION III. ECONOMIC

CHAPTER 8

CHARACTER AND STRUCTURE

OF THE ECONOMY

Most of the country's industries, domestic commerce, and foreign trade are dependent upon a few agricultural products, sugarcane in particular. The processing of sugar was the main industry in 1972, and sugar accounted for more than half of all exports (see ch. 9).

The economy suffered a severe setback from the civil disturbances of 1965, and the process of recovery was hindered by prolonged droughts in 1967 and 1968 that affected agricultural production (see ch. 3). Low world prices for sugar during that period compounded the problem of recovery. Beginning in 1969, however, the economy experienced a period of above average growth because of increased sugarcane production and higher world prices for the sugar exports, increased tourism, growing industrialization, and rising construction activity. By 1972 the government no longer had to concern itself with economic recovery but rather with preventing development of an inflationary spiral.

The gross national product (GNP) growth rate in 1971 of about 7 percent had been the best in more than a decade, and the 1972 rate was expected to be correspondingly encouraging. The political climate during the late 1960s after the election of President Joaquín Balaguer in 1966 had enhanced business confidence and had stimulated private investment. Governmental revenues, expenditures, and public investment also had risen, but the budget was under control and public and private savings were at a high level. In 1971 about one-third of the government's revenues went into infrastructure facilities and the balance for operational expenditures. Additional investment projects were being planned, but these would require external financing, and in 1972 numerous applications for foreign loans were submitted to international lending agencies. The external debt was not burdensome, and the country anticipated receiving and paying off the additional loans with little difficulty.

In relation to the size of its population in 1972, the country's natural resources were promising. It was estimated that the area of arable land could be doubled by better use of irrigation, and climatic and soil characteristics offered opportunities for further crop diversification.

Although sugarcane was the leading export crop, the country also raised coffee, cacao, and tobacco for export in considerable quantities; enough fruits, vegetables, livestock, and cereals and grains were produced to meet domestic needs, but wheat and edible fats and oils were in short supply (see ch. 9).

The noteworthy feature of the country's agrarian structure was an excessive number of small farmholdings contrasted with a few very large farms, most of which were owned by the state. The pattern of tenancy made it difficult to modernize agricultural practices except for those farms that produced export crops.

Industry is closely tied to agriculture because of the processing of sugarcane and other products. Nonagricultural industrial development, however, was a goal of the government in 1972, and an incentive law was in effect that granted benefits designed to attract foreign and domestic investment. The major industrial investment was a nickel-processing plant (see ch. 9).

A central bank headed the banking system and had broad powers to manage bank credit and money supply. There were several state banks, private commercial banks, and a few specialized financial institutions. The national currency was called the Dominican peso, and its symbol was RD$.

NATIONAL ACCOUNTS

The National Office of Statistics (Oficina Nacional de Estadística), a dependency of the presidency, is in charge of preparing all basic statistics. Although the data are considered to be fairly accurate by outside observers, they are frequently published late, thereby losing some of their usefulness. Detailed national account data for 1968 were not published until 1972, and statistics for the 1969-71 period were mainly estimates.

The provisional 1971 GNP was RD$1.5 billion (1 peso equals US$1— see Glossary). GNP had an uneven growth rate during the 1960s; there were some years of very high rates, some years of low rates, and some years, when political crises occurred, of negative rates. Despite the offsetting high years, the average annual growth rate for the 1960-71 period was 3.8 percent, one of the lowest rates in the Western Hemisphere.

Because of population increase, the per capita GNP grew by a much smaller average annual rate than overall GNP—only 1 percent—and was about RD$340 in 1971. The actual income was unevenly distributed, and many rural persons had almost no money income (see ch. 4). The government hoped that income would be more evenly distributed for wage earners beginning in 1972, when a government-decreed profit-sharing scheme was implemented by the private sector. Under this scheme, all firms must distribute 10 percent of their pretax income to all employees.

Agriculture has always been the leading sector of the economy. In 1970 it contributed over 22 percent to the gross domestic product (GDP) (see table 3). Agriculture's relative contribution to GDP had been slowly declining since the mid-1950s as other sectors were growing by faster rates. In 1971, however, overall agricultural production grew by about 7 percent because of generally favorable weather, and its share of the 1971 GDP may have been higher than the 22 percent registered in 1970, because some other sectors grew by smaller percentages.

Manufacturing, a small but dynamic sector of the economy because of the introduction of modern equipment, moved into second place in 1966, displacing commerce as the next leading component of GDP. Public administration followed commerce, but its relative share had been falling, whereas the next leading category, transportation and communications, had seen its share rising. Other sectors contributing to the GDP were rental property, construction, banking and insurance, mining, and utilities, in that order.

GOVERNMENT ROLE

The government economic ideology favors a free economy with a minimum of restrictions. Despite this announced policy, the state is directly involved in agriculture, in industry, and in commerce as a heritage of the Trujillo era. After Trujillo died, the government confiscated the extensive industrial, agricultural, and commercial holdings of his clique. The original purpose of the confiscation was not to establish a managed economy under state ownership but rather to eradicate the influence of the Trujillo family. The state intended to divest itself of these holdings eventually, but in 1972 the government still owned most of the properties it had confiscated.

The confiscated properties have been administered by various government ministries responsible for general policy direction and have been operated by a number of decentralized autonomous or semi-independent agencies established for that purpose.

Originally, the government assumed control of nearly ninety firms, and in 1972 it still owned all or a part of the stock of more than sixty companies, having divested itself of the others by selling them to private interests. Most of the state companies were run by one of two government holding corporations. All of the nationalized sugar estates and sugar mills were placed under the management of the State Sugar Council (Consejo Estatal de Azúcar—CEA). The CEA employed more than 85,000 workers and was the largest single employer in the country (see ch. 9). Most of the other enterprises were turned over first to the Industrial Development Corporation (Corporación de Fomento Industrial—CFI), but were later transferred to a new entity called the State Enterprises Corporation (Corporación Dominicana de Empresas Estatales—CORDE).

CORDE, capitalized at RD$50 million, is completely autonomous and

Table 3. Gross Domestic Product of the Dominican Republic, by Activity, 1955, 1960, and 1964-70.

(in percentages)

	1955	1960	1964	1965	1966	1967	1968	1969	1970
Agriculture:									
Crops	n.a.	n.a.	16.9	18.1	17.4	15.8	15.1	n.a.	n.a.
Livestock	n.a.	n.a.	6.6	7.4	6.9	6.6	6.6	n.a.	n.a.
Forestry and fishing	n.a.	n.a.	0.6	0.6	0.6	0.6	0.6	n.a.	n.a.
Total Agriculture	26.4	27.4	24.1	26.1	24.9	23.0	22.3	22.7	22.4
Manufacturing	15.0	17.5	16.5	14.5	17.0	17.9	17.2	17.3	17.9
Commerce	22.1	19.8	17.6	16.1	16.3	16.4	17.5	17.0	16.9
Public administration	—[1]	—[1]	13.1	15.2	12.7	11.9	11.5	11.1	10.6
Transport and communications	4.7	5.6	6.0	5.2	6.4	6.8	7.4	7.9	8.2
Rental property	—[1]	—[1]	6.2	7.6	6.8	7.0	7.0	6.9	6.7
Construction	6.0	3.0	4.4	3.4	4.0	4.7	4.7	4.9	5.4
Banking and insurance	—[2]	—[2]	1.7	1.2	1.2	1.3	1.5	1.6	1.7
Mining	0.3	1.6	0.9	1.2	1.0	1.3	1.2	1.2	1.2
Utilities	—[3]	—[3]	1.1	1.2	1.2	1.2	1.2	1.2	1.2
Other services	25.5	25.1	8.4	8.3	8.5	8.5	8.5	8.2	7.8
Total	100.0	100.0	100.0	100.0	100.0	100.0	100.0	100.0	100.0

n.a.—not available.

[1] Included in "Other services" category.

[2] Included in "Commerce" category.

[3] Included in "Transport and communications" category.

is run by a board of directors composed of private and public members. Its various enterprises, each of which is permitted a high degree of autonomy, have a total of more than 5,500 employees. CORDE's miscellaneous firms process edible oil; mine salt and gypsum deposits; make paper; manufacture cement, glass, chocolates, tobacco products, shoes, batteries, liquors, flour, paints, textiles, and barbed wire; distribute automobiles; and operate hardware stores, a real estate company, an insurance company, and an airline. In addition to its direct participation in the economy, the government indirectly influences the general economy through the wage, price, and management policies it applies to its own holdings. For example, it was the first to introduce profit sharing with employees of its enterprises.

The government has enacted legislation designed to stimulate private investment in agriculture, livestock, and industry. As of 1972 the Industrial Incentive Law of 1968, which replaced earlier legislation of 1963, provided for varying degrees of fiscal benefits. The greatest number of benefits applied to export firms locating in the two industrial free zones (see ch. 9). Import substituting firms received the next most favorable treatment. The customs duties exemptions granted under the law, however, were coming under public criticism by 1971 because of a belief that such exemptions deprived the treasury of revenue and consequently might force an increase in income taxes.

An Agricultural and Livestock Promotion Law promulgated in December 1969 provided for a number of financial incentives for investments in these two sectors. These included income tax exemptions for new investments and customs duty exemptions for farm machinery. The benefits, however, unlike those granted under the industrial incentive law, were not available to foreign firms or individuals.

With some exceptions, development in the various sectors proceeded until 1970 without any governmental guidelines or policies. A National Development Council, created in 1965, is empowered to advise the president on matters of economic policy, but the council has met infrequently over the years and has deferred policymaking to a wider body, the National Development Commission. This commission was created in 1966 to include all members of the National Development Council plus several private sector members and other public sector members appointed by the president. A National Planning Office (Oficina Nacional de Planificación—ONAPLAN) first established in 1962 as the National Planning Board, a dependency of the presidency, prepares development plans and programs in coordination with other government organizations.

Until 1970 ONAPLAN's principal output consisted of a few regional economic sector or industrial studies. In 1970 the First National Development Plan 1970–1974 was released as part of a longer range general document called the Platform for the Economic and Social Development of the Dominican Republic 1968–1975. Among the principal goals of the First Plan were an average annual GNP growth rate of 6.6 percent during the 1970-74 period; the resettlement of 30,000 peasants on their own land; the creation of 211,000 new jobs by 1974; the provision of education for the entire school age population; the expansion of the water system to provide for 800,000 additional persons; and the building of 27,000 new housing units. The total government investment required to meet all the goals was estimated at RD$477 million.

GOVERNMENT FINANCES

The central government plans and organizes its revenues and expenditures by means of an annual budget. Under the budgetary law in force in 1972, the fiscal year coincided with the calendar year. On the basis of estimates submitted by the ministries and other executive departments a draft budget is prepared by the National Budget Office, a dependency of the Technical Secretariat of the Presidency, which also oversees its implementation. The president is supposed to submit the budget to congress for its approval during its second congressional session, which begins on August 16. Most budgets, however, have been submitted in December because the National Budget Office needs additional time to estimate the following year's revenues based upon current year's actual income.

Congress can only approve or disapprove a budget; it cannot alter one. As of 1972 no budget had ever been disapproved as submitted. If the congress adjourns before it can vote on the proposed budget, the previous budget remains in effect until congress next convenes. Any proposed extrabudgetary expenditures are also submitted to congress by the executive. If the congress is not in session to approve extrabudgetary expenditures, the president may provide for them by decree-law and congress approve them after the fact.

Under the authoritarian Trujillo regime a large but undetermined portion of the government's domestic revenues was either removed from the country by Trujillo and his followers or was devoted to investment in public works and industry. After Trujillo's assassination, budgets increased substantially and government consumption expenditures rose at a high rate until 1966 when tight budgetary principles and an austerity program was initiated, which were still in effect in 1972. As a result, current expenditures for salaries, goods, and services in 1970 were at the same absolute level as in 1964 despite continual budget increases. The budget increases after 1966 were for major capital investments in infrastructure, such as highways and dams.

Because of the austerity program and also because of increased tax revenues and an improved profit position of state enterprises, the government took in more revenue than was budgeted during the latter part of the 1960s. For example, the 1969 budget was set at RD$186 million, but actual income was RD$237 million. The 1970 budget was RD$214 million; RD$240 million income was realized. Nearly RD$304 million was received in 1971 versus a budget estimate of RD$247 million. The 1972 budget was approved for RD$301 million, but, again, revenues were running ahead of estimates. The increased revenues permitted the government to make larger capital investments than were budgeted for and resulted in a smaller need for external financing.

The decentralized agencies have their own budgets that are not included in the national budget. In 1971 the total budgets of some two dozen autonomous and semiautonomous agencies came to RD$294 million. Many of the agencies, such as the Reserve Bank of the Dominican Republic (Banco de Reservas de la República Dominicana), are self-supporting by virtue of their own operations. Others require transfers from the central government budget, or loans, either foreign or domestic, to meet their expenses. The more profitable enterprises, such as the State Sugar Council (Consejo Estatal de Azúcar—CEA) and the National Lottery, contribute tax and dividend income to the central government.

The most important local unit of government in the late 1960s and early 1970s was the municipality, which was granted municipal and fiscal autonomy in 1961. The fiscal autonomy, however, was dependent upon the judgment of the chief of state because the Constitution of 1966, as well as the two previous constitutions, empowered the president to reject any local tax deemed to be contrary to national interests. Municipalities could also be refused authority to negotiate contracts guaranteed by municipal real property or by projected revenues. In the late 1960s the accumulated budgets of all municipalities were between RD$18 million and RD$19 million annually, and more than one-third of the total budget was allotted to the National District. In addition to local taxes and fees, municipal revenue was derived from transfers by the central government and from licenses and fines. Almost all of the municipal income was expended on salaries of local officials.

Central Government Expenditures and Revenues

The budgetary control exercised on the level of current expenditures caused its relative share to fall from nearly 80 percent of the total budget before 1966 to about 70 percent by 1971. From 1966 through 1970 wages and salaries of government employees absorbed between 44 percent and 49 percent of the annual total, goods and services accounted for between 7 percent and 10 percent, transfers to other entities took 16 percent to 19 percent, and amortization of the public debt accounted for between 2.5 percent and 3.5 percent. Capital expenditures took the balance, which had risen to 30 percent in 1971.

A change in the relative share of sectoral expenditures also occurred during the same period. The percentage spent on defense, once the leading sector, dropped continuously while the percentages spent for education and health and social welfare rose (see table 4). Education received the largest share of the budgetary expenditures in 1967 and

167

(in percentages of total expenditures)

	1966	1967	1968	1969	1970	1971*
Education	14.7	14.8	14.8	15.7	17.2	20.4
Health and social welfare	10.6	11.1	11.7	11.1	10.8	13.4
National defense	16.8	14.5	14.0	13.0	12.0	11.4
Transportation and communications	12.6	14.3	14.9	14.8	12.5	10.2
General administration	8.4	6.8	7.9	8.8	8.3	7.8
Justice and public order	8.8	8.8	8.6	7.6	7.3	7.4
Agriculture	6.9	7.2	8.8	7.4	9.6	5.8
Irrigation	2.9	2.5	1.7	4.5	5.5	5.5
Community services	1.7	0.4	0.5	0.3	1.8	3.5
Public debt	2.3	1.8	2.0	2.8	2.8	3.0
Energy	0.0	0.0	0.2	0.8	1.3	1.7
Housing	0.4	2.6	2.1	2.2	1.3	1.6
Water and sewerage	2.0	2.0	2.6	2.0	1.6	1.5
International relations	1.3	1.1	1.1	1.1	1.1	1.1
Urbanization	1.2	2.0	1.8	2.3	1.7	1.0
Industry and commerce	0.9	2.0	0.6	0.5	0.5	0.6
Labor	0.3	0.3	0.2	0.3	0.3	0.3
Others	8.2	7.8	6.5	4.8	4.4	3.8
Total expenditures	100.0	100.0	100.0	100.0	100.0	100.0

*Budget estimate for 1971; previous years are actual expenditures.

for the 1969–71 period, whereas defense received the second-largest share in 1967, and only the third largest from 1968 through 1971. Transportation received from 10 to 15 percent of total expenditures, reflecting the government's intention of improving the highway system. Smaller percentages were spent on other functions.

Taxes brought in from 90 percent to about 94 percent of total current revenue, and nontax sources provided the balance (see table 5). Throughout its independent history the country has placed primary reliance on customs duties as a source of revenue. Initially export and import duties were the only revenue source because the central government exercised too little control over much of the countryside to make the collection of other kinds of taxes feasible. With the progressive integration of rural areas into the mainstream of Dominican life, other levies became part of the tax structure, and nontax devices such as the popular weekly national lottery were introduced.

The tax burden is fairly high. Throughout most of the 1960s it was almost 20 percent of annual GNP, and in 1971 it was 19 percent. Collection of revenue is primarily, but not entirely, a function of the Ministry of Finance. Some minor taxes are collected by other executive agencies. The ministry operates a school of fiscal training, created in 1963, to teach personnel new tax methods, and several hundred persons had received such training by 1972. A national taxpayers register was established in 1972 with the use of electronic data processing equipment,

Table 5. Dominican Republic Central Government Sources of Current Revenue,
1964-70
(in percentages)

	1964	1965	1966	1967	1968	1969	1970
Tax Revenue:							
Import duties	44.2	40.3	44.9	40.5	40.5	41.1	39.6
Income taxes	16.4	17.2	15.3	17.2	16.1	17.4	18.4
Production (excise) taxes	11.4	16.6	13.4	12.3	13.0	13.4	13.8
Export duties	3.8	0.4	1.7	3.6	5.0	4.2	5.3
Sales taxes	5.2	7.6	7.1	6.1	4.8	4.5	4.9
Property and inheritance taxes	3.3	5.1	3.7	4.5	4.4	3.9	4.1
Stamp taxes	2.3	2.5	2.1	2.4	2.4	2.5	2.7
Others	4.8	3.8	3.8	3.7	3.2	2.7	2.7
Total	91.4	93.5	92.0	90.3	89.4	89.7	91.5
Nontax Revenue:							
National lottery	4.8	2.5	4.1	5.4	4.2	3.9	—[2]
Services and royalties	3.1	3.3	3.3	2.7	2.7	2.5	2.4
State sugar enterprise	0.0	0.0	0.0	0.0	0.8	1.3	—[2]
CORDE[1]	0.0	0.0	0.0	0.2	0.4	0.5	—[2]
Other	0.7	0.7	0.6	1.4	2.5	2.1	6.1
Total	8.6	6.5	8.0	9.7	10.6	10.3	8.5
TOTAL CURRENT REVENUE	100.0	100.0	100.0	100.0	100.0	100.0	100.0

[1] State Enterprises Corporation—Corporación Dominicana de Empresas Estatales.
[2] Included in "Other" category.

listing every taxpayer for every type of tax, in order to deter tax fraud and delinquency. The various tax offices also offer taxpayer assistance, and they issue periodic announcements as to when certain tax payments are due. The ministry also issues publicitory material in an effort to convince citizens of their moral obligation to pay taxes.

Import duties accounted for the largest share of revenue during the 1964-70 period—from 40 to 45 percent of the annual total. On January 1, 1972, the Brussels Tariff Nomenclature was adopted to replace the national nomenclature; the new tariff added additional classifications and made import quota controls and duty assessments more operable. Previously, many importers brought in much merchandise classified as miscellaneous under lower rates because the item was not specifically named under the old tariff.

Most imported goods are assessed on a specific basis ranging from RD$0.01 to RD$5 per kilogram of weight, except for luxury goods, which are assessed RD$10.00. For some goods the packing weight is also included. A few items are assessed on the basis of measurement: so much per liter, meter, or dozen. Some commodities are also assessed an ad valorem duty based upon value in addition to the specific rate. Ad valorem rates range from 5 percent to as much as 50 percent of value. Surcharges on the tax assessments are also levied. A surcharge of 4 percent of the assessed duties is charged for all imports except cotton fabrics, which carry a 10-percent surcharge. A second surcharge consisting of a 2-percent levy on the assessed basic duty plus 4 percent of the first surcharge is levied on luxuries.

Income taxation, which yields a much higher percent of revenue in other Latin American countries, only provided between 15 percent and about 18 percent annually from 1964 to 1970. The basic income tax legislation in force in 1972 was Law 5911 of May 22, 1962, plus later amendments. The law was detailed and complicated, and the tax liability often could not be determined by the taxpayer, who had to rely upon the services of a tax attorney or the Dominican Tax Office. The tax was levied upon all income earned in the country, but there were five categories of income, such as personal labor and services, rental, professional fees, investments, and business; and each category had different progressive tax rates, and an individual or a company might be liable under more than one category.

The rates for most individuals were modest, with numerous deductions permitted so that most persons paid little or no taxes. In 1967, for example, out of 50,000 total returns, only 15,000 were from individuals; the rest were from business firms. The minimum taxable annual income in 1972 was RD$1,200 for single persons; RD$2,000, for married persons; and RD$3,000, for married persons with at least two children. Income under those amounts was not taxable. All medical expenses were deductible, and tax rates commenced at 3 percent, rising to a maximum of 70 percent for the highest taxable income.

Most corporations were taxed at rates ranging between 10 percent and 38 percent. In addition, declared dividends were assessed a withholding tax of 8 percent if destined to residents of the country or 18 percent if sent abroad. A tax amendment in 1971 made mining companies liable for a flat 40-percent rate on net income with no allowances permitted for depletion. This amendment should cause an increase in the tax yield once the nickel-mining project is in full operation (see ch. 9).

Production, or excise, taxes were next in order of importance as sources of revenue from 1964 through 1970, accounting for anywhere from 12 to more than 16 percent. Most of this income was derived from taxes on the production of alcohol, beer, wines, cigarettes, and matches. Export duties were next in magnitude in 1970 and accounted for more than 5 percent of total revenue, although they had provided smaller percentages in previous years. Sugar and minerals were the main products liable for export duties; minor amounts were collected from the export of bananas, live cattle, wood, and molasses.

In some years sales taxes brought in more than export duties, although no national general sales tax existed as of 1972. Sales taxes were levied only upon a few commodities; wood products, alcoholic beverages, soft drinks, and amusements. Property and inheritance taxes followed in importance. More revenue was collected annually from the property taxes on vehicles than from inheritances. Stamp taxes and miscellaneous minor taxes yielded the balance of the tax revenue.

Of the various nontax sources of income, the National Lottery provided the largest percentage from 1964 through 1970. In 1971, however, profits from the state enterprises, including the sugar estates, started to increase rapidly as the economy improved; and this source was expected to provide more income in the future. Fees, fines, and the sale of goods and services accounted for the balance of nontax revenue.

Public Debt

The public debt was not considered to be unmanageable in 1972, according to international economists, although it had grown to sizable proportions. The domestic portion of the public debt was about RD$245 million at the end of 1970, owed mostly by the Central Government to the state banks, particularly the Central Bank, but also including some bond issues held by the general public. The domestic debt had accumulated over the years from small annual budgetary deficits and large public infrastructure investments.

The foreign debt still outstanding at the end of 1971 was about RD$340 million, most of which was incurred during the previous ten years. When Trujillo became president in 1930, the country was burdened by heavy foreign debt; but through the introduction of austerity measures, the foreign debt was fully amortized by 1947. New foreign loans contracted from that date onward and outstanding at the time of Trujillo's fall in 1961 totaled only about RD$17 million. Succeeding governments, however, rapidly contracted new debts in an effort to rebuild the economy; but, despite the increase, the country did not face a difficult debt service problem because of advantageous terms it had received. The average rate of interest on outstanding loans in 1970 was only 2 percent. Amortization of the foreign debt could be covered by less than 10 percent of anticipated annual export earnings during the 1970s.

Almost half of the foreign debt had been contracted by the Central Government, and most of the balance by the various autonomous agencies; a small portion had been incurred by the private sector. The United States government was the major creditor followed by the International Bank for Reconstruction and Development—IBRD (commonly known as the World Bank). The Inter-American Development Bank (IDB) and private financial institutions and suppliers in the United States and Europe held the rest of the debt.

Balance of Payments

Prudent fiscal and monetary policies during the 1960s and new incoming capital prevented the balance of payments situation from deteriorating despite some difficult years when large deficits occurred.

During the 1950s, balance-of-payments deficits were encountered only occasionally, but throughout most of the 1960s deficits occurred almost annually; and the country suffered large accumulated losses.

The balance of payments current account was continually negative during the 1960s because imports exceeded exports and large outlays were made for services (such as freight and insurance), for private remittances overseas, and for Dominicans traveling abroad. There was a surplus in the capital account in most years of the 1960s, mainly from new incoming investments and loans, but the surplus was usually not large enough to offset the imbalance in trade and services. In 1969, however, the capital account surplus was high enough to counterbalance the current account, and that year recorded the first overall balance of payments surplus in the decade. A deficit occurred again in 1970, but 1971 was practically in equilibrium with a small deficit under RD$1 million. Increased sugar exports and incoming capital during the first half of 1972 forecast a continued easing of pressure on the balance of payments and a possible surplus. In an effort to encourage the repatriation of dollars held abroad, residents were permitted to open special accounts in dollars in local banks in 1972. Net international reserves grew to about US$45 million in May 1972.

FOREIGN AID AND INVESTMENT

Officially, foreign investment is welcome and is actively encouraged by the Dominican Republic government. No foreign firm had been nationalized since the downfall of the Trujillo regime. Although no sector of the economy is barred to foreign investment, domestic interests have at times been able to prevent a proposed investment by convincing the government that domestic companies may be hurt by the increased competition or that domestic firms could manufacture the same products.

Foreign investment has increased since the promulgation of the 1968 industrial incentives law (see Government Role, this ch.). The law, however, was not as liberal as similar laws of other countries; for example, there were no benefits for investments in commerce, and the number of years for which a tax exemption was granted was shorter than elsewhere. Further, no more than 18 percent of annual profits could be remitted abroad by foreign firms although high-risk ventures might have this ceiling waived on a case-by-case basis.

As of mid-1972 there was no reliable data on total foreign investment in the Dominican Republic. As a percent of total investment in the country, it was believed to be smaller than in other Latin American countries because many firms were eliminated under the Trujillo era and few new ones came in until the 1968 industrial incentive law was passed. The largest single foreign investment as of 1972 was the Falconbridge nickel-mining and -processing facility, installed at a cost of RD$200 million (see ch. 9). Falconbridge, a Canadian firm, was followed in importance by the Gulf and Western Americas Corporation, a United States company, which had varied interests in sugar, a hotel, a finance company, a free zone, cattle, tobacco, and a furfural plant.

From the end of World War II through 1972 the Dominican Republic received nearly US$700 million in assistance from foreign governments and from international lending agencies. The major portion of the assistance was given after 1962 because most foreign aid was cut off during the 1959-62 period in response to economic sanctions imposed against the country by the Organization of American States (OAS) (see ch. 3). The terms of the assistance received by the country were highly favorable; a large proportion was in the form of grants, and loans were provided at low-interest rates or were repayable in local currency.

The United States provided the largest amount of foreign assistance: about US$490 million through 1972, of which about US$215 million of the total was in the form of grants. The aid was for miscellaneous projects and also for budgetary support. The Agency for International Development (AID) and its predecessor agencies provided about US$330 million of the United States aid; the Food for Peace program provided about US$77 million; the Export-Import Bank, about US$40 million; and the balance was provided under various programs, including military assistance.

The Inter-American Development Bank (IDB) lent almost US$70 million for several projects, the two largest loans being US$30 million for electricity and US$21 million for agriculture and industry. Over US$100 million in new loan applications were under study by the IDB in late 1972. The World Bank and its related agencies had lent about US$35 million, the International Monetary Fund (IMF) had provided nearly US$60 million in various standby arrangements to strengthen the peso, the United Nations had supplied about US$10 million for various projects, and European governments had provided the balance.

BANKING AND CREDIT

The monetary unit is the Dominican gold peso (symbol RD$), which was adopted on February 1, 1948. Before that date the currency circulating in the country consisted of United States banknotes and Dominican coins called centavos. All Dominican notes and coins resemble United States bills and coins and are in the same denominations, with one exception: a 30-peso gold coin. The value of the gold peso was set at RD$1 equals US$1. This official rate was still in effect in late 1972, giving the peso one of the longest lifespans of any currency in the world at that time. An active black market is known to operate outside banks on the sidewalks of Santo Domingo but is tolerated by officials and is also known to exist among Dominican residents of New York. The black market rate has fluctuated since its creation in 1960 and was quoted as high as RD$1.25 equals US$1 in June 1971.

The banking system in late 1972 consisted of the Central Bank of the Dominican Republic; three other state-owned banks, one of which was a commercial bank; seven private commercial banks, five of which were foreign-owned; three development finance companies, one of which was state-owned; and a state housing institute. The banking system was controlled by the Monetary Board and supervised by the Office of Superintendent of Banks. There were three basic banking and monetary laws in effect in 1972: The Monetary Law of October 8, 1947, governing money matters; the Organic Law of the Central Bank of the Dominican Republic of December 29, 1962, governing the Central Bank; and the General Law of Banks of February 12, 1963, governing all banks.

The Monetary Board was the policymaking body for the autonomous Central Bank, and its chief officer was called the governor of the Central Bank. The monetary board consisted of the governor, the minister of finance, and five representatives of the public sector. Day-to-day operations of the Central Bank were directed by the manager of the bank, who also acted as chief of personnel.

The Central Bank engages in most of the activities ordinarily carried on by a Central Bank. It acts as a bankers' bank for other financial institutions and holds the legal reserves of the commercial banks. There are two sets of reserve requirements for each type of deposit and banks may select either, depending upon their degree of attractiveness. The Central Bank issues all banknotes and coins; and, in accordance with the decisions of the Monetary Board, regulates the country's credit and money supply. Total money in circulation in mid-1972 was about RD$225 million.

The Central Bank holds and manages the official gold and foreign exchange reserves and controls the foreign exchange transactions of the private sector. It sets the interest rates that banks may offer or charge for deposits and loans. The Central Bank maintains a securities regulation fund to encourage investment of private capital in government securities; the fund may buy part of an unsold government bond issue or repurchase the securities from private holders.

Because of the country's increasing reliance on foreign sources for financing, a Department of International Agreements was added to the structure of the bank in 1965. This department is responsible for coordinating and supervising the negotiation of international loans on behalf of the central government and the autonomous agencies, performing any economic study required by international lenders and administering the Economic Development Investment Fund (Fondo de Inversiones para Desarrollo Económico—FIDE). FIDE is financed from foreign loans and from the Central Bank's own assets, and it relends to other credit institutions for specific projects such as livestock improvement. The fund does not lend directly to the public. The other credit institutions are charged 5-percent interest for FIDE's funds and in turn charge a maximum of 9 percent to the ultimate borrower. As of late 1972 FIDE's capital was RD$63 million.

The Reserve Bank of the Dominican Republic (Banco de Reservas de la República Dominicana), an autonomous institution established in 1941, is a commercial bank but also serves as the fiscal agent and depository for the central government. It may also perform functions assigned to it by the Central Bank and acts as the fiscal agent for municipalities in which it has branch offices. It was the largest commercial bank in the country at the end of 1971, with RD$200 million in assets, 700 employees, and thirty-one branches and agencies throughout the nation.

One important specialized government bank is the Agricultural Bank (see ch. 9). Originally created in 1945 as the Agricultural and Mortgage Bank, its name was changed to the Bank of Agricultural and Industrial Credit in 1948. It was used as a political pawn and was virtually ineffective as a source of credit to small farmers until it was reorganized in 1962 under its present name. Before its reorganization it was also used as a source of funds for state enterprises. Since then it has been working closely with the Dominican Agrarian Institite (Instituto Agrario Dominicano—IAD) in supplying short- and medium-term credit to small farmers. The Agricultural Bank does not accept deposits but obtains its working funds from the central government, bond sales, foreign loans, and repayment by borrowers of previous loans. Because of its increased activity and because many of its older loans were in default, the bank's capital was in danger of being depleted, and in 1972 the government was seeking to recapitalize it by selling agricultural bonds to the private banks.

The National Housing Bank is the most important of several organizations concerned with overcoming the housing shortage (see ch. 5). Created in 1962 as an autonomous government agency, the National Housing Bank serves as a stimulus for home construction by lending to savings and loan associations, which are also required to maintain reserves with the bank. As of 1972 there were eleven such associations with 60,000 members. The National Housing Bank does not lend directly to individuals.

The country's private commercial banking system was well developed in 1972. There were two domestically owned banks, the Credit and Savings Bank (Banco de Crédito y Ahorros), established in 1949, and the Dominican Popular Bank (Banco Popular Dominicano), which opened in 1964. Five banks were subsidiaries of Canadian and United States institutions. The most important was the Royal Bank of Canada, which entered the country before World War I and had eleven branches in 1972. The Bank of Nova Scotia, with four branches, was also a Canadian subsidiary. The United States banks were the Chase Manhattan Bank, the First National City Bank, and the Bank of America, each with two branch offices.

An Industrial Development Corporation (Corporación de Fomento

Industrial—CFI) was established in 1962 as an autonomous government-owned development bank. It will finance machinery, equipment, and some working capital requirements of nonsugar industrial projects. The CFI usually will not lend more than 60 percent of the borrower's total needs as its resources are limited. By mid-1972 the CFI had lent a total of only RD$22 million since its inception.

The first private development financing institution, Dominican Financing (Financiera Dominicana) was established in the middle of 1968 to meet the needs that could not be met by CFI, and it does not restrict itself to industrial investments. Using funds contributed by its 163 stockholders, including local and foreign banks, and by funds lent by the AID it makes medium- and long-term loans to any enterprise or participates in the equity of a company. It also engages in securities transactions and will underwrite new securities issued by private firms. Few securities are actively traded. The most widely held stock in the late 1960s had less than 500 stockholders.

Responding to the success of Dominican Financing, the Gulf and Western Americas Corporation created the Associated Finance Corporation (Corporación Financiera Asociada S.A.—COFINSA) in 1969. COFINSA finances private investment in manufacturing, mining, transportation, and tourism. Several personal loan companies supplement the lending activities of these specialized institutions by financing the purchase of consumer durables. There were about forty insurance companies in 1972, many of which were foreign owned. A certain proportion of insurance premiums must be invested in the Dominican Republic, and the government issued a law in 1971 requiring all insurance on imported goods to be placed only with Dominican companies in an effort to stimulate the local insurance industry.

The government's credit policy has been generally restrictive since 1964 in order to protect the balance of payments and to stem an incipient inflation. With the year 1963 as a base of 100, the overall consumer price index had risen to about 108 by 1971. In 1972 credit rules were tightened even further because bank loans had increased by 23 percent in 1971, despite previous restrictions. Interest rates went to 12 percent, and selective reserve requirements were created in order to alter the makeup of the loan portfolio; smaller reserves were required for agricultural and industrial loans and higher reserves for commercial loans.

Almost 24 percent of the total loan portfolio in the entire banking system in 1970 was for crops and other agricultural purposes, and another 5 percent was for livestock. About 23 percent of the loans were for industry, 16 percent for commerce, 14 percent for construction, and the balance for all other purposes. The high overall percentage for agriculture was because of the loans made by the government's Agricultural Bank. The private banks' loan portfolio actually held a preponderance of loans for industry and commerce: 35 percent and 25 percent, respectively.

Lower income groups who want to purchase major consumer durables, small vendors in markets, and other merchants with limited funds who require capital for purchase of goods do not usually have access to institutionalized credit. They either resort to moneylenders who may charge as much as 1,000 percent annual interest, or, they more usually participate in a loosely formed rotating credit association peculiar to the Dominican Republic and a few other countries in the world. In the Dominican Republic this rotating credit association is called *San*. Each *San* participant contributes a specified sum at regular intervals. At each interval a drawing is held, and the winner collects all or part of the amount contributed. Winners must continue to make contributions but cannot win again until every participant has had an opportunity to win. One member of the *San* group acts as administrator and receives a payment for his services from the contributions; group leadership may also rotate. *San* is effective in mobilizing a large sum of money at a small cost.

An estimated 125,000 persons had benefited as of 1971 from small loans extended by the privately financed Dominican Development Foundation that is associated with a regional organization, the Pan American Development Foundation (PADF). Most foundation loans are small and are used for such things as irrigation pumps, sewing machines, hospital and medical equipment, and machine tools. About 200 Dominican businessmen make monthly contributions to the Dominican Development Foundation to assure its continuity, in addition to funds made available by PADF and other international institutions.

CHAPTER 9

AGRICULTURE, INDUSTRY, AND TRADE

Agriculture and the processing of agricultural products dominate economic activity in the Dominican Republic. During the 1960s agriculture contributed as much as 24 percent to the gross domestic product (GDP) annually, and industrial production, principally sugar processing, accounted for nearly 19 percent of the GDP. The major portion of exports—between 80 and 90 percent—and the greater part of domestic trade also consist of agricultural products.

At least 60 percent of the labor force is in the agricultural sector; it was estimated in 1970 that about 700,000 economically active persons were engaged in agriculture. Of the more than 100,000 persons employed in industry, about 93 percent were engaged in processing agricultural products.

Because of the year-round growing season, generally sufficient rainfall, and relatively fertile soils, a wide range of crops is raised. The only important food crop not grown is wheat, and between 75,000 and 117,000 tons are imported annually to meet the demand. Sugarcane, coffee, cacao, and tobacco are the main export crops, and rice is the most important food crop. Livestock raising is an important part of agriculture, although its growth rate is low. Most cattle are raised on large ranches.

The outstanding feature of land distribution is the existence of a few enormous farms and a multitude of tiny ones. The number of medium-size farms is small; and the largest single landowner is the state, which inherited large tracts belonging to the Trujillo family. A land reform program initiated in 1962 has been moving slowly, and the government's land redistribution goals had not been met by late 1972.

Industry was virtually created by former President Rafael Leonidas Trujillo Molina in the twenty years between 1940 and 1960; he set in motion industrial growth under the aegis of the government for the benefit of his family and followers. At the time of his assassination in 1961, his clique held majority control of nearly every important enterprise. Almost all of these passed to the state, but the succeeding governments, while continuing to operate the confiscated properties, did not acquire majority control of any new ones. Although the government obtained minority share in some of the new enterprises, all new industry was in private hands.

There was a small mining industry, and the initiation of nickel processing in 1972 augured well for the future of this sector. Bauxite mining was another important activity. No mineral fuels were being exploited in 1972, although petroleum prospecting had been going on for several years. Electrical generating capacity was keeping in step with demand, and several major power projects were being completed in the early 1970s.

The outbreak of civil strife in 1965 interrupted expansion of the country's foreign trade, and it took until nearly the end of the decade to surpass the 1964 level. The country's economic relations have been closer with the United States than with any other country, and the United States is the major trading partner by a wide margin.

Roads are the main means of transport, and highway construction in the past has absorbed a substantial share of public investment. Inadequate maintenance of the highways and the lack of farm access roads are the main drawbacks of the road network, and many farmers find it difficult to get their goods to market. One small railroad is not of economic significance, and air transport service is irregular and limited to about fifteen localities.

LAND USE AND TENURE

A national agricultural census was conducted in late 1970, but as of late 1972 only a few scattered statistics from this were available. Most agricultural and land use data obtainable in 1972 stemmed from the census of 1960 and a 1967 agricultural survey. The 1960 data, however, are viewed with caution by most foreign economists because these were compiled during the Trujillo era, when records were deliberately manipulated to conceal land seizures by the Trujillo family, which at one time owned 60 percent of all farmland.

Of the country's total land area of almost 12 million acres, over 6.4 million acres were on farms, according to preliminary data from the 1970 census. The 1967 survey had indicated there were only 5.45 million acres of farmland, including 2 million acres of pastures and 1.6 million acres planted in crops; the balance was either fallow, wooded, undeveloped, or wasteland. More than one-fourth of all farmland was in the two provinces of San Cristóbal and La Vega.

The 1960 census indicated there were almost 450,000 farms, but the preliminary data from the 1970 census enumerated only 300,000 farms in the country. The difference is unexplained but may be accounted for by falsification of data under the Trujillo regime or the abandonment of subsistence farms by migrating families, or a combination of both.

Farm size is highly unequal. Half of all farms in the 1960 census were under 2.5 acres and accounted for only 6 percent of total farmland, whereas at the other extreme 8,000 farms contained more than half of all farmland. The 1967 survey supported the belief that the unequal pattern had changed little by that year, and partial results of the 1970 census confirmed this. In thirteen northern provinces enumerated in 1970, 1 percent of the farms in those provinces accounted for 38 percent of total farm area.

Two special terms are used in the Dominican Republic to denote small landholdings. A subsistence farm is called a *parcela* (plot), and land given to plantation workers for their own use is called *conuco*. The term *conuco*, however, also means a cornfield, possibly because plantation workers usually grew this crop on their land.

Almost 263,000 of the 450,000 farms enumerated in 1960 were classified as being owned by their operators, and they accounted for 73 percent of total farmland. In 1960 about 130,000 of the farm operators rented their land, 31,000 were sharecroppers, and the rest of the farm operators were squatters or operated farms on the basis of some form of mixed management. Over 55,000 farm operators reported that agriculture was not their principal occupation.

The largest landholder and employer of paid agricultural labor in the country in 1972 was the state, which owned about 1.8 million acres. This area was mainly farmland, but it also included unused tracts, part of which could be utilized for agriculture. The state-owned land included sugar estates confiscated from Trujillo and managed by the State Sugar Council (Consejo Estatal de Azúcar—CEA), also known as the Dominican Sugar Commission; land held by the Dominican Agrarian Institute (Instituto Agrario Dominicano—IAD) for redistribution and resettlement; land belonging to the Agricultural Bank and other state entities, including the autonomous agency State Farms (Fincas del Estado), which operates farms growing miscellaneous products for governmental use; and land held by a government agency called National Properties (Bienes Nacionales), which holds all idle property confiscated from the Trujillo family and which controls the largest percentage of public lands.

Land reform in the Dominican Republic began as early as 1905 with the passage of legislation permitting the free use of state-owned land by individuals for a ten-year period, after which rent was to be paid. The 1927 Agricultural Colonization Law shifted the emphasis from individual operation to the establishment of new settlements on public lands, and a 1934 law stipulated that the new settlements must have at least ten applicants and be granted at least 250 acres. The principal reason for the settlement program was the traditional fear of Haitian intrusion into the sparsely settled border region (see ch. 7). The settlement program reached its peak toward the end of the Trujillo era in 1961 when it had a total of over 100,000 Dominican and immigrant colonists.

After the collapse of the Trujillo regime in 1961 the colonization program began to disintegrate. Many of the farm colonies had matured into small urban communities, immigrants had been repatriated or had left for other countries, and the flow of peasants to urban areas increased.

In 1962 the Agrarian Reform Law was passed under which the IAD was created, and the primary emphasis of land reform shifted back to

181

settling landless farm families, particularly squatters, on an individual basis. At the same time new settlements and cooperatives were also to be encouraged by the IAD.

The IAD is a semiautonomous body subordinate to the Secretariat of Agriculture. It is governed by the Directive Council, composed of the ministers of agriculture, public works, labor, and education, the president of the Industrial Bank, and the president of the Industrial Development Corporation. The IAD surveys land, takes a census of the squatters on a project, stakes out farm units, resettles some squatters, settles new farm families, and provides technical assistance, including access roads, potable water, and a small grubstake. Until a five-year test period has passed, the peasant receives only a certificate of provisional assignment; after this, a firm title may be granted.

The progress of land redistribution under the 1962 law has been slow despite the vast amount of state-owned land. Very little private property has been expropriated except to finish a project. From the date of its passage through 1970 (by which date the IAD had hoped to transfer farms to between 45,000 and 50,000 families), only about 11,000 farm parcels totaling approximately 134,000 acres had been distributed. A 1970 report of the Autonomous University of Santo Domingo claimed that only 2 percent of the rural population had received any benefits from agrarian reform. According to a 1967 survey of land reform by agrarian reform experts, it would take 500 years to distribute all the state-owned land at the current rate of redistribution.

It should be noted, however, that the main bottleneck in the progress of land reform is the property survey, the making of which is slow and cumbersome because of the difficulty of determining who holds what rights to land. During most of the colonial era large estates were not divided for inheritance purposes but were kept intact, the heirs receiving shares to the profits from the estate. The shares were negotiable and over the years were sold to outsiders. Certain rights, such as tree cutting, were sold to other persons. Although the land itself passed to the state for one reason or another (Haitian occupation and confiscation of church lands during the nineteenth century and Trujillo estates), many persons still held such shares, and therefore they or their descendants hold some claim to the original land. It then becomes the responsibility of a land court to prove the state's rightful ownership of the land it wishes to redistribute.

Other slowdowns occur in processing applications and in the property survey because of the internal administration of the IAD and because of its small budget. One survey in the late 1960s indicated that, of its 800 employees, only 8 percent were technically qualified to perform their roles. Further, much of the land that had been transferred to the IAD by some other government agency, such as the State Sugar Council, had to be paid for. For example, in early 1972 the sugar council transferred 155,000 acres of land for which compensation had to be made, thereby cutting into the IAD funds available for field operations. Only land acquired from National Properties is transferred free of charge.

The attitude of the landless farmer plays a part in the slow rate of land reform. A survey of rural attitudes in the early 1960s indicated that only 27 percent of the peasants listed ownership of their own farms as their greatest wish. Resistance to change, mistrust of the government, and perhaps even ignorance of what the program has to offer are other possible reasons for the slow response of peasants to the agrarian reform program.

Several agricultural laws passed in 1972 would, if enforced properly, widen the government's agrarian reform program. One of these laws provided for all privately owned ricelands over eighty acres in size and irrigated by government-built irrigation canals to be turned over to the IAD for redistribution; others provided for the purchase of idle or exhausted farmland by the government, the prohibition of certain sharecropping arrangements in order to make absentee landownership unprofitable, and the recovery of state lands being used without permission by private farmers. Many private farmers owning property adjacent to state land were farming some of the state land illegally.

AGRICULTURAL PRACTICES

Indirectly related to the land reform program is the agricultural cooperative movement. A few cooperatives were formed in the 1930s and 1940s, but their activities were limited until the IAD was assigned responsibility for stimulating production, marketing, storing, and processing cooperatives. In addition, the Institute for Cooperative Credit (Instituto de Desarrollo y Crédito Cooperativo—IDECOOP) has funds available for lending to cooperatives. As of 1972 there were four major federations of cooperatives, the largest being the Dominican Federation of Agricultural and Tobacco Cooperatives, with over 8,000 members. All of the federations provide marketing and credit facilities for their members.

During the Trujillo regime there was little incentive or opportunity for the subsistence farmer to acquire skills. The increased emphasis on mechanization that followed the collapse of the regime, coupled with new emphasis on irrigation, soil fertilization, and crop diversification, progressively increased the need for skills; but in 1968 no more than 600 members of the agricultural labor force were reported to have had any formal agricultural training. Of these, no more than forty had received any training at the postsecondary or university level. In 1969, however, nearly 600 students were enrolled in the country's agricultural schools at the secondary level, and the system of higher education conferred degrees on fifteen agronomists, the first ever graduated.

There is a general lack of trained teachers and a low level of rural education. The young farmer is handicapped from the very start by a lack of the rudimentary education necessary for him to make best use of the state's extension services and other technical assistance. The first extension program was undertaken in 1932, but little was accomplished until 1962 when two field agencies were opened as training centers. Experimental research is carried out by several state agencies. The most important is the National Agricultural Investigation Center located at San Cristóbal, which conducts research on soils and all crops except tobacco, which is handled by the Tobacco Institute. The Horticulture Center of Constanza experiments on improving fruits and vegetables, and the Rice Experimental Station at Juma works on rice improvement and also provides seeds to farmers. Several smaller programs are carried out by the IAD, the Agricultural Bank, and the State Sugar Council.

Most of the specialized agencies are under the Secretariat of Agriculture, which is in charge of formulating and carrying out crop and livestock policy. In the late 1960s there were over 8,000 government employees in all the institutions dealing with agriculture, but only about 17 percent were classified as professionals or technicians. Almost half were laborers, one-third were administrators, and the balance was listed as directors.

Farming practices are generally unsophisticated. Although the method has been illegal since 1967, land is still cleared by what is termed the *tumba* method; all standing trees are cut with machetes or axes, and the branches are burned (see Agricultural Production, this ch.). The stumps and roots are removed only if the land is level because such land is more valuable than are hillside plots. Good farmland sold for RD$50 (1 peso equals US$1—see Glossary) to RD$200 per acre in the early 1970s. Plows are used on the level ground but seldom on rolling land, where the hoe and digging stick are preferred.

All farmers, including subsistence farmers, plant the most valuable cash crop on their best soil and food crops for their family on the less fertile ground, rather than planting a crop in the soil best suited to its growth. The hillside plots are more often than not planted in rows running up and down rather than being terraced, and much of the topsoil is lost during heavy rains.

Few farms use mechanized equipment. Horses, oxen, mules, and donkeys are employed by most farmers for plowing, cultivating, hauling, or riding. Only the sugar estates, rice plantations, and some of the larger general crop farms utilize machinery. The 1960 agricultural census indicated that only 10 percent of the farms had some machinery. Oxen are the principal motive power on medium-size farms; donkeys and mules, on smaller ones; and hand labor is mostly used on the smallest plots. Itinerant plowboys who own braces of oxen and plows travel around the countryside contracting their services.

Only about 6,000 farms reported using fertilizers in the 1960 census, and as of 1970 only about 300,000 acres of land under cultivation were being fertilized. Land rotation is the more common method used by most farmers to conserve the soil. Parts of hillside plots, which predominate on most farms, are usually left fallow for as long as five years between plantings, even by the smallest farmers. More level land is generally used as pastureland for two years after having been cultivated for three.

Although rainfall is heavy or adequate in two-thirds of the country, about one-third of the land is too dry to produce crops well without irrigation. A state irrigation service was established in 1932, and by 1972 almost 400,000 acres of land on 33,000 farms were under irrigation. Because of a lack of maintenance, however, only about 270,000 acres were being effectively irrigated. Almost 95,000 acres of irrigated land were ricefields, and 70,000 acres were in sugarcane. The completion of the Tavera dam in 1972 is expected to bring irrigation to about 93,000 acres of formerly unirrigated land in the Yaque del Norte Valley, south of Santiago, in the foothills of the Cordillera Central (see ch. 2; Energy, Mining, and Petroleum, this ch.). A water law permits the state to receive a percentage of irrigated land as compensation. Such land is used for agrarian reform purposes.

Most farmers without access to irrigation systems plant their crops according to precipitation cycles. Some, however, plant in dry periods in the hope that rain will fall out of season and provide them with income ahead of their neighbors. In rural terminology such farmers are called adventurers.

AGRICULTURAL PRODUCTION

Crops

Sugarcane is the backbone of the economy, providing most of the employment and foreign exchange as well as generating other economic activity. It was introduced by Christopher Columbus on the occasion of his second voyage near what is now Puerto Plata. Significant production, however, did not commence until the 1870s, when Cuban emigrants established the first large mills. Production rose even more rapidly during the 1950s as a result of the Trujillo regime's search for additional foreign exchange but fell during the early 1960s after the death of the former president. It started to pick up again in the late 1960s and early 1970s. In 1971 production rose steeply because of excellent climatic conditions (see table 6). Production in 1972 was estimated to have been the largest ever recorded.

The country's climate and soils are favorable to sugarcane cultivation, particularly in the southeast, and the sugar content of the cane is high. The yield is usually between 10 and 12 percent of the volume of cane cut, depending upon the area of the country and the condition of the equipment in the mills. Sugarcane is raised on sixteen large estates, which usually account for 75 to 80 percent of total production. About

Table 6. Agricultural Production of the Dominican Republic, Selected Years, 1966–71.
(in thousand metric tons)

Crop	1966	1969	1970	1971
Sugar	896.0	946.0	984.0	1,246.9
Plantains	n.a.	486.3	580.0	n.a.
Milk	255.0	264.0	283.0	n.a.
Bananas	240.0	267.0	275.0	n.a.
Rice	178.0	195.0	210.0	205.0
Yuca	152.8	165.0	170.0	184.0
Sweet potatoes	77.4	84.0	87.0	n.a.
Peanuts	51.0	73.0	71.0	82.4*
Tomatoes	34.5	36.1	52.0	n.a.
Corn	43.0	43.0	45.0	47.0
Coffee	44.5	43.5	42.0	33.0
Cacao	30.5	30.0	39.0	27.0
Beef and veal	25.0	32.0	32.0	n.a.
Beans	35.0	32.0	25.0	28.0
Peas	21.2	23.0	25.0	n.a.
White potatoes	18.1	22.7	23.0	n.a.
Tobacco	20.5	21.0	21.6	24.4
Onions	17.9	17.0	10.0	n.a.
Pork	9.0	10.0	11.0	n.a.
Cucumbers	n.a.	2.2	5.0	n.a.
Garlic	4.1	3.5	4.0	n.a.

n.a.—not available.
*Estimated.

3,200 small independent growers called *colonos*, loosely organized in the Association of Independent Sugar Growers, supply the balance to the mills owned by the large estates. Some of the mills depend on the small grower for as much as 40 percent of their supplies of cane, whereas other mills make only minimal purchases and produce almost all of their needs themselves.

Twelve of the sugarcane plantations belong to the government-owned State Sugar Council. The sugar council was formed to operate the sugarcane properties expropriated from the Trujillo family, and its mills account for three-fifths of the entire sugar output. Because of a lack of new investment and modernization, its land and equipment deteriorated during the early 1960s, but improvements were made in the latter part of the decade and in the early 1970s. A profit-sharing scheme whereby 40 percent of the net profits is distributed to sugar council employees also helped stimulate improvements and production.

One estate and related mill, La Romana, owned by a United States company, Gulf and Western Americas Corporation, conducts the largest single sugar operation in the republic, accounting for between 25 and 33 percent of total annual production. The remaining three estates and mills belong to one Dominican family, the Vicini family, who were pioneers in the industry.

In the Dominican Republic sugarcane can be planted between March and November, but because the original root structure sprouts new shoots annually—although with decreasing yields—only about 15 percent of the cane is replanted every year. New plantings are made from cane cuttings rather than from seeds, and between fourteen and eighteen months elapse before the new plantings are ready for harvest. Only twelve months are required for succeeding shoots to be ready. The harvest season begins in December and lasts into mid-summer.

Cane-cutting is done with machetes and is extremely arduous. Despite the chronic national unemployment situation, not enough Dominican workers are available during the peak of the harvest season, and large numbers of Haitian fieldhands are employed annually. Many of these remain in the Dominican Republic illegally after the harvest ends, and this has been a continuing source of friction between the two countries (see ch. 7; ch. 2).

Coffee, the second most important export crop, was first introduced on the island in 1715. There are over 93,000 coffee farms, most of them very small, as evidenced by the fact that a total of only 207,000 acres were planted in coffee trees in the late 1960s. During harvesttime, however, the coffee crop provides employment for about 350,000 persons. Most of the coffee farms are located on rolling or steep terrain between 1,000 and 3,000 feet in three major growing areas: the mountain slopes all along the Cibao Valley, the southeastern portion of the Cordillera Central between the towns of Baní and San José de Ocoa, and the northeastern slopes of the mountains south of Barahona (see ch. 2).

Dominican coffee is a variety of arabica, the world's most popular type, and is reportedly of good quality, although, for a number of reasons, the yield is low. About 90 percent of the trees in the late 1960s were between twenty-five and seventy-five years old. Tree density per acre is lower than in most other coffee-growing countries. Cultivation practices are traditional; almost no fertilizer, herbicides, or pesticides are used by most farmers. A few thousand farmers, however, who belong to coffee cooperatives, have received technical advice on how to lower costs and increase yields. The coffee cooperatives have also helped market their members' crops.

The country is ranked as one of the world's leading producers of cacao—usually the third leading export crop. It is raised on more than 50,000 farms and is sometimes interspersed with coffee trees. Most of the harvest comes from small farms in the Cibao Valley between the towns of Moca and San Francisco de Macorís, from farms in the Yuna River valley, and from the humid coastal plain near the towns of Miches and Sabana de la Mar. The cacao trees, like the coffee trees, tend to be overage; in 1969 the majority were over sixty years old. Despite the lack of fertilizers, fungicides, and herbicides, the trees are hardy and relatively free of disease and pests.

Rice is the principal crop for domestic consumption, and acreage and production have been increasing steadily since the end of World War II. Production has been stimulated by a price guaranteed by the government, by better seeds and techniques, and by increased use of irrigation, particularly in the western portion of the Cibao Valley and in the Yuna River valley. Production has increased to the point where government officials in 1972 were predicting possible rice exports in the future.

Tobacco culture provides a livelihood for about 20,000 families, mainly in Santiago and Puerto Plata provinces, where the soil and climate are well suited for tobacco production. Most of the tobacco grown is black and is of two grades. One is a high-quality leaf called *olor*, raised mainly for export for cigarmaking; this is planted in seedbeds and then set out in well-tended rows. The other is a low-quality leaf called *criollo*, planted by seed broadcast and used principally for cigarettes. Some blond tobacco is grown but not enough to meet domestic needs; although one cigarette company has been subsidizing its production, most blond tobacco is imported from the United States.

In response to the growing awareness of tobacco's potential, the government in 1962 created the Tobacco Institute, which operates a tobacco experimental farm and provides technical assistance to growers. Because of the institute's success and the increased use of insecticides, herbicides, and fertilizers by farmers, tobacco yields have been rising rapidly.

Corn, a crop native to the country, is raised to some extent on a majority of the farms, although the principal area is near Luperón in Puerto Plata Province. Consumption of corn is rising steadily as it is being used increasingly as an animal feed grain. Irrigation and better techniques have been helping to increase the yield.

Red beans are the most common bean grown and are nutritionally of great importance to the rural population. They are found either as an intertilled crop on poor land or as a single crop on the best lands. Few farmers use improved seeds; most save their best beans for use as seed. Although yields vary considerably among farms and regions, the yield per acre on some farms is the highest in the hemisphere. Climatic conditions limit production, and imports are required in most years.

For many years the government has desired self-sufficiency in vegetable oils. Housewives have relied mainly on imported soybean oil. Coconut oil is the second most important cooking oil, and the country has more than 1.2 million coconut palm trees under cultivation. Peanut production has been increasing more rapidly than coconut production, however, and peanut oil may eventually become the primary cooking oil. Peanuts have become an important crop for many farmers. A peanut oil factory, which is partly government owned, supplies seeds, insecticides, and other equipment to farmers at cost and guarantees to purchase the entire crop at a fixed price. If the farmer delivers the crop to any one of seven warehouses owned by the factory, he receives a higher price than the guaranteed price.

A number of root crops are grown throughout the country. Yuca, known also as manioc or cassava, is one of the basic elements in the rural diet and is raised on most subsistence farms. It is high in starch content and low in nutritional value. Sweet potatoes are also widely grown. White potatoes are produced in limited quantities in the higher altitudes. Taro, known in the Dominican Republic as *yautia,* is also raised.

A nontraditional crop that is growing in popularity is grain sorghum. It is an alternative animal feed and, although its price fluctuates in relation to the corn crop, more and more farmers are planting it. Another expanding crop is pigeon peas, used domestically and exported, both fresh and canned, to Puerto Rico. There is some vegetable fiber production, particularly cotton, henequen, and sisal. Cotton production, which is small, is stimulated by the tax exemption for imports of any equipment used in cotton production. Sisal and henequen are grown on the poorest land and may be harvested four times a year for twenty years before replanting. Despite low world prices for sisal and henequen, their ability to grow on arid land with large continual harvests provide an incentive for the poorest peasants.

Numerous other crops, mainly fruits and vegetables ranging from tropical to temperate, are grown in varying quantities. Bananas and plantains are grown mainly in the northwest. Plantains are part of the basic rural diet and are raised as a subsistence crop and also for sale to those rural persons who do not grow them. Bananas are produced by numerous small growers, many of whom are receiving government help in improving the quality of the crop. Carrots, radishes, lettuce, cabbage, string beans, tomatoes, scallions, garlic, and onions are grown intensively under irrigation in the Constanza valley.

Livestock

Conditions are advantageous for animal husbandry. The mild climate permits year-round pasturing without protection from the weather, and natural grazing areas are extensive. In fact, livestock raising was the most important economic activity from the colonial period until the beginning of the twentieth century, when sugarcane production surged ahead. During the years of the French and Haitian occupations (1795-1844) the Dominican Republic supplied the entire island with meat, and in rural areas the rancher held the dominant social role over other agriculturists.

The basic difficulty of the cattle industry is the lack of a balanced diet for the livestock. Concentrates with added protein are required, and until the mid-1960s few ranchers were interested in making the needed investment. Because of poor nutrition and partly because of poor practices, most herds have low calving rates, high mortality, and slow weight gains. Those few ranchers who follow proper husbandry methods and who utilize modern technical knowledge have high production levels. Fortunately, the country is free from foot-and-mouth disease, and the only disease generally experienced is brucellosis, which can be treated with vaccines.

The cattle population was estimated at 1.1 million head in 1970, a very slow increase from the 1 million head in 1960. About 35 percent of the total herds are classified as dairy cattle, 30 percent are listed as beef cattle, 10 percent are considered draft animals, and the balance are mixed-purpose animals. A large percentage, perhaps 75 percent, are descended from the cattle introduced by the first Spanish colonists and are smaller in size and produce less milk and beef than do improved breeds. There are a number of pure and crossbreeds, which thrive. A new crossbreed is called the Romana Red, developed by the La Romana sugar estate, which also owns 138,000 acres of pastureland. The Romana Red is recognized as being an excellent draft animal that can also supply beef.

About 5,000 farms are devoted exclusively to livestock raising; and another 5,000, to mixed pursuits of livestock and crops. In addition, most farmers possess a few head of cattle as well as other animals. The biggest herds are found on the sugar plantations, which require large numbers of draft animals for transportation of sugarcane from the fields to the mills or railheads. In addition to the La Romana pastures, the sugar council has almost 150,000 acres in pasturage for its beef and work animals.

Most of the milk from the dairy herds is used to make cheese. Fluid milk consumption is limited, and there is only one pasteurizing plant in the country. Most of the milk for direct consumption is taken to market early in the morning immediately after milking.

Pork is an important source of meat. Only a handful of farms are devoted solely to commercial hog-raising; however, almost every farmer keeps a few such animals. The greatest number of hogs are found in the Cibao Valley near Santiago. Hogs are fed nuts from the royal palm tree, which are rich in fat and protein, but they also forage for edible refuse. Hog cholera and internal parasites take a toll of the animals because of a shortage of veterinarian services and a reluctance of most farmers to vaccinate.

Goats are kept on subsistence farms and by poorer residents on the outskirts of cities. The goats forage for themselves and provide a source of meat and milk. Sheep herds are small and are used mainly for meat rather than for wool because the subtropical climate prevents the development of a good-quality fleece animal. Good-quality sheep require much shade and water. Poultry raising reached a level of national self-sufficiency in the late 1960s; because of the high cost of feed, however, most flocks were cut back in 1970, and large quantities of poultry meat were imported until the flocks could be increased to their former level.

Fishing and Forestry

Fishing is not an important industry despite the extensive coastline and known fishing areas. All fishing craft are small, and of 3,700 registered fishermen in 1968 only 360 had motor-equipped boats. All persons and craft engaged primarily in fishing require licenses and must report the size of their catches. The reported volume of fish caught annually from 1968 through 1970 was about 5,000 tons. Catches by several thousand part-time fishermen, however, probably went unreported.

The most important fishing area is in the Samaná Bay, where mackerel, red snapper, kingfish, and shrimp are caught. Bonito and tarpon are found off the southern coast and have attracted the attention of tourists as game fish. Alligators are hunted in the Yuna River.

In late 1972 there was no forestry industry. Because of indiscriminate cutting by commercial interests and landless farmers and loss of large areas of timber by fires, the felling of trees was prohibited in 1967, and all sawmill activity ceased, forest management and reforestation were placed under the armed forces, and tree felling was made a crime. Nevertheless, many farmers, hoping to escape notice by the authorities, continued to clear land by cutting trees. United Nations experts were asked to help formulate a controlled development plan and undertake an inventory of remaining forest resources. It was hoped that by the mid-1970s cutting operations could resume. Before the prohibition there were seventy-five sawmills in the country, and domestic production met demand; since then, all wood and wood products have been imported.

MANUFACTURING AND CONSTRUCTION

The food and beverage industry accounts for the largest percentage of industrial workers and value of production. Food processing, including sugar refining, accounted for half of all production by value in the late 1960s. Beverages accounted for almost 12 percent, and tobacco, about 7 percent.

Manufacturing comprises a relatively small group of establishments, some of which are state owned. In 1970 there were an estimated 2,400 manufacturing enterprises with a total work force of about 110,000 persons. Under the country's business laws, however, the definition of manufacturing is so comprehensive that any entity making or transforming anything, such as a small neighborhood baker, is included. A 1968 estimate that there were 1,200 industrial establishments probably was more nearly correct. Well over 400 firms in the 1968 survey were located in the constitutional political entity called the National District, 175 firms were in Santiago, and the rest were fairly well scattered throughout the nation.

191

In 1972 there were sixteen sugar mills, twelve of which were owned by the government. Their grinding capacity ranged from 500 tons per day to 15,000 tons daily, and some operate as much as 200 days of the year. Over 75,000 persons are employed in the sugar industry, but some of those counted may not be doing industrial work as such. In addition to the raw sugar, the mills produce molasses, used extensively in the production of domestic rum; bagasse, the crushed cane from which the sugar has been extracted, used for fuel for the mills; and furfural, a chemical byproduct used in making synthetic rubber, pharmaceuticals, and nylon.

Nonsugar food and beverage establishments numbered almost 800 in 1972 and employed about 10,000 persons. These establishments included small rice, corn, and wheat mills, coffee depulping units; chocolate-processing plants; confectioners; meat and meat products plants; fruit and vegetable processors; and ice and ice cream plants. Eight fairly large firms canned food products, and one engaged in frozen-food preparation. The largest firm, with 600 employees, was the Dominican Industrial Society, the prime producer of edible oils and animal feeds and fodder. The 1,600 employees in the beverage industry were the highest paid employees in all industry. The government-owned Dominican National Brewery supplied the country's entire needs and also made soft drinks jointly with another company. About two dozen other firms produced wines and rums.

In 1972 about 4,000 persons were employed in the textile and clothing industries. Many garments are homemade from store-purchased cloth or custom made by tailors. Domestic shoemakers are able to supply the market for low- and medium-priced shoes, but high-grade footwear, as well as factory-made clothing, is usually imported.

One large company manufactures a wide variety of paper and cardboard products. Wood and cork items, including furniture, are produced by numerous small establishments. The chemical industry is fairly well developed. The National Glass Industry, a large firm, specializes in bottles and jars, tableware, plates, and novelties. The metal products industries consist of numerous establishments of limited size. Most important are eight foundries using imported pig iron and domestic scrap.

Many farm families engage in handicraft or small-scale processing activities to supplement their incomes. Some of the more important cottage products include cigars, lime, charcoal, brooms, beeswax, honey, brown or pan sugar, crates, strawhats, cassava starch, coffee-pickers' shoulder sacks, and palm leaves for thatching. Charcoal and lime are usually made by landless peasants in the more arid regions of the country. Handicrafts for tourists are of minor significance; the more popular are home-fashioned needlework, sisal handbags, and mahogany trays and other carved wood items.

There is only one shipyard company, the government-owned Dominican Naval Shipyard, which has facilities in several places for both civilian and military small ship repairing and construction. It is also equipped to produce steel bridges and buildings in addition to naval craft.

The construction industry consists of four major firms and many smaller ones employing more than 20,000 construction workers. The larger firms occasionally form consortia for extensive projects such as dams. During the Trujillo era there was a great deal of construction activity, notably in public works. Since the mid-1960s the construction boom has been stimulated by two new dams, a nickel-processing complex, new housing construction, and the relocation of many firms to the suburbs of Santo Domingo.

Two cement plants, one government owned, produce almost at capacity. An earthquake in September 1971 seriously damaged the government plant and necessitated heavy imports.

ENERGY, MINING, AND PETROLEUM

Until 1972 the mining industry was small, confined to the extraction of bauxite, limestone, salt, gypsum, building stone, and small quantities of iron ore. Fewer than 3,000 workers were employed in the entire industry. A major ferronickel extraction and processing operation started in 1972 however, was expected to employ 1,200 workers and generate US$10 million to US$14 million in foreign exchange earnings annually.

The ferronickel project was undertaken by the Falconbridge Dominicana company, owned by two United States and Canadian firms, the Dominican government, and several private United States and Canadian citizens. The nickel deposits are located near the town of Bonao in the center of the country and contain sufficient known reserves for at least twenty-five years at the planned extraction rate. The investment required to initiate production was nearly RD$200 million, making it the largest single investment project in the country's history.

Until the initiation of the nickel project, bauxite was the most important mineral exploited. Extracted by the Alcoa Exploration Company at the rate of more than 1 million tons annually, it accounted for about 80 percent of all mineral activity. Most of the bauxite comes from an area about twenty miles inland on the southern slopes of the Sierra de Baoruco. The future prospects for bauxite mining appear limited because of the decreasing quality of the known reserves.

Extensive gypsum and salt deposits occur close together about twenty-four miles west of Barahona in the Neiba Valley. Reserves include nearly 1 million tons of almost pure gypsum and an estimated 250 million tons of salt. The largest salt deposit is known as Salt Mountain and is believed to be the largest in the world; it is a ten-mile-long chunk of solid salt. Salt is also recovered from sea water in ponds at Puerto Hermoso on the coast between Santo Domingo and Barahona.

Substantial quantities of granite and marble and other building stone are also mined in the Barahona area. Very high grade marble is mined near Samaná. Travertine and onyx are other ornamental stones of some importance. Amber is found, but a 1969 law restricts its exploitation to the state.

Gold, the first metal to be exploited, has been panned since early colonial days in highland streams in several parts of the country. Gold, as well as silver, may once again become important after 1974, when a gold-silver mine is to be put into operation by the New York and Honduras Rosario Mining Company. Production will commence after a 4,000-ton-per-day processing plant is built. The mine is located near the town of Pueblo Viejo and is known to contain zinc and copper in addition to gold and silver.

No petroleum or natural gas had been found as of late 1972, although three companies have been exploring since 1969. A 30,000-barrel-per-day refinery near the town of Nigua, southwest of Santo Domingo, was scheduled for completion by 1973. Owned jointly by the Shell Oil Company and the Dominican Republic government, the refinery was to process imported crude oil and cut down on costly imports for all domestic needs for gasoline, kerosine, aviation fuel, and fuel oil.

Electrical energy consumption increased at an annual average rate of about 12 percent during the 1960s, and capacity barely kept up with demand until the early 1970s, when two major hydroelectrical projects permitted the government to extend the distribution of electricity to smaller rural communities not previously supplied. The Dominican Electricity Corporation (Corporación Dominicana de Electricidad—CDE), owned by the government, is responsible for the production, distribution, and sale of all electrical energy except that generated by the sugar mills and the Falconbridge nickel plant for their own use. By the end of 1972 CDE's total installed capacity was about 310,000 kilowatts, that of Falconbridge was 198,000 kilowatts, and that of the sugar mills was about 50,000 kilowatts.

The two new projects of the CDE are multipurpose: electricity, potable water, and irrigation. The Tavera dam was completed in late 1972; and the Valdesia project was scheduled for completion in mid-1973. The Valdesia dam on the Nizao River, fifty miles from Santo Domingo, should add an additional 50,000 kilowatts to CDE's capacity. The CDE had about 200,000 customers in 1970, 88 percent of whom were residential. They accounted, however, for only 60 percent of total electricity consumption, and the smaller number of commercial, industrial, and municipal users accounted for the balance. All electric current is sixty-cycle alternating current (AC) with 110–220 voltage.

FOREIGN TRADE

The outbreak of civil strife in 1965 interrupted an expansion of foreign trade that had been in progress for several decades, and it was not until 1969 that the 1964 level was surpassed and steady growth continued (see table 7). Export trade, an important factor in the national economy, is based largely on labor-intensive agricultural production and directly or indirectly constitutes the source of livelihood for a great many people. The foreign exchange earned by exports plays a vital role in the financing of capital goods imports needed for further development of the economy. Also, because the government participates directly in the sugar trade, export earnings are a substantial source of governmental revenue.

The government's trade policy as of 1972 was designed to correct what was becoming a chronic balance-of-payments deficit, to decrease reliance on imported foodstuffs, and to foster industrial growth by restricting certain imports (see ch. 9). As of mid-1972 over eighty categories of goods could not be imported, and many others were subject to import quotas. An export promotion center, the Dominican Center for the Promotion of Exportations, established in 1971, trains commercial attachés, makes foreign market surveys, provides information on export opportunities, and offers credit insurance for exporters. Two industrial free zones have been created whereby firms may locate and receive numerous tax benefits if they produce for export. One is the Herrera Free Zone, located on the outskirts of Santo Domingo and sponsored by the government's Industrial Development Corporation. The other is the La Romana Free Zone, located on the grounds of the La Romana sugar estate. It is jointly owned by the government and the Gulf and Western Americas Corporation.

The country is a member of the General Agreement on Tariffs and Trade (GATT) but, as of 1972, was not a member of any regional economic group, although since 1969 it has expressed an interest in joining either the Central American Common Market or the Caribbean Free Trade Association (CARIFTA). The Central American Common Market is composed of five Central American countries, and CARIFTA is composed of English-speaking countries of the Caribbean. In mid-1972 a special committee began studies to determine if it would be in the country's best interests to join CARIFTA. One objective of the country's foreign policy is to have closer economic ties with Puerto Rico, and a bilateral agricultural and livestock agreement was signed in 1967.

Sugar is the prime export, and the country is the world's third-leading sugar exporter after Cuba and the Philippines. During the 1960s and early 1970s raw sugar accounted for between 48 and 54 percent of total exports annually. Sugar byproducts, such as molasses and furfural, provided an additional 5 percent of total exports. Since few sales are made in the world market, the outlook for continued high sugar exports depends mainly upon the United States sugar import quota. A goal of the government is to obtain an ever-increasing share of the United

Table 7. Foreign Trade of the Dominican Republic, 1964–71.
(in million pesos)*

	1964	1965	1966	1967	1968	1969	1970	1971
EXPORTS:								
Agricultural Products:								
Raw sugar	86.1	57.6	70.3	81.8	82.8	88.1	n.a.	n.a.
Sugar byproducts	9.5	7.2	10.2	12.4	9.0	10.8	n.a.	n.a.
Coffee	30.5	21.2	21.0	17.0	17.9	21.3	n.a.	n.a.
Cacao and byproducts	16.4	7.4	11.1	12.0	13.9	20.1	n.a.	n.a.
Tobacco	14.9	9.5	6.6	10.5	11.3	12.7	n.a.	n.a.
Meat	0.0	0.0	0.0	0.3	3.6	4.0	n.a.	n.a.
Others	11.0	8.8	5.5	7.1	7.6	6.9	n.a.	n.a.
Subtotal	168.4	111.7	124.7	141.1	146.1	163.9	n.a.	n.a.
Mineral Products:								
Bauxite	8.9	11.7	10.3	12.8	12.6	14.6	n.a.	n.a.
Others	0.8	0.4	0.6	0.6	1.2	1.0	n.a.	n.a.
Subtotal	9.7	12.1	10.9	13.4	13.8	15.6	n.a.	n.a.
Manufactures	1.3	1.7	1.1	1.8	3.6	4.5	n.a.	n.a.
TOTAL	179.4	125.5	136.7	156.3	163.5	184.0	217.0	243.0
IMPORTS:								
Consumer Goods:								
Food	38.5	20.9	32.8	33.7	39.8	n.a.	n.a.	n.a.
Clothing	15.2	4.8	11.1	10.6	10.4	n.a.	n.a.	n.a.
Automobiles	12.8	3.8	9.5	7.7	9.4	n.a.	n.a.	n.a.
Others	39.0	45.9	21.0	23.9	26.1	n.a.	n.a.	n.a.
Subtotal	105.5	75.4	74.4	75.9	85.7	n.a.	n.a.	n.a.
Intermediate Goods:								
Fuels	13.3	8.6	13.6	12.8	13.4	n.a.	n.a.	n.a.
Chemicals	10.2	6.1	10.5	10.7	12.0	n.a.	n.a.	n.a.
Fertilizers	4.1	1.5	2.6	4.6	8.0	n.a.	n.a.	n.a.
Others	12.0	5.6	12.9	13.6	16.0	n.a.	n.a.	n.a.
Subtotal	39.6	21.8	39.6	41.7	49.4	n.a.	n.a.	n.a.
Investment Goods:								
Construction materials	5.2	1.4	4.7	5.7	5.0	n.a.	n.a.	n.a.
Transport equipment	2.4	0.6	2.0	2.5	n.a.	n.a.	n.a.	n.a.
Others	49.7	21.8	39.8	48.9	n.a.	n.a.	n.a.	n.a.
Subtotal	57.3	23.8	46.5	57.1	61.7	n.a.	n.a.	n.a.
TOTAL	202.4	121.0	160.5	174.7	196.8	217.0	270.5	311.0

n.a.—not available.
*1 peso equals US$1.

States sugar quota by demonstrating the industry's capability. Under the United States Sugar Act of 1971, the Dominican Republic received an initial basic quota of 634,874 short tons, the second-highest foreign share for the 1972–74 period. Earlier it had the fourth-highest basic quota, although it did receive annual supplemental allotments to cover deficits from unmet quotas of other countries. In some years the supplemental quotas had been considerable and had made the country the second-leading foreign sugar supplier to the United States.

Coffee is usually the second-leading export. Because of stagnating production and increased domestic consumption, exports fell during most of the 1960s until the 1969–70 period, when they stabilized at 12 percent of total exports. The country is a member of the International Coffee Organization, which sets export quotas for member nations. The Dominican quota had been cut several times when the country could not meet its annual quota. For 1972 it received a quota of 360,000 bags.

Cacao is generally the third-leading export, with between 8 and 11 percent of the total. Cacao and its byproducts, cocoa butter and chocolate, are subject to serious price fluctuations on the world market. There is a demand for Dominican cacao, however.

Bauxite exports have been stabilized at about 8 percent of the total and are not likely to increase. The first ferronickel exports began in 1972, and the product was anticipated to become a major export in 1973 or 1974, after full operation of the processing plant had begun.

Tobacco, accounting for 6 to 7 percent of the total, was the only other export product of any significance. Other exports were of minor significance. Meat, fruits, and vegetables were exported, along with some manufactures.

In 1972 detailed import statistics were not available beyond 1968, but consumer goods had been the leading category through 1968 and presumably continued to be so. Food was the predominant consumer item, accounting for about 20 percent of the import bill annually. Wheat, which cannot be produced economically in the country, heads the food list, followed by dairy products, fish, edible oils, and cereals.

Capital, or investment, goods have accounted for nearly 30 percent of annual imports and are headed by miscellaneous machinery and equipment, followed by construction materials. Intermediate goods, which include fuels, chemicals, and fertilizers, make up the balance of imports.

The United States is the country's leading trading partner. Throughout most of the 1960s and through 1970, the United States took as much as 85 percent of annual Dominican exports and supplied more than half of all imports. More than 60 percent of the total exports to the United States is represented by sugar; coffee, cacao, tobacco, meat, and bauxite make up all but a small portion of the remainder. There is a long list of imports from the United States, most importantly foodstuffs, nonelectrical machinery, chemicals, and transport equipment. Most machinery and equipment is of United States origin. Spare parts can be ordered from distributors in Puerto Rico.

Belgium and Spain rotated as the second and third most important export market, each with 3 or 4 percent of the total annually. Belgium took most of the furfural exports. All other countries took the small balance of exports. Imports are received from a wider number of countries. Japan followed the United States as the leading supplier (13 percent in 1970) and in turn was followed by the Federal Republic of Germany (West Germany), Canada, the Netherlands Antilles, and Italy. Other important suppliers are Venezuela, the United Kingdom, Norway, and Spain.

DOMESTIC TRADE AND SERVICES

Domestic businesses are organized in one of several ways. The most common is the sole proprietorship. Others are the general and limited partnership and the limited liability joint stock company, which is similar to a United States corporation. Various symbols are used to denote a limited liability joint stock company: C. por A. or C. x A. (Compañía por Acciones), C.A. (Compañía Anónima), or S.A. (Sociedad Anónima).

Most importers are also wholesalers, and some are retailers. Some importers and wholesalers handle only a single product; others carry a wide range of merchandise. Many, if not most, of the domestic manufacturers are also wholesale or retail merchants maintaining their own outlet stores. Almost 70 percent of all wholesale trade is carried on in the National District, and more than half of the wholesale trade is in food and beverages (see ch. 7).

Retail trade is conducted by a few large establishments and a myriad of small units operated by the owners with the help of their families and perhaps one or two employees. The smallest merchants usually market one or a few commodities. A considerable number of the best stores are operated by Lebanese and Syrians and by some Spanish families. A great many restaurants are operated by Chinese.

Most stores are specialty shops, but some sell textiles, clothing, and notions. About two dozen supermarkets existed in Santo Domingo in 1972, as against only one in 1965; these sell better quality fresh foods than are found in other food outlets. Most urban housewives shop at a variety of retail outlets. The most popular is the *colmado*, a general food store smaller than a supermarket, which handles canned goods, cleaning materials, food staples such as rice and flour, condiments, beverages, and kerosine. General food stores smaller than the *colmado* and carrying more limited supplies are called variously *pulperías* or *bodegas*. Both are roughly equivalent to the North American corner grocery store, but the *pulpería* is usually in the poorer residential districts.

Butchers obtain their supplies from municipally owned slaughterhouses, which may also franchise their operations to private persons. Public markets, although an important part of urban life, are not utilized as frequently by housewives as in most other Latin American countries. There are three public markets in Santo Domingo; all contain mixed retail-wholesale operations. Vendors rent stalls, usually the same ones daily, from the municipality. Street peddlers, almost all women, carry a wide line of food and other household necessities from door to door or station themselves on street corners.

Rural trade is essentially that of moving goods from farm to market; few rural persons are financially able to make purchases of more than basic necessities. Because of inadequate access roads, a great many countrypeople have difficulty in getting their produce to market and little choice of the marketplace. All means of transportation are used: feet, burros, trucks, jeeps, buses, pushcarts, bicycles, and motorcars. Most farmers sell to wholesalers or other intermediaries. Few do their own retailing, except for those farmers located near smaller towns where they can utilize the facilities of the local markets. Market day in the smaller towns is a social occasion; the market area is loud with the voices of vendors hawking their wares, arguments of bargainers, braying of burros, and voices of friends greeting one another.

The independent trucker also plays an important role in farm marketing. He may call upon individual farmers or make stops at prearranged collection points where farmers bring their produce. Some farmers with trucks of their own contract to haul their neighbors' produce. The truckers may either resell to wholesalers or retailers or set up a stall in an urban marketplace.

As of 1972 price supports were maintained by the government for four crops: rice, corn, beans, and grain sorghum. The Institute of Price Stabilization, created in 1970, guarantees to purchase and market price-supported products if the farmer cannot obtain more than the fixed price. The institute also is the sole importer of vegetable oils and allocates the supplies to the processors at a fixed price in proportion to the percentage of domestic oilseeds they have purchased.

In addition to price guarantees to farmers for certain crops, the Directorate General of Price Control sets maximum retail prices for articles of prime necessity. For produce and other items not under guarantee or price control, there is a considerable difference between the payment received by the producer and the price ultimately paid by the consumer. Almost no items are quoted by price in newspapers or on the radio, and prices are obtained only by visits to the outlet or by word-of-mouth.

Rural sales of manufactured and processed goods are handled by the crossroads or village general store or the few specialty shops found in some small towns. The state sugar estates maintain stores on the plantations where the employees can purchase food and a large variety of goods at prices under those charged by private retail establishments.

The lack of rural storage facilities affects farmer, middleman, and retailer. Some wholesalers use rundown, vermin-infested buildings near central markets as food storehouses. The Agricultural Bank operates several warehouses where either food or general merchandise may be deposited. Warehousing facilities at most seaports are considered adequate, and little damage or spoilage occurs there.

The metric system is the official weights and measures standard, but United States units, such as pounds, ounces, inches, feet, gallons, and miles, are frequently used and generally understood. A few old Spanish measures are in use, the most common being the land measure called the *tarea*, equivalent to about 0.16 acres. Quality standards are generally lacking and are applied only in the export of coffee, cacao, tobacco, and a few other products.

The service element in the economy was becoming important during the 1960s and early 1970s. Whereas many of the rural persons migrating to urban areas often could find employment only in service-type jobs, such as servant, gardener, and janitor, those persons with an urban background or some education and training found employment in transportation, storage, communications, utilities, or tourism.

In 1972 the country had a dial telephone network, which provided adequate service between all major cities and towns and direct connection to the United States via underwater cable to the United States Virgin Islands and also via Puerto Rico. The main telephone company was the Dominican Telephone Company, but there were also a few small municipal systems, and the sugar estates maintained their own installations. About 48,000 telephones were in use in 1971, about half of which were located in Santo Domingo.

Domestic telegraph service is provided by the government, but the service is generally voice communicated by telephone from one station to another. A radio telegraph service is also operated by the government to New York City and to some Central American cities. Most international telegraph service is provided by Radio Corporation of America Communications and All America Cables.

The tourist trade was virtually nonexistent until after World War II, and an unattractive political image abroad has kept the country's full tourist potential from being achieved. As of 1972, however, the government was determined to make tourism a major economic activity to counteract the spending of Dominican tourists abroad. In 1970 some 61,500 persons visiting the Dominican Republic spent about RD$15 million, whereas Dominicans spent nearly RD$28 million abroad that year.

As an inducement to invest in tourist facilities the government grants private investors up to 100-percent income tax exemption for ten years, allows exemption from import duties and other taxes, guarantees profit remittance in any currency, and may help finance the project. In 1971 the government opened several tourist offices in the United States in the hope of stimulating visits by middle income tourists and persons seeking to obtain easy divorces under the country's liberal divorce law of 1971. Divorces are permitted after a seven-day residence without regard to nationality. The government also owns several hotels but usually leases them to private interests to manage. Most hotel prices are lower than in other parts of the Caribbean, and the government hopes that this will be another selling point for stimulating tourism.

TRANSPORTATION

The country has a rapidly developing transportation system; although the road network is considered to be among the best in Latin America, it is still inadequate. Before the twentieth century and almost up to the 1930s, surface transportation in parts of the country depended on mule and horse trails, and there had been little improvement since the colonial era. The first major bridge in the country was not built until 1880, and the Río Haina near the capital was not spanned until 1912. Trips between the north and south were lengthy and hazardous, and most travelers actually prepared their last testament before departing. Mule drivers, who were proud of their reliability and honesty, were the prime means used to convey messages, money, and goods from one locality to another. In addition to the horse and mule trails, trade between Santo Domingo and other parts of the country was carried on by small canoes and sailboats, which moved merchandise to and from the capital.

Under Trujillo the surface transportation situation was corrected by an energetic building program—one that was continued by the succeeding governments. As of 1972 there were about 6,600 miles of roads, about one-fifth of which were paved. The base of the highway system is a network of three primary roads emanating from Santo Domingo. The main road is called the Duarte Highway and runs from Santo Domingo through Santiago de los Caballeros to Monte Cristi in the extreme northwest. The Mella Highway runs eastward through San Pedro de Macorís, then north and eastward again through El Seibo to Higüey. The third primary road, the Sánchez Highway, runs westward from Santo Domingo paralleling the coast most of the way up to Azua, whence it runs northwest to Elías Piña at the Haitian border (see fig. 4).

Numerous secondary roads, some paved, branched off from the main highways and provided a good grid of connecting roads, although access roads from the secondary roads to rural communities were generally lacking. About 60,000 vehicles were registered in the country in 1970, of which 22,000 were trucks and buses. Taxi and bus companies were privately owned, numerous, and small. Buses offered irregular service and were overcrowded and poorly maintained, but they provided the main means of intercity passenger connections. Some taxis, called *públicos*, operated like buses and attempted to keep schedules between cities.

Railroads were of little consequence. A government-owned line, the Dominican United Railroads (Ferrocarriles Unidos Dominicanos), ran

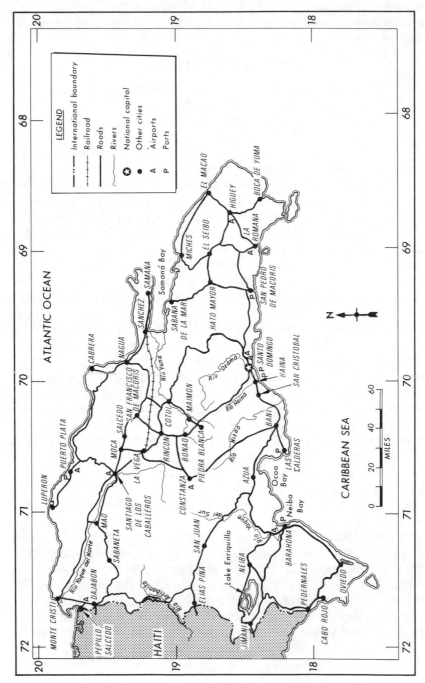

Figure 4. Transportation System of the Dominican Republic, 1972.

from La Vega in the Cibao Valley to the port of Sánchez in Samaná Bay, but it did not carry passengers. Most of the sugar estates operated railroads to carry the sugarcane from the fields to the mills. Together these estate lines totaled approximately 800 miles, but they carried nothing except sugarcane.

Domestic air transportation facilities were limited. There were only about fifteen airfields in the country; the Santo Domingo International Airport, "Airport of the Americas," could accommodate jumbo jets. One airline, the Dominican Aviation Company (Compañía Dominicana de Aviación—CDA), provided passenger and freight service between major cities; it flew three times weekly between Santo Domingo and Santiago. CDA also provided service to Haiti, New York, Miami, Curaçao, and Puerto Rico. Another Dominican airline, Quisqueya Airlines (Aerovías Quisqueya), was engaged only in international service, flying daily to Puerto Rico, Miami, Curaçao, and Haiti. Among foreign airlines offering international service were Air France, Alitalia, Viasa, Iberia, Lufthansa, and Pan American World Airways.

Great effort has been expended on developing the country's seaports. A seagoing dredge was purchased in 1972 to deepen the harbors at several ports and maintain clearance for large ships at others. Santo Domingo is the principal seaport, accounting for 96 percent of total imports by value and 40 percent of total exports. Because sugar is the major export and is shipped from ports nearest the sugar mills, export trade is more widely dispersed. Puerto Plata is the second-leading port, handling 12 percent of exports and 2 percent of imports. Other important ports are Barahona, Boca Chica, Haina, and San Pedro de Macorís.

The country has about 30,000 registered tons of shipping. The privately owned Dominican Steamship Line (Flota Mercante Dominicana C. por A.) is the largest shipping line, with nearly 8,000 tons. The line provides regular sailings between the country and the United States and has fully containerized freight service. Nearly thirty other shipping lines, mostly foreign, also provide service; some of them utilize containers and trailers to move cargo between destinations.

Coastal shipping, although limited, is dominated by the Dominican Steamship Line. Few rivers are navigable except for small craft. Only the Nizao River carries any appreciable amount of inland traffic.

SECTION IV. NATIONAL SECURITY

CHAPTER 10

NATIONAL DEFENSE AND PUBLIC ORDER

In 1972 the Dominican Republic's security forces consisted of the army, navy, and air force, numbering about 19,500 officers and men, and the national police with a strength of about 9,000. These forces had the capability of maintaining internal security and public order and, although the national police was called upon several times during the year to quell riots and control demonstrations, the armed forces were not needed to provide emergency support. The most significant roles of both the armed forces and the police have been those of participants in the competition for political power, or of praetorian guards protecting a government against its opponents. As a legacy of the Trujillo era, both institutions have generally been viewed by the people as agents of repression.

The small size of the security forces did not adversely affect the country's labor force, but the percentage of the annual budget allocated to the armed forces and police was higher than those of most Latin American nations. A large portion of the armed forces annual budget was spent on pay and allowances and on pensions and life insurance for its active and retired members, reflecting the desire of the government to minimize any dissatisfaction on the part of the military personnel.

Units of the army and of the national police were assigned to areas throughout the entire country, with the mission of ensuring the maintenance of public order, and the system of centralized control from Santo Domingo facilitated the dispatching of reinforcements to any needed area. The political system was highly polarized, as the urban poor, many of the educated young, and other groups who supported Juan Bosch and the Dominican Revolutionary Party (Partido Revolucionario Dominicano—PRD) in the early 1960s confronted the more conservative peasants and the spokesmen of entrenched economic interests. These conflicting interests, which had led to civil war in 1965, were still apparent in 1972, and social tension had been manifest throughout the period in a high incidence of political violence. This situation, however, had represented no immediate threat to the government.

NATIONAL DEFENSE

Organization and Control of the Armed Forces

The Constitution of 1966 describes the armed forces as "essentially obedient and nonpolitical and without the right to deliberate. The purpose of their creation is to defend the independence and integrity of the republic, to maintain public order, and to uphold the Constitution and the laws." This description, however, represents an ideal rather than a reality. In fact, the military has always been inextricably involved in domestic political competition (see ch. 7).

The chain of command extended from the president of the republic to the secretary of state for armed forces, and from that individual to the deputy secretaries of state for the army, navy, and air force. The secretary and the three deputies were all military personnel. The secretary, usually an army major general, was appointed by the president; and the deputies, by the secretary with the approval of the president.

Each of the deputies controlled his branch of the service through a chief of staff and a general staff. Each general staff had five principal sections—personnel, intelligence, operations, logistics, and public relations. In addition, there was an administrative judge advocate section for each branch to handle military legal matters. Except in cases of emergency the actual operational control over the three branches of the armed forces was exercised by the chiefs of staff— an army major general, an air force brigadier general, and a navy commodore.

The army had a strength of about 12,000. Its principal combat units were three infantry regimental-type organizations called brigades. Each had from three to five battalions and support units. One brigade was stationed in the Santo Domingo area, and the others were assigned to the northern, southern, and western sectors into which the country was divided for defense purposes. Army forces stationed in the interior were divided into small units—each assigned to a town or village, some of company size and some as small as a squad of eight men commanded by a corporal. In addition to its infantry, the army had field artillery, antiaircraft, and armor units; and support troops consisted of engineer, signal, transportation, medical, and quartermaster units.

The navy had a strength of about 4,000 officers and men. The fleet consisted of one destroyer, three frigates, five corvettes, two minesweepers, three patrol vessels, and twenty-four auxiliary craft. The larger vessels were constructed in Great Britain, Canada, and the United States. The navy operated administratively through three naval zones whose headquarters were in Santo Domingo, Puerto Plata in the north, and Barahona in the south.

The air force had about 3,500 officers and men. Its headquarters was at San Isidro airfield outside Santo Domingo. There were two operational squadrons, each with twenty aircraft. The air force was organized into four commands, all based at San Isidro. These were the Air Command, the Maintenance Command, the Combat Support Command, and the Base Defense Command. The Air Command was responsible for the direction of all flight operations; the Maintenance Command was charged with maintenance and repair responsibilities. The Combat Support Command controlled all base services. The Base Defense Command provided security for the bases, aircraft, and infrastructure and had infantry-type units and parachute squadrons.

The Defense Establishment and the National Economy

Compared with seventeen other Latin American countries, the Dominican Republic, in the 1960s, spent a higher than average proportion of its annual budget for defense. Its expenditures in that period averaged 16.8 percent, contrasted with 11.5 percent for the others. For the Dominican Republic the highest year was 1961 with 22.8 percent, and the lowest was 1969 with 11.7 percent, a total that was still a little more than the average for all the countries. Defense expenditures as a percentage of the gross national product (GNP) for the same number of years averaged 3.2 percent, while the average for all the countries was 1.8 percent.

The United States government has provided the Dominican Republic with military assistance on a continuing basis. From 1946 through 1971 grants totaling US$28.3 million were made in support of the defense establishment of the Dominican Republic. The strength of the armed forces did not adversely affect the country's economy because it represented only 0.5 percent of the total population and 2.5 percent of the total labor force.

Training

The Dominican army, navy, and air force each maintains academies for the training of officer candidates. Conditions for acceptance include a high school diploma and satisfactory completion of a strict physical examination. The army and air force cadets spend the first two years of the four-year course together, after which the air cadets go to the air force school for special training. The naval academy course was also four years. About fifty students graduate yearly from each of the academies.

The army conducted a six-month course for infantry captains and lieutenants—a basic course designed to prepare the students to function efficiently as company commanders. The army also conducted a command-and-staff orientation course for infantry captains, majors, and lieutenant colonels. This was of ten months' duration and was designed to prepare senior infantry officers for battalion and higher command. The armed forces had no other advanced courses in the country, but according to the Military Assistance Agreement of 1962, the United States offered courses on the command and general staff level to Dominican army, navy, and air force officers, both in the United States and in the Panama Canal Zone.

Enlisted men received basic training in training centers established by each of the three branches of the armed forces. The army had a training center near Santo Domingo; the navy operated a training center at Las Calderas, fifty miles west of the capital; and the air force maintained a training center at San Isidro air force base. Subsequent training was performed in army and air force units and on naval vessels.

A training school for all branches was the Vocational School of the Armed Forces and National Police, established in the city of Baní in Peravia Province. The objective of the school was to give manual training to members of the armed forces so that they could be of greater service to the country and society after they finished their tour of active duty and returned to civilian life. Workshops offered instruction in carpentry, electromechanics, and metalworking.

Logistics

In 1972 the nation's industrial base was not developed to the extent necessary for the provision of all items of equipment for the armed forces. Items such as small arms and ammunition, uniforms, subsistence, housekeeping supplies, and personal equipment could be obtained from domestic sources; but all major items, such as ships, aircraft, tanks, artillery, and communications and heavy equipment, had to be obtained from abroad, principally from United States sources. The arsenal constructed at San Cristóbal, fifteen miles west of Santo Domingo, was capable of producing carbines, machine guns, mortars, and antitank guns, as well as rebuilding heavier weapons and manufacturing munitions.

Supply functions were carried out at service level by the Support Command for the army, by the Combat Support Command for the air force, and by a special staff section at headquarters for the navy. There was no central stock-control agency, and supplies were issued directly to the services from domestic suppliers or from the ports of entry.

Military Justice

There was an integrated judicial system for courts martial for officers, and each branch of the armed services conducted courts for minor offenses. The administration of military justice was governed by two documents authorized by the Organic Law of the Armed Forces. These were the Code of Justice of the Armed Forces (Código de Justicia de las Fuerzas Armadas), covering criminal acts, and the Military Disciplinary Regulations (Reglamento Militar Disciplinario), dealing with deliberate disobedience or infractions that adversely affected the morale, discipline, honor, or reputation of the armed forces.

The Code of Justice of the Armed Forces was arranged in three books covering the organization, composition, and jurisdiction of military courts; specific offenses and the punishments for each; and provisions concerning the application of the code. The Military Disciplinary Regulations were contained in a book of eight chapters that outlined the concept of military discipline; stated the standards of obedience expected of all military personnel; specified the punishments that could be imposed, and differentiated between acts that were simple disciplinary violations and those that contravened the Code of Justice of the Armed Forces.

All persons subject to military jurisdiction who committed a crime or misdemeanor while performing military duty were accountable to military authorities, but a military individual not on official business who committed a criminal act in the civilian domain was liable to prosecution by civilian authorities. The system of military justice began to function when information concerning an alleged infraction was brought to the commander in whose jurisdiction it occurred. He was required to launch an investigation by referring the matter to the judicial authorities (military or civil) and, based on their report, to determine future action. If a court-martial was convened, the proceedings were identical to those followed in civilian courts. Decisions were reached by a majority rather than unanimous vote and were announced publicly as soon as the court reconvened. Sessions were public except in cases where national security was at stake and, even then, verdicts and sentences were made public through publication in official orders.

Civic Action

The armed forces were active in carrying out civic action programs. Units of the armed forces dug wells, constructed roads, built houses and schools, provided educational items and sports equipment to rural schools, and gave sewing machines and other needed household articles to poor families. The air force flew medicines, doctors, and food to disaster areas damaged by hurricanes and flew injured personnel to hospitals. One of the army's principal civic action responsibilities was to supervise the functioning of the Directorate General of Forestry, which had been removed from the jurisdiction of the secretary of state for agriculture and placed under the secretary of state for the armed forces. The objective was to regulate the conservation and restoration of the forests, protect against forest fires, and to instill in the minds of the population the very serious need for forest conservation.

Morale Factors

All members of the armed forces who have served honorably for specified lengths of time are entitled to retire with a pension. Officers in certain categories, such as air force pilots and navy engineers may retire after twenty years of service; others must complete thirty years for the maximum pension. Retirement is usually voluntary and granted upon request to individuals who are able to qualify, but it is mandatory for those who become physically or mentally disabled or who reach statutory retirement age. Retirement age differs according to rank but is the same for all branches. General officers must retire at age seventy, colonels and lieutenant colonels at sixty, majors and captains at fifty-five, and all other personnel at fifty. The mandatory retirement age is lowered for personnel required to perform hazardous duty such as flying.

Personnel retiring after the completion of thirty years of active duty receive a pension based on 75 percent of their active duty pay at time of retirement. Those retired for disability receive 50 percent of their base pay if they have completed at least ten years of active duty.

For the benefit of commissioned and enlisted personnel and their dependents, a number of commissaries and exchanges have been established, usually at the locations of the permanent stations of larger units. An armed forces officers' club has been established in Santo Domingo, and each of the three branches has its own officers' and enlisted men's clubs.

Although Article 9 of the Constitution of 1966 authorizes conscription, this has not been necessary because vacancies in the lowest rank have been easily filled by volunteer enlistments.

Uniforms and Insignia

Uniforms of the members of the Dominican Republic armed forces are similar to those of their United States counterparts. Enlisted personnel of the army and air force wear a cotton fatigue uniform for normal duty, whereas navy personnel wear dungarees for work and a middy blouse and trousers when off duty. Army and air force officers also wear the fatigue uniform in the field but, for garrison duty, army personnel wear tan tropical worsted or cotton shirts and trousers and air force officers wear light-blue shirts with blue trousers. Naval officers have blue, white, and tan uniforms. Each branch of the armed forces has a distinctive uniform for dress and formal occasions.

Rank insignia for army and air force company-grade officers is one, two, or three silver laurel leaves. For field-grade officers a metallic national coat of arms is worn with one, two, or three silver laurel leaves. Brigadier and major generals wear the coat of arms with one or two silver stars. Navy rank insignia from ensign to captain are similar to those of the United States Navy. Commodores and rear admirals have gold shoulder boards on which is a metallic-colored device representing the country's coat of arms, with one or two silver stars. Enlisted personnel, regardless of branch, wear a series of olive-green chevrons on the upper sleeve. Officer rank insignia is indicated on shoulder boards worn with the blouse.

Awards and Decorations

The government authorized seven awards for meritorious service. In order of precedence these were: the Order of Merit Duarte, Sánchez, and Mella; the Order of Christopher Columbus; the Captain General Santana Military Order; and the four orders of military, naval, air, and police merit. The first two decorations could be awarded to both military and civilian personnel, both native and foreign, for distinguished service rendered the Dominican Republic. The others were awarded only to military personnel. Each of the three branches of the armed forces had its own awards for marksmanship, and personnel who qualified as aircraft pilots or parachutists were awarded wings on which appropriate devices designating their specialties were superimposed.

PUBLIC ORDER

The National Police

In 1972 the director general of the National Police was an army general officer who was directly subordinate to the secretary of state for interior and police. The director general was assisted by a deputy director and by the two secretariats: internal affairs and planning and public relations. The administration and operations of the National Police were carried out by three sections, each headed by an assistant director general. These were Administration and Support, Police Operations, and Special Operations.

The Administration and Support section supervised personnel, police education and training, and finances and was responsible for the logistical system, communications, transportation, records, and the police laboratory. The operations section carried out normal police operations, including patrolling, traffic control, criminal investigation, rural operations, and prevention of civil disturbances. Patrolling was accomplished on foot and on horseback; by bicycle, motorcycle, and automobile; and for special patrols, by airplanes and boats. The Special Operations section supervised the training and operations of the secret police.

Four regional directors were directly subordinate to the assistant director general of police operations. The headquarters of the regions were Santo Domingo, San Pedro de Macorís, Santiago de los Caballeros, and Barahona. Officially, the principal police functions were the protection of life and property, the maintenance of public order, and enforcement of the country's laws and regulations, but the most significant activity has been cooperation with the armed forces in upholding or opposing governments.

The National Police were active in civic action projects. During 1970 about 3,700 persons were given medical assistance and police dental technicians accomplished over 5,000 extractions. During the same year the police established nine schools in various cities and made donations of composition books, pencils, sewing machines, athletic equipment, and other items to poor people throughout the republic.

Following the violence in the country in 1965, the government requested United States assistance in rebuilding the National Police so that it could assume its proper role in the effort for national reconstruction. A new academy was established, at which members of the police had received training in eight different courses by 1972. Training was given to police stationed in the rural areas, and for the first time a police telecommunication network was developed, and an urban and rural patrol capacity was organized. Between 1961 and 1969 the country received funds from the United States for police training, including training both within the country and in the United States. Between December 1963 and July 1972, National Police students were graduated from courses at the International Police Academy in Washington, D.C.

The public image of the police has improved since the suppression in late 1971 of the terrorist group known as La Banda (The Band). The group, which was responsible for the violence against many opponents of the government of Joaquín Balaguer, was generally believed to have been sponsored by the police. General Neit Nivar Seijas, who was appointed chief of the national police in mid-1971, is credited with having suppressed La Banda.

Internal Security

During 1972 there was no obvious threat to the government of the Dominican Republic from either internal or external sources. Internal unrest requiring police action consisted primarily of teacher strikes for higher pay, followed by student riots for the preservation of university autonomy and open admissions, and unlawful occupation of land by peasants impatient with the slow pace of agrarian reform (see ch. 6). Two years before, the United States Air Force attaché had been kidnapped by members of the leftist Dominican People's Movement (Movimiento Popular Dominicano—MPD) and released after the government had in exchange released twenty political prisoners.

Student riots resulting in police action with some casualties on both sides occurred in November 1969 and March 1971. In September 1972 university students demonstrated outside the university in Santo Domingo, demanding an increase in the national budget allotment for the university. Police using tear gas quelled the disturbance. During November a teachers' strike occurred, which spread all over the country. Student demonstrations in support of the teachers resulted in clashes with the police. In December the Dominican Teachers Association rejected the government's directive to end the strike and refused the president's alternate proposals. Thousands of students at the Autonomous University of Santo Domingo clashed with the police, who were forced to use tear gas.

In March and October 1972 large numbers of peasants illegally occupied privately owned land in the rural areas of Duarte and El Seibo provinces. The government ordered them ejected by the police. This was followed by student demonstrations in favor of the peasants (see ch. 7).

Communist party organizations in the Dominican Republic were fragmented because of widespread dissension over leadership and policy questions. In 1970 it was estimated that the total strength of the several parties was about 1,100 individuals, affiliated with four different organizations. These were the Dominican Communist Party (Partido Comunista Dominicano—PCD), recognized by the Soviet Union; the MPD, which was pro-Chinese; the Revolutionary Movement of 14 June (Movimiento Revolucionario 14 de Junio—MR14J), sympathetic toward Fidel Castro of Cuba; and the Communist Party of the Dominican Republic (Partido Comunista de la República Dominicana—PCRD), which defined itself as a Marxist-Leninist party "created in conformity with the thoughts of Mao Tse-tung."

The parties were organized between 1942 and 1965, and their sources of support included universities, secondary schools, and labor organizations. Direct participation by Communist parties in elections has usually been proscribed by law, but such parties have continued to be active in organizing opposition to rightist groups and supporting programs aimed at redistribution of wealth. The government under President Balaguer, however, by the use of the National Police and the armed forces, has considerably increased its efforts to curb communist activities such as terrorizing and promoting violence and strikes. In 1970 a new law introduced a thirty-year prison term at forced labor for acts of terrorism.

In January 1972 some 4,000 police and troops closed in on a small band of MPD members who had been accused of a bank robbery and of plotting a terrorist campaign. Using small arms, bazookas, and mortars in an all-day battle, the authorities killed four members of the group, which was believed to have numbered only six to begin with. The incident sparked student demonstrations in Santo Domingo, and the government responded by closing all schools and surrounding the Autonomous University of Santo Domingo with police. At the end of 1972 none of the fragmented communist party organizations offered any apparent threat to the stability of the government.

The Penal Code

After the country achieved its independence the French criminal code was adopted in 1845. A Spanish translation was adopted in 1867, and the present code was adopted by the government of President Ulises Heureaux in 1884. The code is composed of four books containing 487 articles. The first book deals with the penalties for crimes; the second, with persons who are punishable, excusable, or liable; the third, with various felonies and misdemeanors and their punishment; and the fourth, with infractions of police regulations and their penalties.

The death penalty, which according to law was executed by a firing squad, was abolished in 1924, and a maximum penalty of thirty years' imprisonment at forced labor was substituted. Punishments included imprisonment with forced labor, imprisonment, jail for specified periods, detention, loss of civil rights, and fines.

The penalty for homicide or for taking up arms against the Dominican Republic is thirty years at forced labor. The same penalty prevails for arson. That for rape is imprisonment for six to ten years; for robbery, imprisonment for five to twenty years. The punishment for crimes against the constitution, such as using force or violence to prevent a citizen from executing his duties, is imprisonment for six months to two years. The same sentence is awarded for any offense committed in public against the chief of state and for premeditated assault resulting in wounds. In the latter case if the victim dies, the sentence is changed to imprisonment for ten to twenty years at forced labor.

In 1970 both houses of Congress passed a law proposed by President Balaguer that denied provisional freedom under bail in criminal cases. The objective was to free Dominican Republic justice from legal mechanisms and allow it to accomplish its mission more quickly. The Congress also passed laws making thirty years in prison the sentence for those convicted for skyjacking, kidnapping, and terrorist acts.

The Prison System

The national penitentiary is La Victoria Penitentiary in Santo Domingo. Twenty other cities have prisons or other facilities where individuals may be confined. Of these, those with the largest annual inmate population are: Santiago, La Vega, Puerto Plata, San Francisco de Macorís, Moca, San Juan, San Cristóbal, and Barahona. All individuals sentenced to more than two years in prison are transferred to La Victoria Penitentiary. This penitentiary has shoe, carpenter, tailor, and barber shops and other facilities to teach the convicts a useful trade. Prisoners who take advantage of these facilities are paid for their labor. Thirty percent of the money earned goes to the family of the prisoner; 25 percent is contributed for the maintenance of prison equipment; 25 percent is placed in the prisoner's personal fund; and 20 percent goes to the prisoner for his personal needs.

Incidence of Crime

The government does not publish statistics indicating the incidence of crime throughout the country, but the daily newspapers of Santo Domingo report criminal acts with great regularity.

Types of crimes enumerated in the newspapers included murder, rape, robbery (including bank robbery), assault with deadly weapons, abduction, fraud, counterfeiting, and suicide. Robbery appeared to be the most often occurring crime, followed by assault and murder. According to the newspaper reports, rural crime is only a small proportion of the total.

BIBLIOGRAPHY

Section I. Social

Alba, Victor. "Why Bosch Fell," *New Republic*, CIL, October 12, 1963, 12-14.

Alexander, Robert J. *Today's Latin America*. (2d ed., rev.) Garden City: Doubleday, (Anchor Books), 1968.

Alliance for Progress. Comisión de la Alianza para el Progreso en la República Dominicana. *Jornadas de la Alianza para el Progreso de la República Dominicana*. Santo Domingo: 1963.

Alonso, Isidoro. *La Iglesia en América Latina*. Bogotá: Oficina Internacional de Investigaciones Sociales de FERES, 1964.

Alonso, Isidoro, and Garrido, Ginés. *La Iglesia en América Central y el Caribe*. Madrid: Centro de Información y Sociología de la Obra de Cooperación Sacerdotal Hispanoamericana, 1962.

American Geographical Society. *Focus: The Dominican Republic*, by John P. Augelli, XV, May 1965.

Andrade, Manuel J. *Folk-Lore from the Dominican Republic*. (Memoirs of the American Folk-Lore Society, XXIII, 1930.) New York: Stechert, 1930.

Antonini, Gustavo A. "El Noroeste de la República Dominicana: Un Modelo morfogenético de la evolución del paisaje," *Revista de Ciencias Sociales* [Río Piedras, Puerto Rico], XIV, No. 2, 1970, 247-259.

———. "Processes and Patterns of Landscape Change in the Línea Noroeste, Dominican Republic." (Ph.D. dissertation.) New York: Columbia University, Department of Geography, 1968.

Arredondo, Alberto, and Campos, Carlos M. "Las condiciones de vida del campesino dominicano," *Panoramas* [Mexico City], IV, July-August 1963, 81-111.

Atkins, G. Pope, and Wilson, Larman C. *The United States and the Trujillo Regime*. New Brunswick: Rutgers University Press, 1972.

Bailey, Norman A. *Latin America in World Politics*. New York: Walker, 1967.

Balaguer, Joaquín. *Dominican Reality: Biographical Sketch of a Country and a Regime*. (Trans., Mary Gilland.) Mexico City: 1949.

———. *Historia de la literatura dominicana*. Ciudad Trujillo: Editorial Librería Dominicana, 1958.

Bateman, Robert H. "Basic Data on the Economy of the Dominican Republic," *Overseas Business Reports* (OBR 68-114.) Washington: GPO, U.S. Department of Commerce, Bureau of International Commerce, December 1968.

Blakemore, Harold. *Latin America.* London: Oxford University Press, 1966.

Bosch, Juan. *Composición Social Dominicana.* Santo Domingo: Colección Pensamiento y Cultura, 1970.

————. "La formación de las clases sociales en la República Dominicana." Pages 130-147 in Instituto de Estudios Sindicales, Sociales y Cooperativos, *Anuario de Sociología de los Pueblos Ibéricos.* Madrid: Gráficos Aragón, 1967.

Burks, David D., and Santana, Arturo. "History: West Indies." Pages 187-199 in Henry E. Adams (ed.), *Handbook of Latin American Studies,* XXXII: Humanities. Gainesville: University of Florida Press, 1970.

Butland, Gilbert J. *Latin America: A Regional Study.* New York: John Wiley and Sons, 1966.

Calderón, Luis; Calle, Arturo; and Sorselaer, Jaime. *Problemas de urbanización en América Latina.* (Estudios Sociológicos Latino-Americanos, No. 13.) Bogotá: Centro de Investigaciones Sociales, Departamento Socio-Económico, 1963.

Campos, Carlos, and Arredondo, Alberto. "Las condiciones de vida del campesino dominicano," *Panoramas* [Mexico City], IV, July–August 1963, 81-110.

Castedo, Leopoldo. *A History of Latin American Art and Architecture from Pre-Columbian Times to the Present.* (Trans. and ed., Phyllis Freeman.) New York: Praeger, 1969.

Clark, Rev. James A. *The Church and the Crisis in the Dominican Republic.* Westminster, Maryland: Newman Press, 1967.

Coleman, William J. *Latin American Catholicism: A Self-Evaluation.* (World Horizon Reports, No. 23.) New York: Maryknoll Publications, 1958.

Considine, John J. (ed.) *The Church in the New Latin America.* Notre Dame: Fides, 1964.

Cooper, Page. *Sambumbia: A Discovery of the Dominican Republic, the Modern Hispaniola.* New York: Caribbean Library, 1947.

Coopersmith, J. M. *Music and Musicians of the Dominican Republic.* (Pan American Union Music Series, No. 15.) Washington: PAU, 1949.

Cordero Michel, Emilio. *La Revolución Haitiana y Santo Domingo.* Santo Domingo: Editora Nacional, 1968.

Corten, André. "Como vive la otra mitad de Santo Domingo," *Caribbean Studies* [Río Piedras, Puerto Rico], IV, No. 4, January 1965, 3-20.

Corten, André, and Corten, Andrée. *Cambio Social en Santo Domingo.* Mexico City: Editora Cultura, for University of Puerto Rico, Instituto de Estudios del Caribe, 1968.

Coulthard, G. R. "Parallelisms and Divergencies Between 'Négritude' and 'Indigenismo'," *Caribbean Studies* [Río Piedras, Puerto Rico], VIII, No. 1, April 1968, 31–55.

————. *Race and Colour in Caribbean Literature.* London: Oxford University Press, 1962.

Crassweller, Robert D. *The Caribbean Community: Changing Societies and U.S. Policy.* New York: Praeger, for the Council on Foreign Relations, 1972.

————. *Trujillo—The Life and Times of a Caribbean Dictator.* New York: Macmillan, 1966.

Crawford, W. Rex. *A Century of Latin American Thought.* Cambridge: Harvard University Press, 1944.

Damboriena, Prudencio. *El Protestantismo en América Latina,* I and II. Bogotá: Oficina Internacional de Investigaciones Sociales de FERES, 1962.

Davis, Harold Eugene. *History of Latin America.* New York: Ronald Press, 1968.

————. *Latin American Thought.* Baton Rouge: Louisiana State University Press, 1972.

Davis, Kingsley. *World Urbanization, 1950–1970,* I: Basic Data for Cities, Countries and Regions. (Population Monograph No. 4.) Berkeley: University of California, Institute of International Studies, 1969.

de Galindez, Jesús. *La Era de Trujillo.* Santiago de Chile: Editorial del Pacífico, 1956.

Demographic Yearbook, 1970. New York: United Nations, 1971.

de Nolasco, Flérida. *La Música en Santo Domingo y otros ensayos.* Ciudad Trujillo: Imprenta Montalvo, 1939.

————. *La Poesía folklórica en Santo Domingo.* Santiago: Editorial el Diario, 1949.

————. *Rutas de nuestra poesía.* Ciudad Trujillo: Imprenta Dominicana, 1953.

Dominican Republic. Banco Central de la República Dominicana. *Estudio Sobre Presupuestos Familiares,* I: Ingreso y gasto de las familias en la ciudad de Santo Domingo, 1969. Santo Domingo: 1971.

Dominican Republic. Secretariado Técnico de la Presidencia. *Estadística demográfica de la República Dominicana,* XXVI. Santo Domingo: 1970.

Dominican Republic. Secretariado Técnico de la Presidencia. Oficina Nacional de Estadística. *República Dominicana en Cifras, 1970,* V. Santo Domingo: 1970.

Dominican Republic. Secretariado Técnico de la Presidencia. Oficina Nacional de Planificación. *Primero plan nacional de desarrollo, versión preliminar para discusión.* Santo Domingo: 1970.

Dominican Republic Election Factbook: June 1, 1966. (Ed., Henry Wells.) Washington: Institute for the Comparative Study of Political Systems, Operations and Policy Research, 1966.

"The Dominican Republic: The Land Columbus Loved Welcomes Tourists and Investors," *New York Times*, Section 14, Advertising Supplement, October 3, 1971, entire section.

"Dominicans Plan Culture Expo for Year's End," *Times of the Americas*, XIV, No. 20, May 20, 1970, 6.

Dorner, Peter, et al. "Agrarian Reform in the Dominican Republic: The Views of Four Consultants." (Land Tenure Center, No. 42.) Madison: University of Wisconsin, LTC, December 1967 (mimeo.).

Dorta-Duque, Francisco. "La Agricultura dominicana: Algunos observaciones socioeconómicos." West Baden: West Baden College, 1962 (mimeo.).

Draper, Theodore. "Bosch and Communism," *New Leader*, XLVI, October 14, 1963, 9–14.

———. "The Roots of the Dominican Crisis," *New Leader*, XLVIII, May 24, 1965, 3–18.

Editor and Publisher International Year Book. New York: Editor and Publisher, 1971.

Engber, Marjorie. *Caribbean Fiction and Poetry*. New York: Center for Inter-American Relations, 1970.

Espaillat, Arturo R. *Trujillo: The Last Caesar*. Chicago: Henry Regnery, 1964.

Etzioni, Amitai. "U.S. Did the Right Thing in the Wrong Way," *Washington Post*, June 13, 1965.

Fagg, John Edwin. *Cuba, Haiti, and the Dominican Republic*. (Modern Nations in Historical Perspective.) Englewood Cliffs: Prentice-Hall, 1965.

Foreign Broadcast Information Service. *Broadcasting Stations of the World*, Part I: Amplitude Modulation Broadcasting Stations According to Country and City. Washington: GPO, January 1971.

———. *Broadcasting Stations of the World*, Part IV: Television Stations. Washington: GPO, January 1971.

Franco, Franklyn J. *Los negros, los mulatos y la nación dominicana*. Santo Domingo: Editora Nacional, 1970.

Free, Lloyd A. "Attitudes, Hopes and Fears of the Dominican People." Princeton: Princeton University Press, for Institute for International Social Research, 1965 (mimeo.).

Gardiner, C. Harvey. "The Japanese and the Dominican Republic," *Inter-American Economic Affairs*, XXV, No. 3, Winter 1971, 23–38.

Gerassi, John. *The Great Fear in Latin America* (Rev. ed.) New York: Collier Books, 1968.

Goldwert, Marvin. *The Constabulary in the Dominican Republic and Nicaragua: Progeny and Legacy of United States Intervention*. Gainesville: University of Florida Press, 1962.

———. *Dominican Republic: History of American Occupation, 1916–1924*. Gainesville: University of Florida Press, 1962.

Goode, William J. "Illegitimacy, Anomie, and Cultural Penetration," *American Sociological Review*, XXVI, No. 6, December 1961, 910–925.

————. "Illegitimacy in the Caribbean Social Structure," *American Sociological Review*, XXV, No. 1, February 1960, 21-30.

Goodsell, James Nelson. "Balaguer's Dominican Republic," *Current History*, LIII, No. 315, November 1967, 298-302.

Greenbie, Sydney. *Three Island Nations: Cuba, Haiti, Dominican Republic.* New York: Row, Peterson, 1942.

Hall, Gwendolyn Midlo. *Social Control in Slave Plantation Societies.* Baltimore: Johns Hopkins Press, 1971.

Harding, Bertita. *The Land Columbus Loved: The Dominican Republic.* New York: Coward-McCann, 1949.

Haring, Clarence H. *The Spanish Empire in America.* New York: Oxford University Press, 1947.

Harman, Carter, and the Editors of Life. *The West Indies.* (Life World Library.) New York: Time, 1966.

Henríques, Fernando. "Color and Contemporary Society in the Caribbean," *Journal de la Société des Américanistes* [Paris], LVIII, 1969, 207-221.

Henríquez Ureña, Max. *Breve historia del modernismo.* Mexico City, Fondo de Cultura Económica, 1954.

————. *Panorama histórico de la literatura dominicana.* Río de Janeiro: Companhia Brasileira de Artes Gráficas, 1945.

Herring, Hubert. "Scandal of the Caribbean: The Dominican Republic," *Current History*, XXXVIII, March 1960, 140-143, 164.

Hicks, Albert C. *Blood in the Streets: The Life and Rule of Trujillo.* New York: Creative Age Press, 1946.

Hitt, Deborah S., and Wilson, Larman C. *A Selected Bibliography of the Dominican Republic: A Century After the Restoration of Independence.* Washington: The American University, Center for Research in Social Systems, September 1968.

Hoetink, H. "The Dominican Republic in the 19th Century: Some Notes on Stratification, Immigration, and Race." Pages 96-212 in Magnus Morner (ed.), *Race and Class in Latin America.* New York: Columbia University Press, 1970.

————. "Materiales para el estudio de la República Dominicana en la segunda mitad del siglo XIX. Parte II: Cambios en la estructura demográfica y en la distribución geográfica de la población," *Caribbean Studies* [Río Piedras, Puerto Rico], VII, No. 3, October 1967, 3-34.

————. "Materiales para el estudio de la República Dominicana en la segunda mitad del siglo XIX. Parte III: Cambios en la estructura de las communicaciones," *Caribbean Studies* [Río Piedras, Puerto Rico], VIII, No. 3, October 1968, 3-22.

Hoffman, James W. "After Trujillo, Trouble. After Trouble, What?" *Presbyterian Life*, April 1, 1962, 6-15.

————. "Outside the Sugarcane Curtain," *Presbyterian Life*, May 1, 1962, 7-11.

Horowitz, Irving Louis (ed.). *Masses in Latin America.* New York: Oxford University Press, 1970.

Horowitz, Michael M. *Peoples and Cultures of the Caribbean: An Anthropological Reader.* New York: Natural History Press, 1971.

Image of the Dominican Republic. (Supplement to *Américas*, XXIII, No. 9.) Washington: Organization of American States, General Secretariat, September 1971.

Inter-American Development Bank. *Socio-Economic Progress in Latin America. Annual Report, 1971.* Washington: 1972.

————. *Socio-Economic Progress in Latin America: Social Progress Trust Fund, Seventh Annual Report, 1967.* Washington: 1968.

————. *Socio-Economic Progress in Latin America: Social Progress Trust Fund, Ninth Annual Report, 1969.* Washington: 1970.

————. *Socio-Economic Progress in Latin America: Social Progress Trust Fund, Tenth Annual Report, 1970.* Washington: 1971.

International Bank for Reconstruction and Development. Economic Program Department. Socio-Economic Data Division. *World Tables, January 1971.* Washington: IBRD, 1971.

International Labor Organization. International Labor Office. *Labour Force Projections, 1965–1985, Latin America.* Geneva: 1971.

International Yearbook of Education, 1968, XXX. Geneva: United Nations Educational, Scientific and Cultural Organization, 1969.

Introduction to Colonial Art in Latin America. (Colonial Art, I.) Washington: Organization of American States, General Secretariat, n.d.

James, Preston E. *Latin America.* (4th ed.) New York: Odyssey Press, 1969.

Kantor, Harry. *Patterns of Politics and Political Systems in Latin America.* (Rand McNally Political Science Series.) Chicago: Rand McNally, 1969.

Lanning, John Tate. *Academic Culture in the Spanish Colonies.* London: Oxford University Press, 1940.

Larrázabal Blanco, C. *Los negros y la esclavitud en la República Dominicana.* Santo Domingo: J. D. Postigo, 1967.

Logan, Rayford W. *Haiti and the Dominican Republic.* New York: Oxford University Press, 1968.

Lowenthal, Abraham F. *The Dominican Intervention.* Cambridge: Harvard University Press, 1972.

Mallet, Alfredo. "Diversification or Standardisation: Two Trends in Latin American Social Security," *International Labour Review* [Geneva], CI, No. 1, January 1970, 49–83.

Mansbach, Richard W. (ed.) *Dominican Crisis, 1965.* (Interim History— Facts on File.) New York: Facts on File, 1971.

Matilla, Alfredo. "Music Festival in Santo Domingo," *Américas*, XXIV, No. 5, May 1972, 35.

Matthews, Herbert L. *A World in Revolution—A Newspaperman's Memoir.* New York: Charles Scribners Sons, 1971.

Mecham, John Lloyd. *A Survey of United States-Latin American Rela-*

tions. Boston: Houghton Mifflin, 1965.

Menton, Seymour. "Literature: Central America and the Antilles," Pages 370–377 in Henry E. Adams (ed.), *Handbook of Latin American Studies*, XXXII: Humanities. Gainesville: University of Florida Press, 1970.

Milne, Jean. *Fiesta Time in Latin America*. Los Angeles: Ward Ritchie Press, 1965.

Minerals Yearbook, 1969, IV: Area Reports: International. Washington: GPO, U.S. Department of the Interior, Bureau of Mines, 1971.

Mintz, Sidney W. "The Caribbean as a Socio-cultural Area," *Cahiers d'Histoire Mondiale* [Paris], IX, No. 4, 1966, 912–937.

————. "The Question of Caribbean Peasantries," *Caribbean Studies* [Río Piedras, Puerto Rico], I, No. 3, October 1961, 31–34.

Monclus, Miguel Angel. *El Caudillismo en la Republica Dominicana*. (2d ed.) Ciudad Trujillo: Impresora Dominicana, 1948.

Moreno, José A. *Barrio in Arms: Revolution in Santo Domingo*. Pittsburgh: University of Pittsburgh Press, 1970.

Morison, Samuel Eliot. *Admiral of the Ocean Sea—A Life of Christopher Columbus*. Boston: Little, Brown, 1949.

Munro, Dana. *Intervention and Dollar Diplomacy in the Caribbean, 1900–1921*. Princeton: Princeton University Press, 1964.

National Council on Marine Resources and Engineering Development. *Marine Science Activities of the Nations of Latin America*. Washington: GPO, 1968.

Needler, Martin C. (ed.) *Political Systems of Latin America*. (2d ed.) New York: Van Nostrand Reinhold, 1970.

Norvell, Douglass G. "Food Marketing in an Urban Place in the Dominican Republic," *Caribbean Studies* [Río Piedras, Puerto Rico], IX, No. 3, October 1969, 104–110.

Norvell, Douglass G., and Wehrly, James S. "A Rotating Credit Association in the Dominican Republic," *Caribbean Studies* [Río Piedras, Puerto Rico], IX, No. 1, April 1969, 45–52.

Norvell, Douglass G.; Billingsley, Ray V.; and McNeely, John G. "The Internal Food Distribution System and Marketing Channels for Plantains and Tomatoes in the Cibao Valley of the Dominican Republic." College Station: Texas A. and M. University, n.d. (mimeo.).

Organización de las N. U. para la Agricultura y la Alimentación. *Informe sobre el proyecto de asentamientos campesinos en el desarrollo regional de San Juan de la Maguana, R.D.* New York: 1969.

Organización de los Estados Americanos. *Datos Básicos de Población en América Latina*. Washington: 1970.

Organización de los Estados Americanos. Instituto Interamericano de Estadística. *América en cifras, 1965: Situación cultural:* Educación y otros aspectos culturales. Washington: 1967.

————. *América en cifras, 1965: Situación social:* Hogar, habitación, mejoramiento urbano, previsión social, asistencia médica y de salud, y trabajo. Washington: 1967.

Organización de los Estados Americanos. *América en cifras, 1970: Situación cultural:* Educación y otros aspectos culturales. Washington: 1971.

————. *América en cifras, 1970: Situación social:* Hogar, habitación, mejoramiento urbano, previsión social, asistencia médica y de salud, y trabajo. Washington: 1971.

Organization of American States. *Statistical Compendium of the Americas.* Washington: 1971.

Organization of American States. General Secretariat. *Dominican Republic.* (American Republic Series, VIII.) (Rev. ed.) Washington: 1970.

————. *Survey of the Natural Resources of the Dominican Republic,* I. Washington: 1969.

————. *21 Latin American Meals.* (641.5-E-7488.) Washington: n.d.

Ornes, Germán E. *Trujillo: Little Caesar of the Caribbean.* New York: Nelson, 1958.

Ortega, Manuel M. "Population Control Problems in the Dominican Republic." (Paper prepared for delivery at the Thirtieth Annual Meeting of the Society for Applied Anthropology.) Miami: University of Miami, 1971.

Osorio, Lizarazo. *The Illumined Island.* (Trans., James I. Nolan.) Mexico City: 1947.

Pan American Health Organization. *Annual Report of the Director, 1969.* Washington: 1970.

————. *Annual Report of the Director, 1970.* Washington: 1971.

————. *Health Conditions in the Americas, 1965–1968.* Washington: 1970.

Pan American Union. *Dominican Republic.* (American Republic Series, No. 8, rev. ed.) Washington: 1969.

Patin, Enrique. *Observaciones acerca de nuestra psicología popular.* Ciudad Trujillo: Editora Montalvo, 1950.

Pattee, Ricardo. *La República Dominicana.* Madrid: Ediciones Cultura Hispanica, 1967.

Paulino, Aliro, Jr. "Manuel Hernández: 28 años sin cantar en Republica Dominicana," ¡*Ahora!* [Santo Domingo], XI, No. 469, November 6, 1972, 74–79.

Pendle, George. *A History of Latin America.* Baltimore: Penguin Books, 1965.

Pepén, Juan F. *La cruz señala en camino: Influencia de la iglesia en la formación y conservación de la nacionalidad dominicana.* Ciudad Trujillo: Editorial Duarte, 1954.

Pérez Cabral, Pedro Antonio. *La comunidad mulata: El caso sociopolítico de la República Dominicana.* Caracas: Gráfica Americana, 1967.

Picon-Salas, Mariano. *A Cultural History of Spanish America.* (Trans., Irving A. Leonard.) Berkeley: University of California Press, 1962.

Population Reference Bureau. "La fuga de talentos: Un círculo vicioso," *Población* [Bogotá], II, No. 8, 1971, 1.

Porter, Charles O., and Alexander, Robert J. *The Struggle for Democ-*

racy in Latin America. New York: Macmillan, 1961.

Publishers' International Directory. (3d ed.) Munich-Pullach: Verlag Dokumentation, 1967.

Revista dominicana de cultura, I. Ciudad Trujillo: Impresora Dominicana, 1955.

Rippy, J. Fred. Latin America: A Modern History. Ann Arbor: University of Michigan Press, 1968.

Robertson, William S. History of the Latin American Nations. (Rev. ed.) New York: D. Appleton, 1930.

Robinson, Harry. Latin America: A Geographical Survey. New York: Praeger, 1967.

Rodman, Selden. Quisqueya: A History of the Dominican Republic. Seattle: University of Washington Press, 1964.

Rodríguez Demorizi, Emilio. Camino de hostos. Ciudad Trujillo: Imprenta Montalvo, 1939.

———. Riqueza mineral y agrícola de Santo Domingo. (Academia Dominicana de la Historia, XX.) Santo Domingo: Editora del Caribe, 1965.

Rodríguez Demorizi, Silveria R. Salomé Ureña de Henríquez. Buenos Aires: Imprenta López, 1944.

Rotberg, Robert I., and Clague, Christopher K. Haiti: The Politics of Squalor. (A Twentieth Century Fund Study.) Boston: Houghton Mifflin, 1971.

Rouse, Irving. "The Arawak." Pages 507–546 in Julian H. Steward (ed.), Handbook of South American Indians. Washington: Smithsonian Institution, 1948.

Rubin, Vera (ed.). Caribbean Studies: A Symposium. Seattle: University of Washington Press, 1960.

Ruddle, Kenneth, and Hamour, Mukhtar (eds.). Statistical Abstract of Latin America, 1970. Los Angeles: University of California at Los Angeles Press, December 1971.

Saint Elmo, Walter. Santo Domingo: Its Commerce, Shipping, Customs Procedures, Port Facilities, and Other Information. Santo Domingo: Garcia, 1926.

Schoenrich, Otto. Santo Domingo: A Country with a Future. New York: Macmillan, 1918.

Smith, Raymond T. "Culture and Social Structure in the Caribbean: Some Recent Works on Family and Kinship," Comparative Studies in Society and History, VI, No. 1, October 1963, 24–46.

Solien de Gonzalez, Nancie L. Black Carib Household Structure. Seattle: University of Washington Press, 1969.

———. "The Consanguineal Household and Matrifocality," American Anthropologist, LXVII, No. 6, Part I, 1965, 1541–1549.

———. "Social Functions of Carnival in a Dominican City," Southwestern Journal of Anthropology, XXVI, No. 4, Winter 1970, 328–342.

Squirru, Rafael. "Dominican Art: A Growing Tree," Américas, XXI, No. 1, January 1969, 32–37.

Stebbins, Richard P., and Amoia, Alba (eds.). *Political Handbook and Atlas of the World, 1970.* New York: Simon and Schuster, 1970.

Stewart, William. "Creole Languages of the Caribbean." Pages 34-53 in Frank Rice (ed.), *Study of the Role of Second Languages.* Washington: Center for Applied Linguistics, 1962.

Suro, Darío. "Sobre artistas y buhos: La escultura taína," *Américas,* XVIII, April 1966, 21-28.

Szulc, Tad. *Dominican Diary.* New York: Delacorte Press, 1965.

Troncoso de la Concha, Manuel de Jesús. "La clase media en Santo Domingo." Pages 57-67 in Theo. Crevanna (ed.), *Materiales para el estudio de la clase media en América Latina,* VI. Washington: Unión Panamericana, 1951.

Troncoso Sánchez, Pedro. *Aspectos de la cultura dominicana.* Ciudad Trujillo: Secretaría de Estado de Educación y Bellas Artes, 1946.

Trujillo, Flor (As told to Laura Bergquist.) "My Life as Trujillo's Prisoner," *Look,* XXIX, June 29, 1965, 52-71.

Turner, Frederick C. *Catholicism and Political Development in Latin America.* Chapel Hill: University of North Carolina Press, 1971.

Unión Panamericana. *Datos básicos de población en América Latina, 1970.* Washington: 1970.

————. *Poesía popular dominicana.* Ciudad Trujillo: Imprenta de la Nación, 1938.

United Nations. *Compendium of Social Statistics, 1967.* (Series K, No. 3.) New York: 1968.

————. *Statistics on Children and Youth in Latin America: Supplement to Statistical Bulletin for Latin America.* Santiago: 1970.

————. *World Economic Survey, 1969-1970.* New York: 1971.

United Nations. Economic Commission for Latin America. *Social Change and Social Development in Latin America.* New York: 1970.

U.S. Agency for International Development. *Population Program Assistance.* Washington: 1970.

U.S. Department of State. *Background Notes: Dominican Republic.* Washington: October 1970.

————. *Foreign Relations of the United States, 1945—Diplomatic Papers,* IX. (The American Republics.) Washington: GPO, 1969.

U.S. Embassy in Santo Domingo. *Post Report.* Santo Domingo: U.S. Department of State, June 1970.

U.S. Department of Labor. Bureau of Labor Statistics. *Labor Law and Practice in the Dominican Republic.* (BLS Report No. 343.) Washington: GPO, 1968.

U.S. Department of the Army. Walter Reed Army Institute of Research. *Haiti and the Dominican Republic.* (Health Data Publications No. 4.) Washington: 1969.

U.S. Agency for International Development. Bureau for Latin America. Office of Development Programs. *Summary of Economic and Social Indicators in 18 Latin American Countries, 1960-1971.* Washington: June 1972.

U.S. Department of Commerce. Bureau of International Commerce. International Marketing Information Service. *Best U.S. Sales Prospects in the Dominican Republic.* (Country Market Digest, IMIS 69-23.) Washington: GPO, October 1969.

University of California at Los Angeles. Latin American Center. *Statistical Abstract of Latin America, 1970.* Los Angeles: 1971.

Véliz, Claudio. *Latin America and the Caribbean.* New York: Praeger, 1968.

Walker, Stanley. *Journey Toward the Sunlight: A Story of the Dominican Republic and Its People.* New York: Caribbean Library, 1947.

Wechsler, Sally (ed.). *Publisher's World 1968/69.* New York: R. R. Bowker, 1968.

Wedge, Bryant. "The Case Study of Student Political Violence: Brazil 1964, and Dominican Republic 1965," *World Politics,* XXI, No. 2, January 1969, 183-206.

Welles, Sumner. *Naboth's Vineyard: The Dominican Republic 1844-1924.* 2 vols. New York: Payson and Clarke, 1928.

Wells, Henry. "Turmoil in the Dominican Republic," *Current History,* L, No. 293, January 1966, 14-20.

White, John W. *The Land Columbus Loved.* Ciudad Trujillo: Editora Montalvo, 1945.

Wiarda, Howard J. "The Changing Political Orientation of the Catholic Church in the Dominican Republic," *Journal of Church and State,* VII, No. 2, Spring 1965, 238-254.

———. "Dictatorship and Development: The Trujillo Regime and Its Implications," *Social Science Quarterly,* XLVIII, No. 4, March 1968, 548-557.

———. *The Dominican Republic: Nation in Transition.* New York: Praeger, 1969.

———. "From Fragmentation to Disintegration: The Social and Political Effects of the Dominican Revolution," *América Latina* [Río de Janeiro], X, No. 2, June 1967, 55-71.

Wiarda, Howard J. (ed.) *Dominican Republic Election Factbook, June 1, 1966.* Washington: Operations and Policy Research, 1966.

Wilgus, A. Curtis. *Historical Atlas of Latin America.* New York: Cooper Square, 1967.

Wilgus, A. Curtis (ed.). *The Caribbean: Contemporary Trends.* (School of Inter-American Studies [Series I] III.) Gainesville: University of Florida Press, 1953.

Wilgus, A. Curtis, and D'Eca, Raul. *Latin American History—A Summary of Political, Economic, Social, and Cultural Events from 1492 to the Present.* New York: Barnes and Noble, 1967 (5th printing; 5th ed. first published 1963.).

Williams, Eric. *From Columbus to Castro: The History of the Caribbean, 1492-1969.* New York: Harper and Row, 1970.

Williams, Mary Wilhelmine; Bartlett, Ruhl J.; and Miller, Russell E. *The People and Politics of Latin America.* (4th ed.) Boston: Ginn, 1958.

227

Wilson, Larman C. "The Foreign Policies of the Dominican Republic and Haiti." Chapter IX in Harold E. Davis and Larman C. Wilson (eds.), *Latin American Foreign Policies: An Analysis.* Washington: The American University, School of International Service, 1971 (Unpublished manuscript.).

Wilson, Peter J. "Caribbean Crews: Peer Groups and Male Society," *Caribbean Studies* [Río Piedras, Puerto Rico], X, No. 4, January 1971, 18–34.

Wiltbank, M. Jay, Jr. *Agricultural Crop Production and Development—Dominican Republic.* Santo Domingo: International Development Services, for Instituto Agrario Dominicano, 1962.

Worcester, Donald E., and Schaffer, Wendell G. *The Growth and Culture of Latin America.* New York: Oxford University Press, 1956.

World and its Peoples: The Caribbean Region and Central America. New York: Greystone Press, 1969.

World Health Organization. *Third Report on the World Health Situation, 1961–64.* Geneva: 1967.

Worldmark Encyclopedia of the Nations, III: Americas. (Ed., Louis Barron.) New York: Harper and Row, Worldmark Press, 1967.

The World of Learning, 1971–72, I. London: Europa Publications, 1972.

World Survey of Education, IV: Higher Education. New York: United Nations Educational, Scientific and Cultural Organization Publications Center, 1966.

World Survey of Education, V: Educational Policy, Legislation, and Administration. Paris: UNESCO Publications, 1971.

Yearbook of Labour Statistics, 1971. Geneva: International Labor Organization, International Labor Office, 1971.

de Zendegui, Guillermo (ed.). "Image of the Dominican Republic," *Américas,* XXIII, No. 9, September 1971, s1–s24.

Section II. Political

Alba, Victor. *Politics and the Labor Movement in Latin America.* Stanford: Stanford University Press, 1968.

Atkins, G. Pope, and Wilson, Larman C. *The United States and the Trujillo Regime.* New Brunswick: Rutgers University Press, 1972.

Bailey, Norman A. *Latin America in World Politics.* New York: Walker, 1967.

Ball, Margaret M. *The OAS in Transition.* Durham: Duke University Press, 1969.

Bethel, Paul D. "The Dominican Republic Goes to the Polls," *Reporter,* XXXIV, June 2, 1966.

Binning, William C. "The Nixon Foreign Aid Policy for Latin America," *Inter-American Economic Affairs,* XXV, No. 1, Summer, 1971, 31–46.

Connell-Smith, Gordon. *The Inter-American System.* London: Oxford University Press, 1966.

Corkran, Herbert, Jr. *Patterns of International Cooperation in the Caribbean, 1942–69.* Dallas: Southern Methodist University Press, 1970.

Crassweller, Robert D. *The Caribbean Community: Changing Societies and U.S. Policy.* New York: Praeger, for the Council on Foreign Relations, 1972.

―――. *Trujillo—The Life and Times of a Caribbean Dictator.* New York: Macmillan, 1966.

"Dominican Chaos," *On Record,* II, No. 10, 1965.

Dominican Republic. *Gaceta Oficial, No. 9250, January 1, 1972 (1972 Budget).* J. R. Vda. García Sucesores, 1972 (entire issue).

Dominican Republic. Dirección General de Estadísta y Censos. *Movimiento postal, telefónico y radiotelegráfico, y carreteras de la república,* XXVII. Santo Domingo: 1963.

Dominican Republic. Laws, Statutes, etc.
"Acta institucional, proclamada el 3 de 1965," *Gaceta Oficial,* No. 8944, September 5, 1965.
Constitution of the Dominican Republic, 1966. Washington: Pan American Union, Organization of American States, General Secretariat, 1967.

Dominican Republic. Secretariado Técnico de la Presidencia. Oficina Nacional de Estadística. *República Dominicana en Cifras, 1970,* V. Santo Domingo: 1970.

Draper, Theodore. "A Case of Defamation: U.S. Intelligence Versus Juan Bosch," *New Republic,* February 19, 1966, 13–19.

―――. "The Dominican Intervention Reconsidered," *Political Science Quarterly,* LXXXVI, No. 1, March 1971, 1–36.

Draper, Theodore. "The Roots of the Dominican Crisis," *New Leader,* XLVIII, May 24, 1965, 3–18.

Edelmann, Alexander T. *Latin American Government and Politics.* Homewood: Dorsey Press, 1969.

Espaillat, Arturo R. *Trujillo: The Last Caesar.* Chicago: Henry Regnery, 1964.

Fagen, Richard R., and Cornelius, Wayne A., Jr. *Political Power in Latin America: Seven Confrontations.* Englewood Cliffs: Prentice-Hall, 1970.

Fagg, John Edwin. *Cuba, Haiti, and the Dominican Republic.* (Modern Nations in Historical Perspective.) Englewood Cliffs: Prentice-Hall, 1965.

Free, Lloyd A. "Attitudes, Hopes and Fears of the Dominican People." Princeton: Princeton University Press, for Institute for International Social Research, 1965 (mimeo.).

Gardiner, C. Harvey. "The Japanese and the Dominican Republic," *Inter-American Economic Affairs,* XXV, No. 3, Winter 1971, 23–38.

Gil, Federico. *Latin American-U.S. Relations.* New York: Harcourt, Brace Jovanovich, 1971.

Goff, Fred, and Locker, Michael. "The Politics of Interventionism: The U.S. in the Dominican Republic." Pages 263–294 in Eric R. Wolf and Edward C. Hansen (eds.), *The Human Condition in Latin America.* New York: Oxford University Press, 1972.

Goodsell, James Nelson. "Balaguer's Dominican Republic," *Current History,* LIII, No. 315, November 1964, 298–302.

Gray, Richard B. (ed.) *Latin America and the United States in the 1970s.* Itasca, Illinois: F. E. Peacock, 1971.

Green, James W. "Local Responsibility in the Dominican Republic: A Report of a Short Investigation into Local Government, Community Development Cooperatives and Agricultural Extension." Santo Domingo: 1965 (mimeo.).

Hennessy, Alistair. "Background to the Dominican Coup," *World Today* [London], XXI, June 1965, 236–239.

Herring, Hubert. *A History of Latin America.* (3d ed.) New York: Alfred A. Knopf, 1968.

Horowitz, Michael M. *Peoples and Cultures of the Caribbean: An Anthropological Reader.* New York: Natural History Press, 1971.

Institute for the Comparative Study of Political Systems. *Dominican Republic; Election Factbook, June 1, 1966.* Washington: 1966.

Kantor, Harry. *Patterns of Politics and Political Systems in Latin America.* (Rand McNally Political Science Series.) Chicago: Rand McNally, 1969.

Kent, Francis B. "Signs of Stability Seen in Dominican Republic," *Los Angeles Times,* April 30, 1972, 7.

Kopkind, Andrew. "The Outlook for Bosch: A Report from the Dominican Republic," *New Republic,* CLIV, No. 21, 1966, 15–18.

———."Politics in Santo Domingo," *New Statesman* [London], May 13,

1966, 676.

Kurzman, Dan. *Santo Domingo: Revolt of the Damned.* New York: Putnam, 1965.

Lange, Ragner. "Was the Dominican Operation Typical and Not an Accident?" *The Sunday Star and Daily News,* July 23, 1972, 10.

Law and Judicial Systems of Nations. Washington: World Peace Through Law Center, 1968.

Logan, Rayford W. *Haiti and the Dominican Republic.* New York: Oxford University Press, 1968.

Lowenthal, Abraham F. *The Dominican Intervention.* Cambridge: Harvard University Press, 1972.

————. "The Dominican Republic: The Politics of Chaos." Pages 34–59 in Arpad von Lazar and Robert R. Kaufman (eds.), *Reform and Revolution: Readings in Latin American Politics.* Boston: Allyn and Bacon, 1969.

Malagon Barcelo, Javier, and Gil Arantequil, Malaguias. *La Constitución y las reformas constitucionales de la República Dominicana, en su premier período como nación independiente (1844–1861).* Panama City: Universidad Interamericana, 1945.

Mallin, Jay. *Caribbean Crisis, 1965.* Garden City: Doubleday, 1965.

Mansbach, Richard W. (ed.) *Dominican Crisis, 1965.* (Interim History — Facts on File.) New York: Facts on File, 1971.

Martin, John Bartlow. *Overtaken by Events: The Dominican Crisis from the Fall of Trujillo to the Civil War.* New York: Doubleday, 1966.

Mecham, John Lloyd. *The United States and Inter-American Security: 1889–1960.* Austin: University of Texas Press, 1961.

Merrill, John C. *A Handbook of the Foreign Press.* Baton Rouge: Louisiana State University Press, 1959.

Moreno, José A. *Barrio in Arms: Revolution in Santo Domingo.* Pittsburgh: University of Pittsburgh Press, 1970.

————. *Sociological Aspects of the Dominican Revolution.* Ithaca: Unpublished Ph.D. dissertation, Cornell University, 1967.

Oglesby, J. C. M. "Haiti and the Dominican Republic." Chapter 6 in Ben G. Burnett and Kenneth F. Johnson (eds.), *Political Forces in Latin America.* Belmont: Wadsworth, 1968.

Pattee, Ricardo. *La República Dominicana.* Madrid: Ediciones Cultura Hispanica, 1967.

Paxton, John (ed.). *The Statesman's Year-Book, 1972–1973.* London: Macmillan, 1972.

Peaslee, Amos J. (ed.) *Constitutions of Nations,* II. The Hague: Martinus Nijhoff, 1956.

Rodman, Selden. *Quisqueya: A History of the Dominican Republic.* Seattle: University of Washington Press, 1964.

Roucek, Joseph S. "The Dominican Republic in Geopolitics (II)," *Contemporary Review* [London], CCVII, July 1965, 12–22.

Simons, Ellen Louise. "Balaguer Takes Over," *Commonwealth,* LXXXIV, July 8, 1966, 437–440.

Slater, Jerome. *Intervention and Negotiation: The United States and the Dominican Republic.* New York: Harper and Row, 1970.

Turner, Frederick C. *Catholicism and Political Development in Latin America.* Chapel Hill: University of North Carolina Press, 1971.

U.S. Agency for International Development. *United States Overseas Loans and Grants and Assistance from International Organizations; Obligations and Loan Authorizations, July 1, 1945–June 30, 1971.* Washington: GPO, May 24, 1972.

U.S. Department of State. "Local Responsibility in the Dominican Republic: A Report of a Short Investigation into Local Government, Community Development Cooperatives and Agricultural Extension," by James W. Green. Santo Domingo: 1965 (mimeo.).

U.S. Congress. 89th, 1st Session. Senate. Committee on Foreign Relations. *Background Information Relating to the Dominican Republic.* Washington: GPO, 1965.

Walker, Malcolm T. "Power Structure and Patronage in a Community of the Dominican Republic," *Journal of Inter-American Studies and World Affairs*, XII, No. 4, October 1970, 485–504.

Walton, Richard J. *Beyond Diplomacy. A Background Book on American Military Intervention.* New York: Parents Magazine Press, 1970.

Wedge, Bryant. "The Case Study of Student Political Violence: Brazil 1964, and Dominican Republic 1965," *World Politics*, XXI, No. 2, January 1969, 183–206.

Wells, Henry. "The Dominican Experiment with Bosch," *Orbis*, X, Spring 1966, 274–280.

———. "The OAS and the Dominican Elections," *Orbis*, VII, Spring 1963, 150–163.

———. "Turmoil in the Dominican Republic," *Current History*, L, No. 293, January 1966, 14–20.

Wiarda, Howard J. "The Changing Political Orientation of the Catholic Church in the Dominican Republic," *Journal of Church and State*, VII, No. 2, Spring 1965, 238–254.

———. "The Development of the Labor Movement in the Dominican Republic," *Inter-American Economic Affairs*, XX, No. 1, Summer 1966, 41–46.

———. "The Dominican Republic: Dictatorship, Development, and Disintegration." Chapter 10 in Martin C. Needler (ed.), *Political Systems of Latin America.* New York: Van Nostrand Reinhold, 1970.

———. *The Dominican Republic: Nation in Transition.* New York: Praeger, 1969.

———. "The U.S. and the Dominican Crisis: Background to Chaos," *Caribbean Monthly Bulletin*, II, July 1965, 1–4.

Williams, Eric. *From Columbus to Castro: The History of the Caribbean 1492–1969.* New York: Harper and Row, 1970.

Wilson, Larman C. "The Foreign Policies of the Dominican Republic and Haiti." Chapter IX in Harold E. Davis and Larman C. Wilson (eds.), *Latin American Foreign Policies: An Analysis.* Washington:

The American University, School of International Service, 1971 (Unpublished manuscript.).

(Various issues of the following periodicals were also used in the preparation of this section: *Américas* [Washington], August 1972–January 1973; *Christian Science Monitor*, August 1972–January 1973; *Evening Star* [Washington], February 1972; *Evening Star and Daily News* [Washington], August 1972–January 1973; *Guardian Weekly* [Manchester], August 1972–January 1973; *Latin America* [London], January 1968–November 1972; *New York Times*, August 1971–August 1972; *Quarterly Economic Review* [London], No. 3, 1969–No. 1, 1972; *Times of the Americas* [Miami], May 1968–October 1972; *Wall Street Journal* [New York], August 1972–January 1973; *Washington Post*, April 1970–November 1971.)

Section III. Economic

Adela Investment Company. *Annual Report, 1971.* Luxembourg: 1972.

American Geographical Society. *Focus: The Dominican Republic,* by John P. Augelli, XV, May 1965.

Andic, Fuat; Andic, Stephan; and Dosser, Douglass. *A Theory of Economic Integration for Developing Countries, Illustrated by Caribbean Countries.* (University of York Studies in Economics, No. 6.) London: Allen and Unwin, 1971.

Antonini, Gustavo A. "El Noroeste de la República Dominicana: Un Modelo morfogenético de la evolución del paisaje," *Revista de Ciencias Sociales* [Río Piedras, Puerto Rico], XIV, No. 2, 1970, 247–259.

———. "Peasant Agriculture in Northwestern Dominican Republic," *Journal of Tropical Geography* [Singapore], XXXII, June 1971, 1–10.

———. "Processes and Patterns of Landscape Change in the Línea Noroeste, Dominican Republic." (Ph.D. dissertation.) New York: Columbia University, Department of Geography, 1968.

Augelli, John P. "Agricultural Colonization of the Dominican Republic," *Economic Geography,* XXXVIII, January 1962, 15–27.

Balance of Payments Yearbooks, 1959–1963, XVI. Washington: International Monetary Fund, 1964.

Balance of Payments Yearbooks, 1960–1964, XVII. Washington: International Monetary Fund, 1965.

Balance of Payments Yearbooks, 1966–1972, XXIII. Washington: International Monetary Fund, 1972.

Bateman, Robert H. "Establishing a Business in the Dominican Republic," *Overseas Business Reports* (OBR 70–92.) Washington: GPO, U.S. Department of Commerce, Bureau of International Commerce, 1970.

Bloomquist, Aldrich C. (ed.) *The Gilmore Puerto Rico-Dominican Republic Sugar Manual, 1970.* Fargo, North Dakota: Bloomquist Publications, 1970.

Bosch, Juan. *The Unfinished Experiment.* New York: Praeger, 1965.

Brookings Institution. *Refugee Settlement in the Dominican Republic.* Washington: 1942.

Campos, Carlos, and Arredondo, Alberto. "Las condiciones de vida del campesino dominicano," *Panoramas* [Mexico City], IV, July–August 1963, 81–110.

Centro Interamericano de Administradores Tributarios. *Documentos y Actas de la Primera Asamblea General 1967, Panamá.* Buenos Aires: Compañía Impresora Argentina, 1968.

———. *Documentos y Actas de la Segunda Asamblea General 1968, Buenos Aires.* San José, Costa Rica: Instituto Centro Americano de Administración Pública, 1969.

Cole, J. P. *Latin America: An Economic and Social Geography.* London: Butterworth, 1970.

Conway Research. *Latin America's Industrial Incentives.* Atlanta: 1967.

Corten, André. "Como vive la otra mitad de Santo Domingo," *Caribbean Studies* [Río Piedras, Puerto Rico], IV, No. 4, January 1965, 3–20.

Díaz Santana, Arismendi. *Desarrollo y Descomposición de la Economía Dominicana.* Santo Domingo: Impresiones, M.D., 1969.

Dominican Republic. *Antología de la literatura dominicana,* II: De la vida campesina. (Colección Trujillo Publicaciones del Centenario de la República.) Ciudad Trujillo: Impresora Dominicana, 1944.

——. *Gaceta Oficial, No. 9250, January 1, 1972 (1972 Budget).* J. R. Vda. García Sucesores, 1972 (entire issue.).

——. "Jornadas de la Alianza para el Progreso." Santo Domingo: August 1963 (mimeo.).

Dominican Republic. Banco Agrícola de la República Dominicana. *Boletín Estadístico, 1970.* Santo Domingo: 1971.

——. *Memoria Subre las Actividades Desarrolladas Durante el Año 1970.* Santo Domingo: n.d.

Dominican Republic. Banco Central de la República Dominicana. *Memoria Anual, 1960.* Santo Domingo: 1967.

Dominican Republic. Banco de Reservas de República Dominicana. *Informe Anual, 1971.* Santo Domingo: Impresora Nacional, n.d.

Dominican Republic. Camera de Cuentas. *Informe, 1970.* Santo Domingo: n.d.

Dominican Republic. Corporación Dominicana de Electricidad. *Memoria, 1968.* Santo Domingo: 1969.

Dominican Republic. Dirección General de Estadística. *Quinto censo nacional agropecuario, 1960:* (cifras provisionales). Ciudad Trujillo: Sección de Publicaciones, 1961.

——. *21 años de estadísticas dominicanas, 1936–56.* Ciudad Trujillo: Impresora Dominicana, n.d.

Dominican Republic. Dirección General de Estadística y Censos. *Estadística industrial de la República Dominicana, 1962,* XIII. Santo Domingo: Sección de Publicaciones, 1965.

——. *Movimiento postal, telefónico y radiotelegráfico, y carreteras de la República, 1963,* XXVIII. Santo Domingo: Sección de Publicaciones, 1965.

——. *Primer censo nacional de comercio, 1955.* Ciudad Trujillo: Sección de Publicaciones, 1960.

——. *Producción agrícola de la República Dominicana, 1950–1959.* Ciudad Trujillo: Sección de Publicaciones, n.d.

Dominican Republic. Dirección General de Información y Prensa. *Evolución de la Industria Azucarera en la República Dominicana.* Santo Domingo: Editora del Caribe, 1968.

Dominican Republic. Laws, Statutes, etc.

Código del trabajo—1964. Santo Domingo: 1964.

Income Tax Law: Law No. 5911 (Unofficial translation.) Santo Domingo: Secretary of State for Finance. General Directorate for Income Tax, 1968.

Dominican Republic. Oficina Nacional de Estadística. *Comercio Exterior de la República Dominicana, 1969.* Santo Domingo: n.d.

———. *Estadística Industrial de la República Dominicana, 1968.* Santo Domingo: December 1970.

———. *Quinto Censo Nacional Agropecuario, 1960.* Santo Domingo: 1966.

Dominican Republic. Secretariado Técnico de la Presidencia. Oficina Nacional de Estadística. *Estadística de los Negocios de Seguros, 1968,* XXXII. Santo Domingo: 1970.

———. *República Dominicana en Cifras,* 1970, V. Santo Domingo: 1970.

Dominican Republic. Secretariado Técnico de la Presidencia. Oficina Nacional del Presupuesto. *Ejecución del Presupuesto, 1969.* Santo Domingo: 1970.

Dominican Republic. Secretariado Técnico de la Presidencia. Oficina Nacional de Planificación. *Primero plan nacional de desarrollo, versión preliminar para discusión.* Santo Domingo: 1970.

Dominican Republic. Secretaria Técnica de la Presidencia. Oficina Nacional de Planificación. *Plataforma para el desarrollo económico y social de la República Dominicana, 1968–1985.* Santo Domingo: 1968.

"Dominican Republic." Pages 275–282 in Eugene Fodor (ed.), *Fodor's Caribbean, Bahamas and Bermuda, 1971.* New York: David McKay, 1971.

"Dominican Republic." Pages 514–530 in Barclay's Bank, D.C.O., *West Indies and Caribbean Yearbook, 1965.* London: Thomas Skinner, 1965.

Dorner, Peter, et al. "Agrarian Reform in the Dominican Republic: The Views of Four Consultants." (Land Tenure Center, No. 42.) Madison: University of Wisconsin, LTC, December 1967 (mimeo.).

Dorta-Duque, Francisco. "La Agricultura dominicana: Algunos observaciones socioeconómicos." West Baden: West Baden College, 1962 (mimeo.).

Federación Latinoamericana de Bancos. *Capacitación bancaria en Latinoamérica.* Bogotá, Colombia: Editorial Kelly, 1972.

Fernández, Diógenes H. *Objectivos e Instrumentos de la Política Monetaria Nacional.* Santo Domingo: Banco Central de la República Dominicana, 1970.

Financiera Dominicana. *Financiera Dominicana Introduces You to Dominican Figures.* Santo Domingo: 1972.

Food and Agriculture Organization. *Government Marketing Policies in Latin America.* Rome: FAO, 1967.

Free, Lloyd A. "Attitudes, Hopes and Fears of the Dominican People." Princeton: Princeton University Press, for Institute for International Social Research, 1965 (mimeo.).

Furtado, Celso. *Economic Development of Latin America.* (Cambridge Latin American Studies.) Cambridge: Cambridge University Press, 1970.

García Aybar, José E. *El presente, futuro de la industria azucarera dominicana.* Santo Domingo: Asociación de Industrias de la República Dominicana, 1965.

Haidar, Walter. "Foreign Trade Regulations of the Dominican Republic." *Overseas Business Reports* (OBR 72-022.) Washington: GPO, U.S. Department of Commerce, Bureau of International Commerce, 1972.

Hirschman, Albert O. (ed.) *Latin American Issues, Essays and Comments.* New York: Twentieth Century Fund, 1961.

Hitt, Deborah S., and Wilson, Larman C. *A Selected Bibliography of the Dominican Republic: A Century After the Restoration of Independence.* Washington: The American University, Center for Research in Social Systems, September 1968.

Hoetink, H. "Materiales para el estudio de la República Dominicana en la segunda mitad del siglo XIX, Parte I: Agricultura." *Caribbean Studies* [Río Piedras, Puerto Rico], V, No. 3, October 1965, 3–21.

──────. "Materiales para el estudio de la República Dominicana en la segunda mitad del siglo XIX, Parte III: Cambios en la estructura de las comunicaciones," *Caribbean Studies* [Río Piedras, Puerto Rico], VIII, No. 3, October 1968, 3–22.

──────. "Materiales para el estudio de la República Dominicana en la segunda mitad del siglo XIX, Parte IV: Cambios en la estructura del poder económico," *Caribbean Studies* [Río Piedras, Puerto Rico], VIII, No. 4, January 1969, 3–37.

Hurt, Leslie C. "U.S. Sugar Act Extended—New Quotas Established," *Foreign Agriculture,* IX, No. 43, October 25, 1971, 12.

Instituto Interamericano de Ciencias Agrícolas. *Organización Administrativa del Sector Agropecuario de República Dominicana.* Turrialba, Costa Rica: 1969.

Inter-American Development Bank. *Actividades por países, 1961–1964.* Washington: n.d.

──────. *Annual Report, 1971.* Washington: 1972.

──────. *Fifth Annual Report of the Social Progress Trust Fund, 1965.* Washington: 1966.

──────. *Fourth Annual Report of the Social Progress Trust Fund, 1964.* Washington: 1965.

──────. *Proceedings: Special Meeting of the Board of Governors, March 1, 1971.* Washington: 1971.

──────. *Socio-Economic Progress in Latin America: Social Progress Trust Fund, Ninth Annual Report, 1969.* Washington: 1970.

──────. *Socio-Economic Progress in Latin America. Social Progress Trust Fund, Tenth Annual Report, 1970.* Washington: 1971.

──────. *Third Annual Report of the Social Progress Trust Fund, 1963.* Washington: 1964.

Inter-American University. Center for the Study of Interpretation of Contemporary Latin America. *A Bilingual Report on the Dominican Republic Today.* San German: Inter-American University Press, 1964.

International Bank for Reconstruction and Development. *El grupo del Banco Mundial en las Américas.* Washington: IBRD, 1970.

―――. *Trends in Developing Countries.* Washington: IBRD, 1971.

International Bank for Reconstruction and Development. Development Services Department. *List of National Development Plans.* (2d ed.) Washington: IBRD, September 1968.

International Bank for Reconstruction and Development. International Development Association. *Addendum to List of National Development Plans.* Washington: 1970.

―――. *World Bank International Development Association Annual Report, 1972.* Washington: IBRD/IDA, 1972.

International Coffee Organization. *Informe de la misión sobre la República Dominicana.* London: 1967.

International Development Services. "Agricultural Crop Production and Development." Santo Domingo: Instituto Agrónomo Dominicano, 1962 (mimeo.).

International Finance Corporation. *IFC in Latin America.* Washington: 1971.

―――. *International Financial Statistics, November 1972.* Washington: International Monetary Fund, 1972.

―――. *1972 Annual Report.* Washington: International Bank for Reconstruction and Development, 1972.

International Labor Organization. International Labor Office. *Labour Force Projections 1965–1985, Latin America.* Geneva: 1971.

International Monetary Fund. *Twenty-Third Annual Report on Exchange Restrictions, 1972.* Washington: IMF, 1972.

International Monetary Fund. International Bank for Reconstruction and Development. *Direction of Trade, June 1972.* Washington: IMF/IBRD, June 1972.

James, Preston E. *Latin America.* (4th ed.) New York: Odyssey Press, 1969.

―――. "A Natural Resources Survey of the Dominican Republic," *Geographical Review,* LIX, April 1969, 287–289.

Kurzman, Dan. *Santo Domingo: Revolt of the Damned.* New York: Putnam, 1965.

Lowenthal, Abraham F. *Hydraulic Resource Development in the Dominican Republic.* (Committee on Dominican Studies, Studies in Development and Administration, No. 3.) Santiago de los Caballeros: Asociación Para el Desarrollo, 1965.

May, Stacy, and Plaza, Galo. *The United Fruit Company in Latin America.* Washington: National Planning Association, 1958.

Minerals Yearbook, 1969, IV: Area Reports: International. Washington: GPO, U.S. Department of the Interior, Bureau of Mines, 1971.

Nehemkis, Peter. *Latin America: Myth and Reality.* New York: Knopf, 1964.

Norvell, Douglass G. "Food Marketing in an Urban Place in the Dominican Republic," *Caribbean Studies* [Río Piedras, Puerto Rico], IX, No. 3, October 1969, 104–110.

Norvell, Douglass G., and Billingsley, Ray V. "Traditional Markets and Marketers in the Cibao Valley of the Dominican Republic." Pages 391–400 in Michael M. Horowitz (ed.), *Peoples and Cultures of the Caribbean.* Garden City: Natural History Press, 1971.

Norvell, Douglass G., and Wehrly, James S. "A Rotating Credit Association in the Dominican Republic," *Caribbean Studies* [Río Piedras, Puerto Rico], IX, No. 1, April 1969, 45–52.

Norvell, Douglass G.; Billingsley, Ray V.; and McNeely, John G. "The Internal Food Distribution System and Marketing Channels for Plantains and Tomatoes in the Cibao Valley, Dominican Republic." College Station: Texas A. and M. University, n.d. (mimeo.).

Organización de los Estados Americanos. Instituto Interamericano de Estadística. *América en cifras, 1970: Situación cultural:* Educación y otros aspectos culturales. Washington: 1971.

———. *América en cifras, 1970: Situación económica,* IV: Balanza de Pagos, Producto e Ingreso Nacional y Finanzas. Washington: Secretaría General de la OEA, 1971.

Organization of American States. *Characteristics of the Demographic Structure of the American Countries.* Washington: 1964.

———. *Image of the Dominican Republic.* Washington: Pan American Union, 1971.

———. Inter-American Economic and Social Council. "First Annual Meeting." Mexico City: 1962 (mimeo.).

———. *Inventory of Information Basic to the Planning of Agricultural Development in Latin America.* Washington: 1964.

———. *Physical Resource Investigations for Economic Development: A Casebook of OAS Field Experience in Latin America.* Washington: OAS, General Secretariat, 1969.

Organization of American States. Department of Legal Affairs. General Legal Division. *Mining and Petroleum Legislation in Latin America.* (2d ed.) Washington: Pan American Union, 1969.

Ornes, Germán E. *Trujillo: Little Caesar of the Caribbean.* New York: Nelson, 1958.

Pan American Development Foundation. *Annual Report, 1971.* Washington: n.d.

Pan American Union. *Cacao. The Chocolate Tree.* (Commodity Series.) Washington: 1968.

———. *Dominican Republic.* (American Republic Series, No. 8.) Washington: 1964.

———. *A Statement of the Laws of the Dominican Republic in Matters Affecting Business.* (3d ed.) (Ed., Antonio Tellado.) Washington: 1964.

Pan American Union. Department of Statistics. *Cost of Living Indexes of the American Nations, 1965,* Nos. 21 and 22. Washington: 1965.

Pan American Union. Inter-American Committee for Agricultural Development. *Inventory of Information Basic to the Planning of Agricultural Development in Latin America—Dominican Republic.* Washington: 1964.

Pan American Union. Inter-American Economic and Social Council. *Minutes of the Subcommittee of the CIAP on the Dominican Republic.* (OEA, Ser. H, XIII CIAP, 127.) Washington: 1964.

Parsons Corporation. *The Dominican Government Sugar Industry.* Los Angeles: 1967.

Pendle, George. *A History of Latin America.* Baltimore: Penguin Books, 1965.

Pflaum, Irving Peter. *Arena of Decision: Latin America in Crisis.* Englewood Cliffs: Prentice-Hall, 1964.

Pick's Currency Yearbook, 1971. New York: Pick, 1971.

Puga, William B. (ed.) *Electrical World: A Directory of Electric Utilities in Latin America, Bermuda, and the Caribbean Islands, 1969-70 Edition.* New York: McGraw-Hill, 1969.

Quintano Ripollés, Antonio. *La Influencia del derecho penal español en las legislaciones hispano-americanas.* Madrid: Cuadernos de Monografías; Ediciones Cultura Hispánica, 1953.

Rambo, A. Terry. "The Dominican Republic." Chapter IX in Martin C. Needler (ed.), *Political Systems of Latin America.* Princeton: Van Nostrand, 1964.

Ravelo, Sebastián R. *Proyecciones de la balanza de pagos de la República Dominicana.* Santo Domingo: n.pub., 1966.

Remick, Jerome, and Almanzar, Alcedo. *The Coinage of the Dominican Republic.* (2d ed.) San Antonio: Almanzar's, 1972.

Robichek, E. Walter, and Sansón, Carlos. "The Balance of Payments Performance of Latin America and the Caribbean, 1966-1970," *Staff Papers,* XIX, No. 2, July 1972, 286–343.

Rodman, Selden. *Quisqueya: A History of the Dominican Republic.* Seattle: University of Washington Press, 1964.

Rodríguez, Rafael, and Lowenthal, Abraham. "The Dominican Republic: An Informal Handbook." Santiago de los Caballeros: Asociación Para el Desarrollo, 1965 (mimeo.).

Rogers, Gifford. *Land Tenure in the Dominican Republic.* (International Development Services.) Santo Domingo: n.pub., 1963.

Russin, Jonathan, and Brown, Ronald L. "Automatism vs. Discretion: The Industrial Investment Incentive Law of the Dominican Republic," *Law and Policy in International Business,* III, No. 2, 1971, 366–385.

Schmidtt, Karl L., and Burks, David D. *Evolution or Chaos.* New York: Praeger, 1963.

Schurz, William Lytle. *Latin America.* New York: Dutton, 1964.

Solving Latin American Business Problems. New York: Business International Corporation, 1968.

The Statesman's Year-Book, 1972–1973. London: Macmillan, 1972.

Statistical Yearbook, 1964. United Nations, Department of Economic and Social Affairs. Statistical Office. New York: 1965.

Stopelman, Francis. *Quisqueya: Threshold of the Americas.* Leiden: Nederlandsche Rotogravure Maatschappii, n.d.

Tamames Gómez, Ramón. *La República Dominicana y la integración económica de América Latina.* Buenos Aires: Instituto para la Integración de América Latina, 1968.

Thiesenhusen, William. C. *Technological Change and Income Distribution in Latin American Agriculture.* (Land Tenure Center, No. 78.) Madison: University of Wisconsin, LTC, August 1971.

Troncoso, Moises Poblete, and Burnett, Ben G. *The Rise of the Latin American Labor Movement.* New York: Bookman Associates, 1960.

Unión Panamericana. Departamento de Estadística. *América en cifras, 1963.* Washington: 1964.

United Nations. *The Economic Development of Latin America During the Post War Period.* New York: 1964.

United Nations. Department of Economic and Social Affairs. *Panel on Foreign Investment in Latin America, Medellín, Colombia, 8–11 June, 1970.* New York: 1971.

————. *World Economic Survey, 1969–1970: The Developing Countries in the 1960s and the Problem of Appraising Progress.* New York: 1971.

U.S. Agency for International Development. *U.S. Foreign Aid in Latin America: Proposed Fiscal Year 1973 Program.* Washington: June 1972.

U.S. Department of Labor. *Directory of Labor Organizations, Western Hemisphere,* I. Washington: GPO, 1964.

U.S. Embassy in Santo Domingo. *Post Report.* Santo Domingo: U.S. Department of State, June 1970.

U.S. United States Information Agency. "Dominican Republic: A Communications Factbook." Washington: 1962 (mimeo.).

U.S. Department of Agriculture. Economic Research Service. *Agriculture and Trade of the Dominican Republic.* (ERS-Foreign 330.) Washington: GPO, 1972.

————. *The Latin American Farmer.* (ERS-Foreign 257.) Washington: GPO, 1969.

————. *U.S. Foreign Agricultural Trade Statistical Report, Calendar Year 1971.* Washington: 1972.

U.S. Department of Agriculture. Foreign Agriculture Service. *Agricultural Geography of Latin America.* Washington: GPO, 1958.

————. *The 1965 Western Hemisphere Agricultural Situation.* (ERS-Foreign 113.) Washington: 1965.

————. *World Agriculture Production and Trade, Statistical Report.* Washington: March 1965.

U.S. Department of Commerce. Bureau of International Commerce. "Dominican Republic." Washington: GPO, 1965 (mimeo.).

————. "Market Indicators for Latin American Republics." *Overseas Business Reports*. (ERS-65-41.) Washington: GPO, 1965.

U.S. Department of Labor. Bureau of Labor Statistics. *Labor Law and Practice in the Dominican Republic*. (BLS Report No. 343.) Washington: GPO, 1968.

U.S. Embassy in Santo Domingo. Foreign Agricultural Service. *Dominican Republic: Agricultural Situation, 1970*. Santo Domingo: January 25, 1971.

U.S. Agency for International Development. Bureau for Latin America. Office of Development Programs. *Summary of Economic and Social Indicators in 18 Latin American Countries, 1960–1971*. Washington: June 1972.

U.S. Agency for International Development. Bureau for Program and Policy Coordination. Office of Statistics and Reports. *A.I.D. Economic Data Book: Latin America*. Washington: July 1971.

————. *Selected Economic Data for the Less Developed Countries*. Washington: June 1972.

U.S. Department of Commerce. Bureau of International Commerce. International Marketing Information Service. *Best U.S. Sales Prospects in the Dominican Republic*. (Country Market Digest, IMIS 69-23.) Washington: GPO, 1969.

U.S. Department of Commerce. Bureau of International Programs. American Republics Division. "Background Data on the Economy of the Dominican Republic," by William P. Wadbrook. Washington: 1962 (mimeo.).

Vega, Bernardo. "Charla dada en la Universidad Católica Madre y Maestra de Santiago de los Caballeros." Santo Domingo: Banco Central de la República Dominicana, January 1966 (mimeo.).

————. *Política monetaria y cambiaria en la República Dominicana 1957–1967* (Speech given in Palace of Fine Arts, 25 November 1967, Santiago.) Santo Domingo: n.pub., 1967.

Westbrook, John T. "Socio-economic Factors Related to Success and Failure in Agrarian Reform: The 'Caracol' Project, República Dominicana." Pages 293-325 in F. M. Andic and T. G. Matthews (eds.), *The Caribbean in Transition: Papers on Social, Political, and Economic Development*. Río Piedras, Puerto Rico: University of Puerto Rico, 1965.

World and Its Peoples: The Caribbean Region and Central America. New York: Greystone Press, 1969.

Worldmark Encyclopedia of the Nations, III: Americas. (Ed., Louis Barron.) New York: Worldmark Press, Harper and Row, 1967.

Yearbook of Labour Statistics, 1971. Geneva: International Labor Organization, International Labor Office, 1971.

(Various issues of the following periodicals were also used in the preparation of this section: *Alliance for Progress Weekly Newsletter* [Washington], March 15, 1971–October 23, 1972; *Américas* [Washington], August 1972–January 1973; *Boletín Mensual* [Santo Domingo], January 1972–May 1972; *BOLSA Review* [London], January 1968–August 1972; *Business Latin America* [New York], February 20, 1969–October 26, 1972; *Christian Science Monitor,* August 1972–January 1973; *Evening Star and Daily News* [Washington], August 1972–January 1973; *Guardian Weekly* [Manchester], August 1972–January 1973; *Inter-American Bulletin on Taxation* [Washington], July 1971–September 1971; *Inter-American Center of Tax Administrators Newsletter* [Panama], December 1968–August 1972; *Latin America* [London], January 9, 1970–November 2, 1972; *Monthly Bulletin of Agricultural Economics and Statistics* [FAO, Rome], June 1972–September 1972; *New York Times,* October 3, 1971–October 25, 1972; *Noticias: Weekly Digest of Hemisphere Reports* [New York], January 15, 1969–October 25, 1972; *Quarterly Economic Review: Cuba, Dominican Republic, Haiti, Puerto Rico* [London], July 1969–July 1972; *Times of the Americas* [Washington], May 29, 1968–October 11, 1972; *Translations on Latin America* (U.S. Department of Commerce, Joint Publications Research Service, [Washington]), December 14, 1966–September 19, 1972; U.S. Embassy in Santo Domingo, various reports, January 20, 1970–May 24, 1972; *Wall Street Journal* [New York], June 27, 1972–January 1973; *Washington Post,* August 1972–January 1973; and *World Agricultural Production and Trade: Statistical Report* [Washington], July 1972–September 1972.)

Section IV. National Security

Bishop, Crawford M., and Marchant, Anyda. *A Guide to the Law and Legal Literature of Cuba, the Dominican Republic and Haiti.* Washington: Library of Congress, 1944.

Blackman, R. U. B. (ed.) *Jane's Fighting Ships.* London: Sampson Low Marston, 1972.

Burnett, Ben G., and Johnson, Kenneth F. *Political Forces in Latin America.* Belmont, California: Wadsworth, 1968.

Crassweller, Robert D. *The Caribbean Community: Changing Societies and U.S. Policy.* New York: Praeger, for the Council on Foreign Relations, 1972.

de Beasault, Lawrence. *President Trujillo: His Work and the Dominican Republic.* Washington: Washington Publishing Company, 1936.

Dominican Republic. Laws, Statutes, etc.
  Código de justicia de las fuerzas armadas. Santo Domingo: Ministerio de las Fuerzas Armadas, n.d.
  Código Penal de la República Dominicana. Santo Domingo: Editora del Caribe, 1962.
  Constitución de la República Dominicana. Santo Domingo: Ministerio de Educación, Bellas Artes y Cultos, 1963.
  Reglamento militar disciplinario. Santo Domingo: Ministerio de las Fuerzas Armadas, n.d.

Dominican Republic. Secretaría del Estado de Agricultura. *Organización Administrativa del Sector Agropecuario de la República Dominicana,* II, Santo Domingo: 1969.

Espaillat, Arturo R. *Trujillo: The Last Caesar.* Chicago: Henry Regnery, 1964.

Goldwert, Marvin. *Dominican Republic: History of American Occupation, 1916–1924.* Gainesville: University of Florida Press, 1962.

Hechos, 1966–1968: Dos Años de Progreso. Santo Domingo: Ediciones "Alpa," July 1, 1968.

Hicks, Albert C. *Blood in the Streets: The Life and Rule of Trujillo.* New York: Creative Age Press, 1946.

James, Preston E. *Latin America.* (4th ed.) New York: Odyssey Press, 1969.

Lieuwen, Edwin. *Survey of the Alliance for Progress: The Latin American Military.* Washington: GPO, U.S. Senate, Committee on Foreign Relations, Subcommittee on American Republic Affairs, 1967.

Logan, Rayford W. *Haiti and the Dominican Republic.* New York: Oxford University Press, 1968.

Lowenthal, Abraham F. *The Dominican Intervention.* Cambridge: Harvard University Press, 1972.

Mecham, John Lloyd. *A Survey of United States-Latin American Relations.* Boston: Houghton Mifflin, 1965.

Mejía, J. Thomás. *Memoria.* Santiago: Editorial el Diario, 1946.

Moreno, José A. *Sociological Aspects of the Dominican Revolution.* Ithaca: Unpublished Ph.D. dissertation, Cornell University, 1967.

Needler, Martin C. (ed.) *Political Systems of Latin America.* (2d ed.) New York: Van Nostrand Reinhold, 1970.

Pan American Union. *Dominican Republic.* (American Republic Series, No. 8.) Washington: 1964.

————. *A Statement of the Laws of the Dominican Republic in Matters Affecting Business.* (3d ed.) (Ed., Antonio Tellado.) Washington: 1964.

Rodman, Selden. *Quisqueya: A History of the Dominican Republic.* Seattle: University of Washington Press, 1964.

U.S. Agency for International Development. "Public-Safety Assistance Programs in Latin America," *Inter-American Economic Affairs,* XXVI, No. 3, Winter 1972, 92–96.

U.S. Agency for International Development. Bureau for Latin America. Office of Development Programs. *Summary of Economic and Social Indicators in 18 Latin American Countries, 1960–1969.* Washington: June 1970.

————. *Summary of Economic and Social Indicators in 18 Latin American Countries, 1960–1971.* Washington: June 1972.

U.S. Agency for International Development. Bureau for Program and Policy Coordination. Office of Statistics and Reports. *U.S. Overseas Loans and Grants.* Washington: May 24, 1972.

Welles, Sumner. *Naboth's Vineyard: The Dominican Republic, 1844–1924.* 2 vols. New York: Payson and Clarke, 1928.

Wiarda, Howard J. "The Politics of Civil-Military Relationships in the Dominican Republic." *Journal of Inter-American Studies,* VII, October 1965.

Wilson, Larman C. "United States Military Assistance to the Dominican Republic" (Paper prepared for delivery before the Seminar on the Dominican Republic, Center for International Affairs, Harvard University, April 20, 1967.) N.pl.: n.pub., 1967.

Wood, Davis. *Armed Forces in Central and South America.* (Adelphi Papers No. 34.) London: Institute for Strategic Studies, 1967.

Yearbook on Latin American Communist Affairs, 1971. Stanford: Stanford University, Hoover Institution Press, 1971.

(Various issues of the following periodicals were also used in the preparation of this section: *El Caribe* [Santo Domingo], October 1972–December 1972; *El Nacional* [Santo Domingo], October 1972–December 1972; *Listín Diario* [Santo Domingo], October 1972–December 1972; *Ultima Hora* [Santo Domingo], October 1972–December 1972.)

GLOSSARY

bachillerato(s)—Secondary school baccalaureate; required for admission to a university.

bodega(s)—Generally, a warehouse but, as used in the Dominican Republic and a few other Latin American countries, refers to a small grocery store.

bohio(s)—Taino (*q.v.*) Indian name for their thatched houses; now applied to the dwellings of the poorer countrypeople.

CARE—Cooperative for American Relief Everywhere.

CARIFTA—The Caribbean Free Trade Association. As of 1972, an economic grouping of most of the English-speaking Caribbean countries.

CARITAS—Catholic Relief Services. A national Roman Catholic charity organization affiliated with Roman Catholic relief services in the United States.

colono(s)—As used in the Dominican Republic refers to a small independent sugarcane grower. In other Latin American countries the word usually designates a settler or a tenant farmer.

compadrazgo—Literally, "copaternity." A system of ritual coparenthood linking parents, child, and godparents in a close social or economic relationship.

Constitutionalist—Name adopted by the faction that during the civil strife in 1963 called for restoration of the government of Juan Bosch and the Constitution of 1963.

conuco—Originally meant a very small patch of ground assigned to slaves to cultivate for themselves. Later denoted a small farm and, specifically, a cornfield.

criollo—In colonial times designated a person of presumably pure Spanish descent born in America.

de primera—Term derived from *la clase de primera* (literally, "the first class"). Used to describe the upper stratum of elite families.

IAD (Instituto Agrario Dominicano)—Dominican Agrarian Institute. Principal government agency for agrarian reform.

licenciado(s)—Licenciate; a person who has received a university degree roughly equivalent to a bachelor's degree in North America.

machismo—Literally, "maleness." Complex of beliefs and attitudes defining the concept of masculinity.

merengue—Popular dance.

patrón—Literally, "patron"; also boss, sponsor, protector, or master. Traditionally, an employer or social superior who forms paternalistic ties with someone of lower status, rewarding deference and loyalty with protection and an active personal interest.

personalismo—Literally, "personalism"—a complex of belief and behavior stressing personality, individuality, and interpersonal relations more than ideology and institutionalism.

peso—Popular name of currency; official name is Dominican gold peso. Symbol is RD$ and official rate in 1972 was RD$1 equals US$1.

pulpería(s)—A retail store that sells all sorts of provisions and liquors.

Taino—The Arawak people who occupied Hispaniola and the other islands of the Greater Antilles at the time they were discovered by Christopher Columbus.

Triumvirate—The three-man junta, composed of civilians but backed by the armed forces, that governed the country between the overthrow of President Juan Bosch in September 1963 and the outbreak of civil war in April 1965.

World Bank Group—Consists of the International Bank for Reconstruction and Development (IBRD, commonly known as the World Bank), the International Development Association (IDA), and the International Finance Corporation (IFC).

INDEX

England. *See* Great Britain
English language: 55
Enriquillo: 118
Enriquillo Basin: 13
enrollments: 104, 108, 110, 113
Estrella Ureña, Rafael: 43
"ethiopianization": 51
ethnic patterns: 50–54
executive branch: 134–135, 140; economy, 162, 165, 166, 167, 168; national security, 206
export crops: 81, 162
Export-Import Bank: 173
exports (*see also* export crops): 165, 195–198

family (*see also* children, marriage, women): 62–66, 141; elite, 61, 63; lower classes, 64; patrilineal structure, 63
family planning: 25, 26, 65; Dominican Evangelical Church, 71
farming (*see also* agrarian reform, agriculture, land, landownership, peasants): 20, 23, 38, 39, 57, 58, 91, 162, 180–191; coffee, 187; credit, 175; income, 95, 192; peasants, 150; practices, 184; ranches, 189, 190; state, 179, 181; trade, 199; transportation, 180
Ferdinand VII of Spain: 37
Fiallo, Fabio: 120
fiestas: 97
Figueres, José: 156
financial difficulties. *See* foreign debt.
fine arts. *See* cultural life
fishing: 19, 191; coastline sovereignty, 9; gross domestic product, 164; imports, 197; legislation, 19
food and beverage industry: 191, 192, 198
food supply (*see also* crops): 80–82, 195; cost, 95; donated, 93, 173; imports, 196, 197; and income, 94; peddlers, 199; processing, 91; *sancocoho*, 82
foreign aid (*see also* United States): 172–173; loans, 174
foreign debt: 40–41, 153, 161, 171; under Trujillo, 44
foreign exchange: 195
foreign investments: 172–173, 197; ferronickel project, 193
foreign relations (*see also* individual countries): 152–159, 195; economy, 168
forestry: 191; armed forces, 209; gross domestic product, 164
forests: 7, 17, 18
Fourteenth of June movement: 142, 143, 213
France: 39, 51, 100, 117, 120, 121, 128, 129, 133, 137, 158; occupation, 31, 36–37, 189;

schools, 62
freedom of expression: 125–126
Freemasonry: 71
French West India Company: 35
Frias Sandoval, Luis: 123
Friends of Family Planning (Amigos de Planificación Familiar—APL): 25, 26
fruits: 162, 184, 189; export, 197; industry, 192

Galván, Manuel de Jesús: 118
García Godoy, Héctor: 47, 145, 146, 156
García, José Gabriel: 119
García, Juan Francisco: 120
Garrido, Edna: 124
General Agreement on Tariffs and Trade (GATT): ix, 195
Germany (West Germany): 93, 128, 129, 158; imports, 198
Gil de Liendo, Rodrigo: 116
gold: 32, 33, 35, 194
Government of National Reconstruction: 47
governors: 137, 138–139
grains (*see also* corn): 189; imports, 197
Gran Colombia, Republic of: 37
Great Britain: 37, 39, 51, 133, 158, 198, 206
gross domestic product (GDP): 163, 179
gross national product (GNP): 161, 162, 166; defense, 207; and taxes, 168
guerrilla warfare: v, 39, 42
Gulf and Western Americas Corporation: 195
gypsum: 19, 20, 193

Haina: 203
Haiti: 1, 7, 10, 11, 12, 13, 15, 16, 31, 46, 117, 118, 133, 153, 156, 157; air service, 203; border, 8, 9, 10, 24, 25, 35, 49, 52, 181; fieldhands, 187; language, 55; migration, 52; occupation, 51, 67, 100, 137, 182, 189; prejudice, 54, 56, 65; priests, 69; voodoo cult, 71–73
handicrafts: 192
Hapsburg dynasty: 36
health and welfare: 79–93; and economy, 167, 168
Henríquez Ureña, Camila: 121
Henríquez Ureña, Max: 122
Henríquez Ureña, Pedro: 122
Henríquez y Carvajal, Federico: 118
Henríquez y Carvajal, Francisco: 41–42
Hérard-Rivière, Charles: 38
Herrera Free Zone: 195
Heureaux, Ulises: 39–41, 60, 120, 213
Higher Institute of Agriculture: 108

highway system: 44, 180, 201; and economy, 166
Higüey: highway, 201
Hispaniola: 1, 31, 32, 33, 35, 51, 115, 117
holidays: 94, 97
Honduras: 154, 156
Horticultural Center of Constanza: 184
hospitals (see also clinics): 86-87, 177; private welfare, 93; social security, 92; venereal disease, 89
housing: 57, 82-85, 141; cost, 95; and economy, 168, 174, 175
hurricanes: 17, 43, 84

illiteracy: 57
Imbert Barrera, Antonio: 46, 47
immigration: 24, 25, 36; Haitian, 24, 65, 71; Italian, Armenian, Syrian, and Lebanese, 61
import crops: 81
imports: 85, 95, 193, 195-198; and economy, 165; oil, 194
Incháustegui Cabral, Héctor: 121
income: 110, 162, 177
Independence Day: 38
Independent Democratic Action (Acción Democratica Independiente—ADI): 149
Indianism (indigenismo): 116, 118
Indians. See Taino (Arawak) Indians
Industrial Bank: 182
Industrial Development Corporation (Corporación de Fomento Industrial—CFI): 163, 175-176, 182
Industrial Incentive Law of 1968: 165, 172
industry (see also manufacturing): 2, 44, 91, 179-180, 191-203; and economy, 161, 162, 163, 165, 176
infant mortality: 22, 88
inflation: 176
Institute for Cooperative Credit (Institute de Desarrollo y Crédito Cooperative—IDECOOP): 183
Institute of Price Stabilization: 199
Institutional Act of August 31, 1965: 133, 148
Inter-American Development Bank (IDB): viii, 5, 88, 171, 173
Inter-American Peace Commission: 45
Inter-American Peace Force: 47, 132, 144, 154
Inter-American Treaty of Reciprocal Assistance: viii, 158
International Atomic Energy Agency (IAEA): 159
International Bank for Reconstruction and Development (IBRD): 159, 171

International Civil Aviation Organization (ICAO): 159
International Court of Justice: 159
International Development Association (IDA): 106, 159
International Finance Corporation (IFC): 159
International Labor Organization (ILO): 27, 28, 158, 159
International Monetary Fund (IMF): 159, 173
International Planned Parenthood Federation: 26
International Police Academy: 212
International Telecommunications Union (ITU): 159
Iran: 158
irrigation: 7, 13, 15, 21, 177, 183, 185, 188; and economy, 161, 168
Isabella of Spain: 33
Isabella II of Spain: 39
Israel: 93, 128, 158
Italy: 128, 129, 158; imports, 198

Japan: 129, 158; imports, 198; Japanese, 53
Jerónimo de Alcocer, Luis: 116
Jesuit Order: 21, 149
Jews: 24-25, 53, 81
Jiménez, Juan Isidro: 41
Johnson, Lyndon B.: 154, 155
judiciary: 137-138; and economy, 168

Kennedy, John F.: 154
kinship: 62-63; interpersonal relations, 77; lower class, 64

La Altagracia: 72, 83
La Banda: 146, 147, 212
labor force: 27-29, 32, 113, 131, 132; agriculture, 8, 27, 179, 183, 184; Bosch, 46; church influence, 70; and economy, 168; industry, 8, 27, 191, 192; mining, 193; security forces, 205, 207; service jobs, 27; working hours, 94
labor organizations (see also peasants, teachers): 149, 150-151; American Institute for Free Labor Development (AIFLD), 150; Autonomous Confederation of Christian Unions (Confederación Autónoma de Sindicatos Cristianos—CASC), 150, 151; Constitutional Action (Acción Constitucional—AC), 151; Labor Front for Union Autonomy—Labor Center for Dominican Workers (Frente Obrero Pro-Sindicatos Autónomos—Central Sindical de Trabajadores Dominicanos—FOUPSA-CESITRADO), 150, 151;

253

257

PUBLISHED AREA HANDBOOKS

550–65	Afghanistan	550–58	Laos
550–98	Albania	550–24	Lebanon
550–44	Algeria	550–38	Liberia
550–59	Angola	550–85	Libya
550–73	Argentina	550–163	Malagasy Rep.
550–20	Brazil	550–45	Malaysia
550–61	Burma	550–161	Mauritania
550–83	Burundi	550–79	Mexico
550–96	Ceylon	550–76	Mongolia
550–159	Chad	550–49	Morocco
550–60	China, People's Rep. of	550–64	Mozambique
550–63	China, Republic of	550–35	Nepal, Bhutan and Sikkim
550–26	Colombia	550–88	Nicaragua
550–91	Congo (Brazzaville)	550–157	Nigeria
550–67	Congo (Kinshasa) Zaire	550–94	Oceania
550–90	Costa Rica	550–48	Pakistan
550–152	Cuba	550–46	Panama
550–22	Cyprus	550–156	Paraguay
550–158	Czechoslovakia	550–92	Peripheral States of the Arabian Peninsula
550–54	Dominican Republic		
550–155	East Germany	550–42	Peru
550–52	Ecuador	550–72	Philippines
550–150	El Salvador	550–162	Poland
550–28	Ethiopia	550–160	Romania
550–29	Germany	550–84	Rwanda
550–153	Ghana	550–51	Saudi Arabia
550–87	Greece	550–70	Senegal
550–78	Guatemala	550–86	Somalia
550–82	Guyana	550–93	South Africa, Rep. of
550–164	Haiti	550–95	Soviet Union
550–165	Hungary	550–27	Sudan
550–151	Honduras	550–47	Syria
550–21	India	550–62	Tanzania
550–154	Indian Ocean Territories	550–53	Thailand
550–39	Indonesia	550–89	Tunisia
550–68	Iran	550–80	Turkey
550–31	Iraq	550–74	Uganda
550–25	Israel	550–43	United Arab Republic
550–69	Ivory Coast	550–97	Uruguay
550–30	Japan	550–71	Venezuela
550–34	Jordan	550–57	Vietnam, North
550–56	Kenya	550–55	Vietnam, South
550–50	Khmer Rep. (Cambodia)	550–99	Yugoslavia
550–81	Korea, North	550–75	Zambia
550–41	Korea, Rep. of		

☆ U.S. GOVERNMENT PRINTING OFFICE: 1973 O541–134 (P.O. 9)